W9-CNA-908

Praise for eGov

"Developing effective e-government is an enormous technical, managerial and political challenge. But it must be done. If you are a change agent in government or want to do business with the new e-government, this globe-spanning and example-laden book is invaluable."
Don Tapscott, Chairman of Itemus Inc., and co-author of Digital Capital

"E-Government is about using technology to reinvent relationships and put citizens at the center. This book provides valuable ideas to implement more efficient government operations and to build more effective relationships with core constituencies. With great examples from around the world it offers a workbench to elected officials and a blueprint to government employees."
Davide Vigano, General Manager, Public Sector, Microsoft

"The Internet has transferred power to the people. Not in the sense of anarchy but in the sense of rising expectations for e-convenience. The new economy is not just about business transformation. Governments also need to look beyond the recent burst of the dot-com bubble and realize that the gauntlet is set down: major new and innovative ways are now possible to handle almost any kind of transaction, and this book shows them how."
John Patrick, Chairman, Global Internet Project
Vice President, Internet Technology, IBM

"A definitive account of where e-government is now, and where it's going. It deals with the real issues governments and citizens face. Highly recommended."
Tim Field, Chief General Manager, Government Online,
Australian Government National Office for the Information Economy

"Douglas Holmes has given us a compass for the next great cyber frontier—a guide for e-government. A bible for the modern political leader, a heady mix of history, best practices, vision and direction, Holmes takes over where Osborne and Gaebler leave off."
Frank McKenna, former premier of New Brunswick, Canada

"Douglas Holmes has captured that rare mix of the promise of e-government with the pragmatic realities of implementation."
Chris Yapp, ICL Fellow, Lifelong Learning

eGov

eBusiness Strategies for
Government

Douglas Holmes

NICHOLAS BREALEY
PUBLISHING

LONDON

First published by
Nicholas Brealey Publishing in 2001
Reprinted 2002

3–5 Spafield Street
Clerkenwell, London
EC1R 4QB, UK
Tel: +44 (0)20 7239 0360
Fax: +44 (0)20 7239 0370

PO Box 700
Yarmouth
Maine 04096, USA
Tel: (888) BREALEY
Fax: (207) 846 5181

http://www.nbrealey-books.com

ISBN 1-85788-278-4

Library of Congress Cataloging-in-Publication Data
Holmes, Douglas, 1960–
    EGov, an EBusiness plan for government / Douglas Holmes.
        p. cm.
    ISBN 1-85788-278-4
    1. Internet in public administration. 2. Electronic government information. 3.
Electronic public records. 4. Public administration--Computer network resources.
Includes bibliographical references and index.

JF1525.A8 .H65 2001
352.3/8/02854678 21

British Library Cataloguing in Publication Data
A catalogue record for this book is available from the British Library.

Printed in Finland by WS Bookwell.

Contents

Acknowledgments

The many dedicated public-sector employees whom I've had the pleasure of interviewing over the years are the most important sources of knowledge for this book. Further reference points are the government computer press, the web, the countless conferences through which I have managed to stay awake, and many good people within the scores of innovative technology companies working to make e-government happen. I am especially grateful to Andrew Hawkins for his continuing support and encouragement. Special thanks also to Connie Dean, Mike Cassidy, and everyone at Nicholas Brealey Publishing. Above all, this is for you, Dominique.

eGov Headlines

◆ 75 percent of Australians file their income tax returns over the internet.

◆ Singapore provides 150 public services from one portal.

◆ 8,000 shipping consignments are cleared online through Dubai Customs every day.

◆ The US federal government annually makes four million online purchases for goods and services worth $17 billion.

◆ Administrative costs in the US Department of Agriculture dropped from $77 per transaction to $17 after the introduction of an e-procurement system.

◆ It takes 25 seconds for police in Scandinavia to transmit a fingerprint image to another force.

◆ A traffic website for commuters in Minneapolis/St. Paul is viewed 300,000 times a day.

◆ One billion annual health insurance claims in France are now submitted electronically rather than on paper.

◆ Residents of Uppsala, Sweden can access their medical records online over a WAP phone.

◆ University students in Germany register for exams and search for library books using wireless devices.

◆ Multimedia mobile units drive around Costa Rica, providing internet access, email, and computer training to rural citizens.

◆ Monterrey Tech is the world's most geographically dispersed educational system, providing online courses to 43,000 students throughout Mexico and Latin America.

◆ Estonia had no privately owned computers in 1991. Today it is among the top 20 most connected countries in the world.

◆ Public petitions to the Scottish Parliament are created and submitted online.

◆ Brazilians vote electronically in all national and local elections.

Introduction

THE WEB AS ENABLER

Public-sector managers, government contractors, civic reformers, and socially concerned businesspeople all took notice in 1992 when *Reinventing Government*, by David Osborne and Ted Gaebler, argued for a "customer-driven" government that empowered citizens by pushing control out of the bureaucracy and into the community. The book was both a call to arms against bureaucratic malaise and a guide for those who wanted to build more effective public administrations. The authors foresaw a more entrepreneurial, mission-driven government with a civil service composed of knowledge workers who functioned as a team focused on outcomes not inputs. At last somebody was saying, "We don't need more government or less government, we need *better* government."

A reinventing government movement took hold in many countries, leading to some major behind-the-scenes transformations: public services were put out to competitive tender, outsourced, and privatized. The focus was primarily on reducing costs. Yet little attention was paid to the ability to meet the needs of individual citizens and businesses, government's customers. The inflexible bureaucrats, the long waits and the multiple complex forms—they're all still there. Dealing with government remains a hassle.

Public administration has not become more customer focused largely because little effort was ever made to induce culture change within government so that employees would share information, work as a team, and become knowledge workers. The people at the top who set the political agenda—politicians, press, pressure groups—have also never taken much notice of calls to reinvent government and remain stuck in the old political ways of personalized confrontation, left versus right, right versus wrong. Nor should anyone underestimate the significance of public apathy and the low expectation of initiative in government. Why change when nobody cares?

The reinvention of government is badly in need of an enabler. Something that fosters teamwork and the sharing of information. Something that excites the politicians and press. Something that's useful to business. Something that's relevant to citizens' everyday lives and addresses their personal needs and circumstances. Something like the internet.

It is easy to be cynical about new technology as a cure-all for society's ills, and it is sometimes difficult to separate the internet from other types of technology solutions. Government especially has a history of putting its faith in large IT projects only to see them run late and over budget, and in the end failing and even shaking public confidence. In *Reinventing Government*, Osborne and Gaebler hardly gave computers a mention. But that was a decade ago, before everyone took off into cyberspace. The internet is proving to be something unique and different. It is enabling new ways of communicating, working, shopping, learning, and playing. Now it can enable a new way of governing.

Electronic government, or e-government, is the use of information technology, in particular the internet, to deliver public services in a much more convenient, customer-oriented, cost-effective, and altogether different and better way. It affects an agency's dealings with citizens, businesses, and other public agencies as well as its internal business processes and employees. The e-government movement is being driven by the need for government to:

➢   cut costs and improve efficiency
➢   meet citizen expectations and improve citizen relationships
➢   facilitate economic development.

While many agencies have made great strides to reduce costs, too often this has come at the price of cutting programs. Today, agencies are under pressure to save money while maintaining or even increasing their level of services to citizens and businesses. By using the internet, the cost of processing transactions is greatly reduced, with savings in paper and printing, mailing, and personnel. Online transactions can streamline processes and lead to greater efficiencies with less human interaction. One of the primary reasons for inefficiency is that the basic model of government remains entrenched in the industrial age with a continued reliance on the centralized mass production of public services delivered through vertical "stovepipe" channels. Citizens today have diverse needs that must cut across the underlying structures, so the internet can be used as a collaboration tool for employees and departments.

The most publicly visible way for the internet to improve the public sector is through its ability to reduce the time and effort required for citizens and businesses to comply with government rules and regulations. As people become aware of the power of the web and experience good service in the private sector, they will become less tolerant of poor, impersonal service in the public sector. If people can buy an airplane ticket over the internet, they will want to renew their vehicle registration the same way. If they can go online to check how their stocks are doing, they will want to go online to check their medical records. In the digital age, public services need to be instantly accessible, around the clock, from home or work.

Ultimately, e-government is more than selling public licenses over the internet. It's about making the transition from the industrial society to the emerging information society. Businesses are already moving their services and transactions online, and increasingly they are choosing to invest only in areas that offer the infrastructure and business climate needed to succeed in the new knowledge economy. By embracing the web itself, governments can make their municipalities, states, or countries more appealing to inward investment and help their own firms step out and become part of the world's major markets, contributing to their region's prosperity.

The internet started as a government project. Its origins can be traced back to 1969 and a US Defense Advanced Research Projects

Agency (DARPA) program to develop techniques and technologies that would allow computers to communicate across multiple networks. The result was ARPANET, which connected 40 computers at its first public demonstration in 1972. Private enterprise, university researchers, non-governmental organizations, and individual behavior—just about every-body but government—have led most of the subsequent internet phenomena: electronic mail, news groups, bulletin boards, the World Wide Web, browsers, surfing, domain names, search engines, spam, hack-ing, intranets, extranets, broadband, video streaming, multicasting, por-tals, e-commerce, e-business, and the wireless internet and m-commerce. ARPANET struggled through the 1980s and by 1990 had ceased to exist. While the US government still legally owns the internet's root server that forms the basis for top-level domains, the internet today is largely a government-free zone.

Many public-sector organizations do have websites. These are used primarily as marketing devices to promote the image of a particular department or to raise public awareness with general administrative information. They are cheaply designed and the content is renewed infre-quently. The information is sometimes simply a scanned reproduction of already printed material, so-called brochureware. Some organizations provide more comprehensive and dynamic information, with searchable databases and email reply services. Very few provide a variety of inter-active transactional services. Rarely can a person log on to a government website and submit a form, make an appointment, inquire about a job, apply for social benefits, purchase a license or permit, pay a tax bill or a parking fine.

While the private sector entered the twenty-first century trans-formed by e-commerce and e-business, until now the usefulness of the internet has not crossed the minds of most public officials and politi-cians. Government was more distracted than any other sector by the Y2K threat, and prior to 2000 most of the IT funding and expertise that could have gone into developing web infrastructure and applications were siphoned off to prevent a millennium disaster. However, even without the Y2K anxiety, the public sector has not had the same incentive as the private sector to embrace the web. Specifically, competition hasn't driven it online. Businesses have to make sudden decisions to stay ahead of competitors and increase profits, whereas no equivalent market pressures bear down on public agencies. In government, making a right decision takes priority over making a fast decision. Government is generally slower to adapt to technological change because, out of necessity, it operates in a more risk-averse culture. The impact on society would be disastrous if dot-govs failed at the same rate as dot-coms. The public sector is more accountable than the private sector for the money it spends and is bound by more and different laws, in areas of procurement for example. It has to be more conscious of integrity, transparency, and openness. It must seek political support for its projects, and ideology is often involved. Finally, the sheer size and complexity of government completely dwarf most private companies.

AN E-BUSINESS PLAN FOR GOVERNMENT

As tempting as it might be, an agency cannot take a private company's e-business plan and implement it because there are simply too many differences between government and industry. An e-strategy doesn't come shrink-wrapped in a box. Governments must establish their own visions, considering all the ways to deliver quality, cost-effective public services in ways that citizens and businesses want to receive them. An e-business plan for government must strategically detail how the internet will be used to integrate service delivery across agencies, shift the mindset and culture within the civil service, and apply the "faster, better, cheaper" values of e-commerce to public services.

The first place an e-business plan ought to go is government's own backyard, from A to A, or administration to administration (also known as G2G, or government to government). Instead of merely talking to their boss and the person in the next cubicle, government employees can use the web to communicate, share knowledge, and work with other employees in their department, other departments, other levels of government, other governments. Next, an e-business plan should take government from A to B, or administration to business (also known as G2B, or government to business). The internet can help government improve the way it deals with the business community, conducts its own business with suppliers, and works with private-sector partners to deliver public services. Finally, it's all the way from A to C, or administration to citizen (also known as G2C, or government to citizen), where all public transactions and form filling are done over the internet. The first part of this book looks at each of these three communication flows, but in reverse order, because the citizen must always come first.

The journey from A to A, B, and C is already being embarked on by a small band of enthusiastic agencies from around the world. Perhaps not moving quite as fast or as willingly as some would like, these trailblazers are nonetheless working hard to link organizational change with the establishment of portals, websites, intranets, call centers, and one-stop shops. They are acquiring new technologies and integrating old ones, forging new kinds of alliances and partnerships, sharing knowledge, and working as teams.

In Australia, for example, three-quarters of all income-tax forms are now filed over the internet. Truck drivers passing through the Czech Republic and ships entering the port of Dubai make their customs declarations electronically. Federal procurement officers in the US arrange online auctions and conduct billions of dollars worth of e-commerce transactions. Canada was the first country to connect all its schools and public libraries, while Sweden has used the web to advance telemedicine. Rural telecenters are becoming an important mode of government access throughout Africa and the Indian subcontinent. Brazil is a pioneer in electronic voting, helping the country become a vigorous democracy after decades of military dictatorship.

Innovation is not limited to a specific jurisdiction or region, and e-government isn't the preserve of wealthy and developed nations. While

America may be well beyond reach in its private and commercial use of the internet, its use in the public sector isn't any further ahead or behind other countries. If a trend exists at all, it is that smaller governments and organizations have been the quickest to embrace the e-government concept. Often being smaller makes it easier to work across departments, and there may already have been a tradition of doing so. Smaller governments also tend to be more naturally citizen centric.

In the Baltics, Estonia introduced new technologies to quickly "leapfrog" its larger industrialized European neighbors and become one of the world's most wired countries. Costa Rica invests more per capita than most developed countries on school computers and internet training for teachers. Belgium used technology to put its social welfare house in order. The city-state of Singapore is the most advanced in providing full online services to its citizens.

In countries with federal systems, modernization usually starts at the state level. The state of Victoria in Australia and the province of New Brunswick in Canada were two of the very first jurisdictions to get the e-government ball rolling. While Washington DC stumbles, many US states have raced ahead to issue birth certificates or renew driver's licenses through government portals. In the area of education, small campuses such as Mayville State and Valley City State universities in North Dakota were fully wired before the major state colleges. Locally, the remote north Canadian city of Yellowknife, population 17,000 or so, has a "smart community" initiative involving dozens of public, private, and nongovernmental organizations and voluntary agencies. The similarly sized Parthenay, in rural France, could teach Paris a thing or two about online public services.

Each example represents an island of best practice. When you put them all together, as this book sets out to do, you get a fairly good picture of how a government of the future might look. The book considers what each successful e-government project shares, what links the islands, and what are the common ideas, approaches, and beliefs.

Emerging from the various e-government strategies and action lines are five underlying principles:

> ➤ *Put everything (information and services) online and do everything online.* All forms and documents are published initially in digital form, and printed on paper afterward only if necessary. Information is stored on an intranet or data warehouse, not in filing cabinets and boxes, because digital information is more efficient to create and maintain, and can more easily be analyzed, searched, updated, and shared. Rather than entering the same data multiple times, information is input just once. Agencies should establish a timetable and set target dates for putting services online and justify, on a case-by-case basis, any business areas that cannot go online for operational or policy reasons.

> ➤ *Ensure easy and universal access to online information and services.* Government has a moral obligation to ensure that all citizens have equal access to public services, including online services, regardless of their location, income, ethnicity, age, or education. In the information society, internet access is not a luxury, it's a necessity. Public services should be available 24 hours a day irrespective of location, and they should be accessible through a single contact point that is self-explanatory and easy to use. Services will be clustered into common themes or "life events" rather than displayed by government office. They will use everyday terms such as "my car" or "registering to vote" rather than government jargon.

> ➤ *Skill government employees to be knowledge workers.* Most public servants are hard working and dedicated, but often demoralized with the presumption that they're not as good as the private sector. So success in the civil service needs to be rewarded, restrictions that stifle innovation suspended, and employees given the opportunity to learn new skills throughout their careers. Front-desk staff should have fingertip access to the accurate and up-to-date information they require to deliver quality public services. Web-based technologies facilitate culture change by creating a workplace where data is organized across departmental boundaries, making it easy for employees to access information intuitively, share it, and work as a team.

➤ *Work in partnership to make it happen.* While government cannot be run like a business, it can learn from business and adopt private-sector techniques. The private sector should play a greater role in the delivery of public-sector services, and other societal players such as trade unions and the voluntary sector should also be involved in the governing process. There needs to be better cooperation between central and local governments, rather than one dictating to the other and one beating off the other. By adopting best-value policies and keeping an open mind about which kind of supplier—public, private, or partnership—can deliver the best service, different organizations bring together their respective skills and knowledge and, in the process, learn from each other.

➤ *Remove barriers and lead by example.* In the information society, government should proactively encourage business and consumer confidence by helping key sectors go online. It should set in place the legal frameworks needed to underpin the new economy, but avoid imposing unnecessary regulations and burdens that can stifle innovation. It should invest in people—education and training, health, mobility, culture, and quality of life—to ensure that the new economy does not compound existing social problems of unemployment, social exclusion, and poverty. And finally, government should lead by example by conducting its own business online, including e-procurement and the acceptance of electronic filing and electronic payments.

NOW THE HARD PART

Given its complexity and scale, the actual implementation of an e-business plan for government can seem like a daunting task, and many organizations risk trying to do too much too fast. IT industry marketing types often say that it's like eating an elephant: the only way to manage it is one bite at a time and eventually you'll finish.

The approach taken by most of the trailblazers is to "think big, start small, and scale fast." Thinking big is the vision and plan itself. Starting with small projects limits risk and avoids high-profile disasters, allowing organizations to be more innovative and realize faster results. This will help win support for future projects from politicians, employees, businesses, and citizens. It is best to start with transactions that are repetitive (anything a person might have to do more than once a year) or prone to cause frustration (such as simple license renewals, for which people currently have go to an office and stand in line). For larger projects, it is best to pilot an online application in one region before rolling it out nationwide. Government must then operate on internet speed to chalk up and take advantage of its successes. As soon as a pilot project has achieved the desired result, it has to be quickly scaled up to a full online service, and new services must be added constantly until there is full e-government.

Most of the problems in delivering e-government are organizational and political rather than technical. Left solely to an IT department, e-government will only automate existing processes. It is not a techie's job to reinvent government. The public sector needs web-savvy central visionaries, but unfortunately most government leaders still don't look on technology as a priority. Few use technology personally on a daily basis and not many people are able to picture their president or prime minister, governor or mayor, surfing the web. Policy makers don't view the online community as voting constituents and many believe that there isn't a large demand for electronic services, since only 25 percent of their country's population has web access. That was last week. This week it's 30 percent, next week it'll be 40 percent, and soon the internet will be as common as televisions and telephones. Indeed, as digital television and third-generation cellphones enter people's lives, the internet will converge with televisions and telephones.

E-government is nonpartisan. It does not favor left or right, one party or another. But astute politicians understand the mileage to be gained by talking about technology, and the internet is a gift horse for any public official wishing to portray a modern, visionary, and dynamic image of government. Sometime soon, politicians will not be re-elected if they have not incorporated the internet in their vocabulary. Public officials—both elected and appointed—must take the initiative to understand the way cyberspace works and adjust their public duties in line with current trends.

The second part of this book looks at how the early leaders are applying technology to address the traditional areas of government activity, such as the environment, healthcare, social welfare, employment, education, criminal justice, and defense. It is about using the internet to deal with those issues that simply won't go away.

The digital age also throws up a raft of new issues that policy makers will have to grasp in order to make the right decisions for their constituents. The third part of the book considers some of the new challenges that are already coming to the fore and how some governments are reacting. Emerging issues include cyberterrorism and cybercrime, privacy, data protection, jurisdiction over cyberspace, e-commerce taxation, and the problem of "electronic emigrants." The discussion covers the various digital divides in society, and addresses how local communities can find their place in an increasingly global world. Finally, it looks at how the internet affects politicians themselves, and how the web can transform an ailing system of representative democracy into a more robust form of participative democracy.

In time, the internet will affect the public sector much more profoundly than it has the private sector, for the simple reason that people like to go out shopping whereas they dread the thought of making a trip down to a stuffy old government office and do so only out of necessity. The reaction of citizens and businesses any time a public service is put online is almost always overwhelmingly positive. Success by today's trailblazing agencies will eventually bring all the others along, so the march to e-government can't be stopped. Governments that stick to the old ways of doing business will further open themselves to ridicule and accusations of incompetence and corruption. Citizens will want to know why they have to stand in line for a service when people in the neighboring town, region, or country can carry out transactions online and without fuss. This generation will be the last to tolerate standing in line; the next will expect to be online.

Part One

The ABCs of eGovernment

1 Getting from A to C: Administration to Citizen

DON'T STAND IN LINE, GET ONLINE

An American soldier renewed his Virginia state driver's license one Tuesday in December 1999. No big deal—except that it was six o'clock in the morning and he completed the procedure in seconds without leaving the army base where he was stationed, across three state boundaries in Fort Benning, Georgia. In so doing, he became the first Virginian to renew his driver's license over the internet. His other option would have been to request leave to drive 500 miles to Virginia (on a potentially expired license) and stand in line at an inconvenient hour to conduct the business face to face.'

People's perceptions of government are based largely on this kind of interaction with bureaucracy, and most see dealing with government as a dismal experience, somewhere below having to look after the neighbor's cat. Either you're confronted by an unresponsive, nay-saying bureaucrat, or you're put into an endless telephone loop. You're told to fill in Form 123 by hand and then some other agency will require you to provide the exact same information all over again on Form XYZ. You stand in line for hours only to be told that your documentation is incomplete. Then you're told to conclude the transaction at another government office clear across town. That office closes at 4.15 and there's no way you're going to get there in time. So you'll have take time off work the next day as well. All this to accomplish a menial task like renewing a car registration. People today value their time too much to put up with the hassles of a slow and unreliable public service.

Motor vehicle agencies provide a quick and easy barometer for the effectiveness of the public sector because so much of their work is devoted to paper processing, document handling, and error correcting. They are also in direct daily contact with the public and are normally characterized by long queues and unanswered phone calls. But a growing number of motor vehicle agencies, such as the state of Virginia's, are turning to the internet to make themselves more customer focused and to give people a faster, simpler and more convenient way of doing their government business.

Toward the end of 1999, Andersen Consulting (now Accenture) surveyed the motor vehicle agencies of all 50 US states and found that 47 had websites. This seems reasonable, except that only 13 offered any kind of transaction service. Nine provided the ability to renew vehicle registrations, seven issued license plates, two issued driver's licenses, and only one allowed people to make an online inquiry. The others simply provided basic information like fees and documentation required for registration processes. The Maine Bureau of Motor Vehicles website dourly suggested: "If you do not find your answers here, please contact us at our main office in Augusta or any one of our 13 conveniently located branch offices."

A branch office is conveniently located only if you happen to live next door to one. People ought to be able to find all their answers from home or work. If for some extraneous circumstance they can't, then they should be able to send an inquiry from home or work. Citizens ought to be able to communicate with government any way they want, and in the digital age most will want to communicate through the web or by email. Public-sector agencies often already have performance targets for handling communications by post, phone, and fax. These should be extended to cover online inquiries.

In their 1992 book *Reinventing Government*, David Osborne and Ted Gaebler suggested that the best way for public service providers to respond to the needs of citizens was by putting resources (vouchers, cash grants, other funding systems) into the hands of individuals and give them a choice—a choice of school for their children, a choice of recreation facilities, even a choice of police services. The idea was boldly attempted by some governments, perhaps too often driven by dogma, but people still had to wait in long queues to register their child at the school of their choice. They still had to go across town to register at their chosen recreation facility, and they still had to fill in multiple forms for all their chosen police service providers.

Rather than apply the basic private-sector consumer-choice approach of *who* should provide a public service, the emphasis today is on giving citizens and businesses a choice of *where* and *when* they can access public services. Banks, supermarkets, travel agents, and dot-coms are making services and products available around the clock, so why shouldn't government? Increasingly, people want to access public services "right here, right now." Right now is any time—24 hours a day, 7 days a week. Right here is from any place—home, work, school, or the palm of their hand.

The cost of developing online services is modest compared to other delivery channels, and the marginal cost of someone accessing a website is virtually zero. Using the internet won't just make people's lives easier, it will change the way they think about government: Modern rather than institutional. Efficient rather than bureaucratic. On message rather than off base. *Cool* rather than *it sucks*. The web has the ability to reinvent government in a way that nobody could have imagined in the early 1990s, and in a way that matters most to the citizens and businesses who receive public services and to the taxpayers who pay for them.

THE TAXMAN, AT YOUR SERVICE

So what about taxes? Nobody likes paying them, but they're more inclined to do so if it's a relatively easy and painless process. Tax time is currently a headache for most citizens and it's no picnic for the tax collector either, since processing endless paper forms is an expensive and time-consuming exercise. The data on every form has to be checked manually and then keyed into a computer system for further processing and inspection. The administration of business taxes, such as sales tax or value-added tax, is especially costly because returns are made monthly or quarterly. Given all this, it should not be surprising that tax offices the world over have been among the first public agencies to embrace electronic government and put their transactional "services" online.

France allows individuals and companies to file and pay all income taxes, local taxes, property taxes, corporate taxes, and social security contributions over the internet. Ireland collects VAT and employers' tax over the web and allows taxpayers to view an up-to-date statement of their account at any time. And all the functions of Spain's tax administration agency are online, offering access to individual tax returns and payment, applications, the processing of tax refunds, information and consultation, and assistance programs for the preparation and presentation of tax refunds. The Internal Revenue Service has the most frequently visited US public-sector website, and about one-third of American tax returns were filed electronically in 2000. US tax refunds are electronically deposited into people's bank accounts and tax payments can be made online with a credit or debit card, so people can pay their taxes the same way they pay for commercial items.

The error rate for electronic tax returns is less than 1 percent, compared to 20 percent for those that are paper based. A computer can check an e-filer's math for mistakes and a tax return program can give advice, ask questions, and remind taxpayers to include certain information like their zip code or social insurance number. Those who owe money can authorize direct debits from their bank accounts on a selected date, so that they can file early but still make the payment closer to the deadline. With digital signatures now becoming recognized in law, in future taxpayers should be able to include a personal identification number with their return so they don't have to mail in a signed document afterward. Another problem for American taxpayers is that they must pay $20 or more for the software that's required to file a tax return via the internet, but the IRS plans to make it possible for Americans to file online for free starting in 2003.

Governments are so eager to shift away from paper-based tax returns that many are offering incentives to people to go digital. The US and Canadian governments promise that anyone due a tax refund will receive it within two weeks if they file electronically. The British government offers cash—a £50 rebate to companies that file VAT returns online and another £50 for submitting their employer's tax that way. Individual taxpayers get £10 off for e-filing their income tax. This raises questions about social inequality based on access to technology, but in many countries the majority of electronic tax returns are filed by professional tax preparers, and their biggest customers are lower income earners. (Promotions such as offering loans against an anticipated refund are highly popular.)

In the end, it will be added value and convenience, rather than financial carrots, that will bring people around to filing returns and paying taxes online. In this respect, no country is further ahead than Australia, where 75 percent of all income tax forms are submitted electronically through the Australian Tax Office (ATO) website. Of these, 60 percent are processed without any human intervention, using the so-called zero touch approach. The ATO website features calculators, "smart forms," online assistance and interactive feedback. The agency also provides free "e-records" software, tailored especially for small businesses, to assist them in managing cash flow, business planning and, of course, ensuring tax compliance.

In the early days of taxes, the collector's primary responsibility was enforcement, usually at the point of a sword. Once it became accepted that paying tax was as inevitable as death, their duties shifted more to administration and accounting. Once again, the tax office's role and the way it interacts with the taxpayer are changing. In the digital age and global economy, faced with tax competition from other jurisdictions and concerned about securing a reliable stream of revenue, the taxman is about to become a service provider. Now there's a new concept.

PORTAL DEFINITION #1:
A MAGNET IN THE HAYSTACK

The sheer size and complexity of government form a major barrier for anyone trying to access public-sector information and services. Most central governments have about 70 different departments or agencies, each of which nowadays has its own website with a URL that's impossible to guess or remember. There can be just as many additional organizations at the state, regional, and local levels. It's a nightmare trying to figure out which official in which department at which level is responsible for which program. A number of agencies may be involved in providing a service, each requiring the completion of different forms. They all expect people to communicate with them in turn rather than taking the initiative to deal with each other.

One of the most compelling arguments for e-government is the opportunity it presents to provide seamless services arranged, not from a bureaucratic viewpoint, but by subject or life event, such as a birth in the family, a marriage, a death, moving house, starting school, setting up a business, declaring bankruptcy, being accused of a crime, or whatever.

Say someone loses his job. That's a life event; not a pleasant one, but it happens. The guy feels bad enough as it is without having to battle the bureaucracy. But first he'll have to contact and provide a mountain of personal information to the benefits agency to claim and collect unemployment insurance allowance, and then he'll have to contact and provide the same information to the job center to register for work, to the tax office to claim a tax rebate, to the local authority to claim local tax benefits, to the housing office to claim housing benefits, and maybe also to a retraining program or a local charity to attend a job club. It's painfully obvious that all these services are related, so rather than have the demoralized jobseeker traipse off or phone around to a half dozen different offices, it would be much more dignified to cluster all these functions and make them accessible through a single access point.

History will look back on the formative e-gov years as dominated by the rise of the "single window to government," the "government gateway" or, the emerging favorite, the "government portal." Through a portal, the information systems of all departments and agencies can be linked to deliver integrated services in a way that avoids citizens having to understand the complicated internal organizational structures of government. People who want to renew their vehicle registration or book a driving test shouldn't need to know the name of the government department that delivers this service; they should just be able to go to the government portal and click the life-event option for "my car." Portals can feature specific areas for specific people—workers, businesses, students, war veterans, cat owners—and they can be accessed from various devices—home and office PCs, public kiosks, web-enabled call centers, one-stop shops, digital TV, third-generation cellphones, intelligent appliances, game consoles.

The Australian state of Victoria was an early visionary of portal technology when, in May 1998, it published its *Online Government 2001* strategy paper, which recognized: "An integrated approach to electronic service delivery—sometimes referred to as a *single window*—has the potential to offer multiple services and therefore provide more convenient dealings with government for the community, including the business sector." The Victoria government's Multi-service Express (*me*) portal now offers citizens more than 80 interactive services ranging from ordering a birth certificate to registering on the electoral roll. The site gives a choice of three ways to access services and information: by service type (paying bills, applying for a grant, etc.); by life event (moving house, having a baby, etc.); or by location (government agency or department). The *me* portal is connected to the state's *maxi* network, which offers both public and private services organized around the life events of citizens and customers.

Most administrations are now embracing the portal concept. The US federal government jumped on the bandwagon on June 26, 2000 when Bill Clinton, looking relaxed and informal in a red open-neck shirt during his first webcast to the nation, announced that the FirstGov portal would be created within 90 days. Sure enough, in another webcast, the president launched the site on September 22. Using technology that searches 500 million documents on 27 million web pages in less than one-quarter of a second, FirstGov serves as a single point of entry to a wide range of life-event services, such as applying for student loans or planning for retirement. Citizens can see the progress of their application for social security benefit and get advice on buying a home or starting a business. They can also use the site to reserve a national park campsite, apply to watch a space shuttle launch, and conduct research at the Library of Congress. The FirstGov "brand" is available for use by commercial and non-commercial organizations, including the likes of Yahoo! and Jeeves, so that people can continue using their familiar consumer portals while benefiting from the full-text search of all government web pages. Marty Wagner, associate administrator for government-wide policy at the General Services Administration, the federal agency that administers the portal, says: "Government information on the web is like having many needles in the haystack. FirstGov gives citizens the magnet to find the needles."

Meanwhile, back in the state of Virginia, the government portal concept is being taken a step further with "My Virginia Homepage," which lets citizens tailor online government services to their particular tastes. Launched in July 2000, the personalized portal allows users to add, update, or remove links to such services as public meeting announcements, legislative sites, local government, local media, state government agencies, and traffic information. Further phases provided the ability to complete tasks involving multiple government agencies and gave people the option to request electronic reminders to renew government permits. There is also an automated legislative tracking service linked to the Virginia general assembly, with email notification of government-related announcements.

PORTAL DEFINITION #2:
A COMPLEX, GROWING ORGANISM

With everything that was once a search engine or even just a dusty old website now calling itself a portal, the US National Electronic Commerce Coordinating Council (NEC3) has put forward definitions for government portals based on five levels. Each level becomes increasingly difficult to master, rather like playing Nintendo. Many governments are already at level one or will be very soon, and some are approaching levels two and three. Levels four and five are mostly still visions.

➢ The first-level portal provides information or services easily with relatively few mouse clicks. It is functional, hiding organizational complexity and showing government as the citizen wants to see it.

➢ The second level offers online transactions such as vehicle registration, business licensing, tax filing, and bill payment.

➢ The third-level portal lets people jump from one service to the next without having to authenticate themselves again. This requires collaboration between departments and the sharing of services such as authentication, security, search, and navigation.

➢ The fourth-level portal draws out data needed for a transaction from all available government sources. This requires collaboration between organizations, as well as data warehousing and middleware technology so that different databases can interface with each other. The federal government of Canada is accomplishing this with what it calls a "federated architecture," comprising both shared departmental and government-wide components separate from the systems that individual departments use for their own needs. All departments will be able to rely on the new architecture to share information and provide integrated services directly to Canadian citizens.

➢ The fifth- and highest-level portal adds value and allows people to interact with government on their own terms, providing aggregated and customized information and services in subject areas corresponding to the citizen's own particular circumstance. Taking the vehicle registration scenario, rather than logging on to the motor vehicle agency's website, the URL for which nobody knows, citizens can go to the government portal and click a "my car" icon. This gives them access to their vehicle registration as well as a listing of their traffic citations, insurance company ratings, recall notices on their car, and more. They could be reminded to renew their car registration and request updates on traffic conditions via a pager, cellphone, or email. "A level-five portal will be a complex, growing organism, rich in data, transactions and multimedia—it will almost replicate a society," says P.K. Agarwal, past chairman of the NEC3 and now CIO of the California Franchise Tax Board. "It is hard to visualize because it will be nothing like today's websites."

Singapore's e-Citizen Center portal is perhaps the closest there is to level-five integrated online services. When logging on to the site, the user's connection speed (high or low bandwidth) is automatically detected and the graphics are adjusted accordingly before the citizen is led down a road of life, along which he or she can stop at signs indicating a series of life events. At the first stop, Singaporeans can order a birth certificate and find out about immunizing their child. Subsequent life events involve attending school, registering for national service, looking for a job, pursuing a "first-class" career, going overseas, employing people and, finally, retiring from the workforce.

Across the road from each life event is a corresponding virtual town or building that citizens can enter with a mouse click. In Education Town, students can sign up to attend schools, register for national exams, request a place in student residences, and apply for government grants. At the nearby Housing Town, people can apply for a TV license, get their telephone and utilities connected, inform government of a change of address, and have their mail redirected. They can also receive information on renting or buying publicly subsidized apartments. At Health Town, patients can book appointments with a doctor or dentist, register for admission at the Singapore General Hospital, obtain weight and height charts, and even purchase handbooks and cassette tapes on health and fitness. Employment Town integrates work-related services such as applying for jobs, recruitment, retirement, and training. People can also post job vacancies, file income tax returns, and request social security statements. In Business Town, companies can apply for patents, submit applications for industrial facilities and foreign housing, and apply for research and training grants for IT professionals and students. The three agencies responsible for overseas travel are joined together in Transportation Town, along with organizations dealing with domestic transport. Here, citizens can apply for a passport, notify the authorities of an overseas trip and apply for an exit permit (remember, this is Singapore), as well as order a taxi, take an online driver's test and, yes, renew their vehicle registration.

The e-Citizen Center started in 1997 as a pilot to demonstrate to government ministers what was meant by "integrated" and "citizen-centric" electronic services. From a single education services package, the portal grew gradually and by April 1999 it included 49 life events with 150 transactions. In comparison to Singapore's approach, to pilot and then scale up, the Australian state of Victoria's *maxi* system, probably the most advanced government portal after Singapore, was launched on a large scale and with a big bang. Its biggest problem has been securing sufficient online content to attract a critical mass of citizens to the portal. In retrospect, Victoria government officials feel that a phased approach on a smaller scale would have been more appropriate.

CREDIT CARDS ACCEPTED, NOT BAKSHEESH

Singapore is able to deliver a high level of integrated, transactional public services more easily than most governments because it's a small city-state with a single layer of government and a highly developed technological infrastructure. Its population of 3.8 million is homogenous, financially secure, educated, and computer literate. But what about an ethnically and geographically diverse, overpopulated developing country where people are poor and illiterate, where the basic infrastructure is a shambles and the government must operate within a limited budget—a country like India? About 700 million of India's one billion people live in small rural villages and are dependent on farming and agricultural industries. Most are not even connected to the electricity grid, let alone the internet. Just 20 people out of 1,000 have telephone access and only 3 out of 1,000 have access to a computer. Annual income is barely $400 per capita.

Farmers would earn more if they didn't have to rely on middleman traders who have a habit of quoting commodity rates far below the market price and pocketing the difference. Every year Indian farmers must also obtain a copy of their public land records to apply for crop loans, which involves traveling to a faraway government office to submit applications or expedite them, meet officials, obtain information, and so on. They lose a day's income plus transportation costs, and once there they face discomfort, harassment, and corrupt behavior by public officials. The relevant official might be unavailable, forcing a repeat visit. The officer in charge might say that the records are lost or destroyed, but for a bribe he will redraw the map to the detriment of the farmer's neighbor. The government official works from paper files over which he has a monopoly, adding to the inefficiency and lack of transparency.

So what can information-age government possibly do for these beleaguered people? Quite a lot, actually. Senior officials in the district *panchayat* (council) of Dhar together with the state government of Madhya Pradesh, in the soya and cotton belt of central India, decided that the best way to ease their farmers' plight was to wire up the villages. In January 2000, the Gyandoot intranet—Gyandoot means "messenger of knowledge" in Hindi—was commissioned to connect Dhar district headquarters to a network of rural cybercafés called *soochanalayas,* located at village council offices, bazaars, local shops, bus depots, and along the roadside in central villages to which people frequently travel. Since most rural villagers are barely literate and electronic financial transactions were not yet legally provided for in India, an operator with a physical presence was required to assist people and take payments. To ensure sustainability, local acceptance, and low staff costs, local youths were trained as *soochaks* to own and operate the kiosks. The *soochak* is not a government employee but rather a volunteer who takes out a bank loan to buy a computer, modem, and printer while the district council covers the telephone costs. Villagers pay a nominal amount—less than 50 cents for any service—and there is a published price list. The *soochak* retains 90 percent of the fees, while a 10 percent commission is passed back to the government to fund the development of new online services and build greater capacity on the system. Some *soochaks* earn extra money by offering computer classes.

Repeated meetings with villagers determined the initial services to be made available and the local youths to be trained as *soochaks*. Official land records were among the first documents to be put online and the local banks gladly accept the printouts duly issued by the *soochaks*—there is no longer any possibility of feud or corruption. Villagers also use the intranet to apply for caste, income and domicile certificates, and demarcations. The system allows Hindi email communication between connected villages, and public grievances may be sent to district headquarters with an email reply assured within seven days. (Common complaints include broken handpumps, absent school teachers, and poor-quality seed.)

Commodity prices and volumes are also provided daily, so farmers are cutting out the middlemen and simply going to the market where they can fetch the highest prices. This at times has meant trucking their produce 400 miles to Bombay to earn 40 percent more than they would at home. Or else they decide to hold on to their produce and wait until local prices improve. And don't shed any tears for the traders: they benefit as well. A grain merchant wanting to check produce prices across

India used to pay $2.50 per phone call to survey market centers. The same service for all markets costs 10 cents from Gyandoot.

This community-based approach is giving India's marginalized tribal poor their first ever chance to access technology. It empowers them to take greater control of their lives and is the sort of project that Bill Clinton had in mind on his presidential visit to India in March 2000, when he urged government leaders to make sure their booming IT industry benefited the country's impoverished masses and not just its western-educated élite. Impressively, the whole Gyandoot system was developed, and the initial 21 *soochanalayas* connected, in just 51 days at a cost to government of only $57,000. It uses commercial software, and a small Bhopal-based e-commerce firm, rather than a big global systems integrator or consultancy, was hired for the implementation. An editorial in the influential *Times of India* said: "This model should ideally be replicated in as many rural areas as possible. The only people complaining will be super-fatted bureaucrats and lethargic politicians rendered increasingly irrelevant by the spreading web of information."

CRM = BIG BROTHER?

Citizens of western countries typically go through a sequence of events when contacting a government office: first they phone, then they write, and then they visit in person if their query is still not resolved. It's not unusual for government offices to leave telephones ringing unanswered or for someone to say "I'll put you through" and then the line goes dead. Citizens rarely know the right person or right number to dial, which results in their being bounced around different departments and being provided with inaccurate and out-of-date information. If a citizen does happen to know who to talk to, that person is inevitably in a meeting.

In the future, a website, most likely a portal, will be a citizen's initial contact and moment of truth with government. The internet will soak up the repetitive calls for general information that currently jam departmental switchboards and distract government staff from their regular work. Phoning will become the second stage of the process, although even then people may well prefer to send an email.

In Sweden, where the majority of citizens are already internet users, government agencies undertake regular customer satisfaction surveys that include specific questions about electronic services. All the surveys show high expectations and demand for online services. In surveys about tax, for example, the most common question is: "When will I be able to file my return over the internet?" Some agencies are having difficulty handling the sheer volume of email queries on such subjects.

Going digital doesn't mean everything has to be zero touch like the Australian Tax Office. Computers aren't very good at calming distressed people in emergency situations, nor can they go out and collect the garbage on Wednesday mornings. And somebody has to reply to all the email queries. Some level of human intervention will always be required and, as such, call centers and counter service at one-stop shops are becoming an important part of most governments' overall plans to improve public service delivery. While these are not regarded as true online services because they're not fully automated, they do benefit from online support. Call centers should use the same information sources and technology as a government portal, ensuring a standard approach to dealing with inquiries, whether online, over the phone, or face to face. When call center staff answer the phone, they should be able to call up all relevant data on their computer and have an informed discussion with the caller. In future, government websites and call centers could work in tandem: a call button on the website could initiate an immediate return call by phone or video link, and the citizen and call center agent could have the same website in front of them while they discuss an issue.

The London Borough of Newham created a small team to handle direct customer contact for local council tax and tax benefits. The team was given full access to the authority's council tax and benefits systems and could use the information to answer just about any citizen query. Within six months the number of personal visits to the tax office reduced from several hundred per day to about 60. The success of this initiative encouraged the council to establish its Newham 2000 call center to deal with all council business. In its first year of operation, 80 highly trained multilingual staff, working in four shifts between 8 am and 8 pm, were handling an average of 2,000 calls a day, rising to around 3,000 during peak periods. The waiting time for calls to be answered averages five seconds; data is collected on how long each inquiry takes and how long inquiries remain outstanding. Clear and simple security checks are used to confirm a caller's identity and all information about residents is kept confidential and secure. The technology monitors services and records information about which services residents need, what services they are interested in, and areas where they are experiencing problems. So, as well as allowing it to deal with complaints and enquiries, the council gets an overall picture of how it provides its services.

By getting a more integrated view of interactions with citizens through correlating database information about people's location, status, dependants, and so on, governments are more able to identify individuals' current situation and, by implication, gain an understanding of their future needs. This is the principle behind customer relationship management (CRM), which is moving to the top of private companies' IT investment lists with the aim of helping them get to know their customers and enabling direct personalized marketing. Many governments are looking to use the same practice, redubbed citizen relationship management, to make better use of the considerable amounts of data they collect from their constituents. By extracting hidden patterns in large amounts of data through techniques such as data warehousing and data mining, governments can develop one-to-one relationships with citizens and provide tailored public services such as those available on the My Virginia Homepage portal. Conversely, the technology can be used to keep tabs on people, for example to determine if their tax claim might be fraudulent or if a business's VAT return might be late.

Governments have always tracked citizens from birth to the grave, compiling records on just about everything they do: where they work and how much they earn, where they bank and how much they're in debt, where and with whom they live, where and when they travel, what they drive, their health status and treatment, whether they have a criminal record, and so on. But all these files are usually kept from different perspectives, so government's view of the citizen is historically fragmented and information concerning any one individual is tucked away in different filing cabinets or, more recently, scattered across hundreds of unconnected and technically incompatible databases. Information collected by one agency has been kept locked away and inaccessible to other agencies. This frequently leads to accusations that government's left hand doesn't know what its right hand is doing, but in a perverse way the chaotic situation has served to protect people's privacy by ensuring that data isn't used for purposes unrelated to the reason it was obtained.

CRM doesn't require more information to be obtained from people; if anything, it means getting less because the amount of duplicate information is reduced to make the data more manageable. Most governments legitimately want to make public services more efficient by limiting the number of times a citizen has to give out the same information to different departments: a change of address, for example. So the dilemma is to figure out how processes can be made simpler, without at the same time making it easier for government to acquire and misuse power over the citizen by aggregating all the information held by different agencies into a single, virtual superdatabase.

There was a public outcry in May 2000 over the Canadian government's so-called Longitudinal Labor Force Files, a database containing information on 33 million citizens. The data was derived from different departments and different levels of government, but was held centrally by the federal Department of Human Resources. File data included people's ethnicity, movements in and out of the country or between Canadian provinces, and sensitive information about individuals' health and taxes. The government said the files were needed for policy research purposes and assured the public that the information was closely guarded and would not fall into the wrong hands. But then newspapers, which had dubbed the database the "Big Brother files," reported that police and the security service had gained access to the files. Quebec's provincial government demanded that files on its residents be destroyed, and thousands of people from across the country jammed government phone lines as they tried to find out what information was being held on them.

Bowing to public pressure, the government dismantled the database and the information was sent back to the agencies and provincial governments from where it had originally come. The government's information-sharing arrangement between agencies was put under review and the human resources department's own policy analysis and research data was henceforth kept as "separate, secure, and unlinked files." Jane Stewart, the government minister responsible, acknowledged that there had been "public concerns about privacy in this era of constantly changing technology."

When accessing services, people generally don't care if the information they require is held in a different computer system and by another department, or even by a private-sector company. But when they talk about privacy on the internet, there is unease about the potential misuse of personal information. People want convenience and simplicity in electronic dealings with government coupled with privacy protection. They want to be able to trust the new ways of doing business.

In many countries, personal information is becoming a commodity that can be bought, sold, and traded. Public registers are becoming widely accessible over the internet and companies working in partnership with the government are using public data for private gain. There is at best a patchwork of laws, regulations, and codes concerning the collection, use, and disclosure of personal information, and most private-sector industries are subject to no rules at all. Obviously, there needs to be a balance between people's right to privacy and the need for public and private-sector access to information on which to base decisions and provide services. That balance will vary from country to country as each considers its own values and cultures. The Singapore government doesn't worry too much about privacy and civil liberties, which has helped it race ahead with the development of its level-five e-Citizen Center portal. This style of e-government probably wouldn't be acceptable in a country such as the UK, where even the idea of putting a photograph on a driver's license is considered an attack on privacy and a potential area for the abuse of data.

The internet enables government to provide better public services, and it should also allow more transparency and accountability, so there is ample justification for driving the digital government agenda forward. In doing so, however, it's worth bearing in mind that the internet also gives government the potential to collect and connect much more information about people, posing new risks for personal privacy. While governments aren't necessarily spying on their citizens, it might be worth recalling that in *Nineteen Eighty-Four*—George Orwell's definitive literary work on the abusive power of technology and the loss of privacy resulting from living in an overly transparent society—Big Brother watched through a ubiquitous two-way "telescreen" located in public and private buildings.

2 Getting from A to B: Administration to Business

A CAPTIVE AUDIENCE

It's inconceivable that any company sales rep today would hand out a business card that didn't include a website and email address. Even the smallest firms these days use computers in their professional activities, and most are connected to the internet. Companies are adjusting their strategic thinking to conduct business-to-business e-commerce and are finding it useful for quickening their turnaround times, lowering costs, keeping inventory, tracking orders, replenishing consumables, anticipating the next requirement, upgrading systems, and planning maintenance. If only they could also use the web to reduce red tape and simplify their transactions with government, their e-business life would be complete. The earliest e-gov successes should come in dealing with the business community, because here government has a captive audience.

People don't like standing in line in their jobs any more than they do in their free time. Rather than driving down to city hall to fill in forms, a building contractor would find it easier to apply for and receive building permits and schedule inspections over the web. Public-sector efficiency is especially important to businesses in areas of the economy where government must be involved through regulation or the provision of infrastructure. This is especially the case in international trade where, in the age of economic globalization, the clearance of consignments at border crossings has become a time-sensitive matter. Industry places a growing importance on express and just-in-time delivery systems, yet customs checks remain a lengthy process requiring much effort and incurring costs for both government and trader.

Typical is the truck driver who sits idle for up to 12 hours waiting to cross from Germany into the Czech Republic. And he only wants to drive through the country, *en route* to points north, south, or east. Landlocked in the center of Europe with four neighbors and a good highway infrastructure, the Czech Republic has become an important transit country. Some 2.5 million trucks enter and leave the country every year, compared to half a million that drive into Britain. This is new administrative territory for the Czechs; prior to the Velvet Revolution in 1989, all foreign trade was conducted by a handful of state-owned companies and the national customs directorate was staffed with no more than 500 people skilled primarily in the art of keeping out unwanted literature. Now Czech customs has 9,000 employees responsible for registering all goods entering the country, collecting customs duties, and supporting national trade policies for tariffs, quotas, and licenses. Customs officers also collect data for the compilation of national trade statistics.

Even this number of staff was not enough to keep up with demand; the queues at the borders kept growing longer, shipping companies and other businesses were growing frustrated with the delays, and it soon became impossible to physically examine the majority of consignments. So Czech customs turned to the web. The internet now allows the country's 200 customs offices, including 75 border posts, to connect internally with each other and externally to traders through a "One Window to Customs" website. By 2000, about 80 percent of all customs declarations were being submitted electronically, with traders monitoring the progress of their goods as they went through the customs process. The collection of customs duties is fully automated, with audit trails preventing fraud and ensuring accuracy.

Just about every government has a similar, growing need to improve relations with importers and exporters. In the US, the biggest trading nation in the world, most exporters are small companies and many are eligible for federal assistance, but to get it they have to approach up to 30 different agencies. So the Department of Commerce opened a special web portal to act as a one-stop government shop for American exporters.

Trading services and associated businesses are also of major importance to the economy of the United Arab Emirates, where Dubai is the major commercial center of the Middle East with one of the world's largest artificial deepwater ports. The Dubai Department of Ports and Customs deals with more than 26,000 companies, including importers and exporters, clearance and forwarding companies, shipping companies, air agents, warehousing companies, banks and financial institutions, airlines, numerous transportation and trucking firms, and duty-free business operations in the Jebel Ali free-trade zone and at the airport. These companies were coping daily with reams of paper documents such as air and sea bills, vehicle clearance, and exit–entry certificates. The customs agents were drowning in their own red tape, until one day in 1998, when Dr. Obaid Suqer Busit, the department's director general, dictated: "We will go to a messaging-based scenario. If someone sends me a fax I will reject it; likewise if someone sends me a memo, I will reject it."

To carry out the director general's orders, Dubai Customs integrated previously isolated applications for administration, goods inventory, bill of entry, accounts tracking, statistics, and inspections—and put all them online. By June 2000, about 8,000 customs clearance transactions were being conducted online. The website automatically calculates duties and fees, allowing companies to pay using either a standing order or a credit account. The system automatically determines whether a counter visit is required for each shipment based on its contents, customer history, and any intelligence gathered about the shipment that may render it suspect.

THE TOUGH GO SHOPPING, ONLINE

Since the public sector operates in the same business venues and accesses goods and services from the same suppliers as the private sector, there are many immediate gains to be made for government in the area of online procurement. Indeed, the e-commerce activity that's now reshaping private industry's trading habits will seem minute once government plugs in and plays. General Electric, the world's biggest company, does $1 billion of web-based business annually. The US federal government, only just starting, spent more than $10 billion online in 2000, mostly on high-quantity, low-cost purchases for rudimentary consumable items such as office supplies. Even the online procurement of computer equipment tends to be for small threshold items available in open markets, things like keyboards and off-the-shelf software. Most agencies still use a pen and paper to place orders for bigger and more complicated purchases. Nevertheless, this is changing quickly and the General Services Administration (GSA) expects that more than $17 billion of US federal transactions, encompassing four million items and services, will soon be conducted electronically each year. This is about as significant a move to e-business as you can get, private or public.

For most public-sector organizations, the first step to online procurement is to send out tenders and receive bids for government contracts electronically. A universal public-access system for carrying out public-sector tendering over the internet will expand supply and demand, improve the quality of information, make the tendering process easier and faster, impose transparency, and reduce transaction costs. It will also make interactions clearer and easier for businesses, thereby reducing their costs and making it easier for them to bid for contracts. Requests for proposals can be put on the web or emailed to contractors, eliminating the need for traditional postal waiting periods, often up to four weeks, between the announcement of a contract and the acceptance of bids. Bidders can be notified immediately by email.

Accepting proposals is a little more difficult, because governments have to ensure that proposals come from the source they state and that they have not been tampered with ahead of the opening date. But technologies such as date stamping and encryption are becoming well established, and government procurement will get a boost from the private sector, where consumer risk is increasingly being reduced by better technology and internet security. In Europe, the bigger problem for government e-tenders is European Union procurement rules that require the acceptance of paper submissions without discrimination. The Australian government and some US states, on the other hand, encourage e-business by charging a fee to companies that submit paper proposals.

Linking together online catalogs with credit or procurement cards is the easiest and quickest way for governments to streamline high-volume, low-cost purchases. Many governments are establishing online shopping centers, or e-malls, where online catalogs from approved suppliers are assembled and from which government purchasers can buy everything from stationery to vehicles to energy. The GSA Advantage e-mall sends out email updates to US government buyers whenever the status of their order changes. There are also privately initiated e-malls or procurement portals where procurement officers can log on and make credit-card purchases. These portal companies make money through traditional reseller models, collecting a percentage of the products they sell. With payments made online, procurement cycles are shortened, the double or triple rekeying of data into a financial management system is eliminated, and the paper purchase order is replaced by an electronic file that is born with the placement of an order and lives through to the receipt and distribution of the purchased item.

The Department of Natural Resources and Environment (NRE) in the state of Victoria, Australia, was a typical government agency, with procurement carried out by more than 2,500 field staff using paper requisition forms. Once purchases were approved by an authorized officer and the goods had arrived, staff would wait for an invoice to appear before sending it to the accounts payable office, where the details were manually entered into a computer system and the payment processed. Accountability and responsibility were blurred because the process was so lengthy and labor intensive. In July 1998, a paperless procurement process was put on the departmental intranet covering requisition, approval, checking, payment, and reconciliation. A bookmark takes staff directly to the purchasing system where they log on with a personal identification and password. The staff member completes an electronic requisition, which is emailed to an authorized officer who approves or rejects it electronically. If approved, the order is transmitted directly to the supplier and when the goods arrive, the staff member acknowledges receipt electronically and the supplier is paid electronically with no delays and no invoicing.

Previous purchase approvals took several days to process; now they rarely take more than 24 hours and are often instant. The system automatically performs the relevant checks, eliminating the need for extra signatures and paperwork. With the expanded use of electronic catalogs as an effective means of sourcing goods and services, no part of NRE's procurement process is conducted manually. In less than a year, the department was buying half its products electronically and had saved $1.3 million due to increased efficiency.

The potential to reduce processing costs dramatically is perhaps the greatest attraction of e-procurement. When the US Department of Agriculture introduced a purchase card system, its transaction costs dropped to an average $32 per order from $77 using the traditional paper purchase order and writing a check. The department believes that, with reengineering to a better online system, processing costs can be further reduced to about $17 per transaction. These numbers are based on 18,000 daily purchases, so the money saved is staggering—potentially more than $1 million a day. The Marine Corps Air Station in Beaufort, South Carolina, and the Beaufort Naval Hospital were able to lower supply procedure costs and reduce inventory by half as a result of an integrated supply program developed by a company called ProcureNet. For this, ProcureNet became the first private company to receive a Hammer Award, generally given only to teams of federal employees who make significant contributions to government reform.

Online procurement systems create further opportunities for cost savings by automatically gathering the management information needed to be informed purchasers. With the right information, purchasers can look at usage and ask why a particular office is spending more on pencils, for example, than one further down the corridor, or whether a department really needs a dozen different brands of pencil. Armed with this information, departments can reduce the number of appropriate suppliers and reap the benefits of bulk buying.

For smaller government agencies and local authorities, which traditionally lack buying clout and don't have the time to go looking around for the best deal, the internet allows them to pool resources and set up online intermediaries that can negotiate volume discounts. Los Angeles-based ECitydeals facilitates transactions between hundreds of US city governments and private companies, and enables cities to purchase goods and services, post competitive public works bids, trade taxes with other cities, and advertise job opportunities. It generates its revenue through transaction fees, advertising and sponsorships, economic development services, and consulting. In the UK, 12 hospital trusts use an electronic requisition and purchase order system called Supply Stream, developed by IBM and the National Health Service (NHS), with another 70 hospitals operating a limited version of the system. The system interfaces with a trust's existing financial system and automatically converts requisitions to purchase orders. IBM offers Supply Stream as a managed service that can be accessed through the NHS intranet so a hospital does not require any additional IT investment to use it.

Recognizing that an organization's ability to make savings could be severely curtailed by a supplier's lack of investment in e-commerce, Supply Stream will load a company's product details on to a hospital trust's online catalog if the company can't provide the information digitally itself. The hospital purchaser can then print out an order form and send it in by fax. By no means an ideal situation, this nevertheless sends suppliers a clear message to get connected without precluding them from the marketplace.

As in the private sector, governments are also getting excited about the possible benefits of online reverse auctions, where sellers bid down against one another for specific orders. The Postal Service was the first US public agency to conduct a reverse auction, receiving bids for supplies of pre-stamped envelopes, fuel, and leased truck trailers. FreeMarkets, a pioneer in business-to-business online auctions, "hosted" the auctions from its headquarters in Pittsburgh, while companies from across the country submitted their bids over the web. Post Office officials remained passive participants, watching the action of steadily dropping prices on their computer screens at headquarters in Washington DC.

Auctions present a major departure from the standard public procurement process in which contracts are awarded on the basis of sealed envelopes and companies have only one chance to make a winning bid. With online auctions, bidders typically make several submissions over the course of an hour or two. However, the problem with auctions is that they are driven almost solely by price and are therefore inconsistent with many government policies on source selection based on best value. To address this concern, the US Army's Communications-Electronics Command has tested online procurement software that selects the seller with the lowest price, and then searches the web for more information about the supplier and performs a value analysis of the company, its prices, its performance, and compliance with previous contractual agreements.

While e-procurement undoubtedly makes government purchasing more efficient, there are concerns that a reduction in the overall number of government suppliers could lead to less choice and competition in the long run. Small businesses in particular fear that e-commerce could leave them out of the running for government contracts. To level the playing field, the US federal government has launched a SmallBizMall.gov site to give small firms a place where they can fulfill online orders. It provides a central location for government purchasers to find small business vendors, compare their prices, and receive quantity discounts, and where online account management and personalized accounts can be supplied.

COMBINING INNOVATION WITH VALUES

The procurement of information technology and information services is one of government's biggest headaches. Because day-to-day computer needs vary dramatically from one year to the next, it is difficult to determine how much of an IT budget can be channeled into projects such as developing portals or online services. Organizations often have no idea how much money they spend on computer maintenance and desktop management. Outsourcing such relatively routine IT tasks can provide a more predictable and accurate accounting of costs, giving agencies more control over their IT budgets.

By signing a deal with Wang for the management of 1,600 workstation seats, the US Treasury Department was able to draw on a staff of contractors devoted to everyday IT maintenance issues, while freeing internal IT staff to work on mission-critical projects that had a greater direct impact on its public and financial institution customers. The Treasury still has to spend new money to upgrade its seat-managed technology, but it knows ahead of time when and how much will have to be allocated.

Seat-management contracts usually cover all an organization's desktop computers and related software, hardware, network services, maintenance, upgrades, helpdesk, training, and consultancy. And increasingly, under the application service provider (ASP) outsourcing model, an external vendor will deploy, host, and manage enterprise applications over a private network or the internet. The ASP owns all the equipment and software, while the government agency essentially rents the system, paying per hit, per user, or per month for such services as human resource management, security management, and payroll and accounting. The Florida Department of Motor Vehicles, for example, uses an ASP to process and store its vehicle registration documents.

For an ASP or seat-management contract, an agency defines the level of service it needs to support its users and missions, while the contractor proposes the level of technology needed to meet the request. A tightly defined service-level agreement usually includes financial incentives to guarantee network performance and availability, user access speeds, and desired response times for helpdesk support. In the UK, a consortium led by ICL took over total operational responsibility for HM

Customs and Excise's desktop, telephony, and data network for 24,000 staff. At the same time, the consortium was given the job of implementing and managing an entirely new state-of-the-art secure IT and telecommunications infrastructure, ensuring a smooth transition from the old to the new systems.

For the past decade, the British government has routinely awarded major contract work under its private finance initiative (PFI), in which departments and agencies move away from being the owners and operators of assets to become purchasers of services from the private sector. The contractor is given responsibility for the design, build, finance, and operation of the assets required by the public-sector client, becoming a long-term provider of services rather than simply an upfront asset builder. This means that increasingly the British government no longer builds roads, it purchases miles of maintained highway. It no longer builds prisons, it buys custodial services. And it no longer buys computers and software, it pays for managed IT services.

In most private finance deals the underlying asset outlasts the contract, but when IT is involved the contract tends to outlast the asset. The average length of an IT contract is seven to ten years, during which there is normally allowance for at least one "technology refresh." Because technology changes so quickly and it is expensive to stay current, the UK government likes privately financed IT projects. Much of the risk is transferred to the private sector (for which the government pays through higher service charges) and PFI suppliers only start to receive their service payments when the flow of services actually begins. Continued payment depends on meeting performance criteria, so risk and reward go hand in hand.

PFI procurement is only practicable where there are suppliers able to deliver the required service and willing to accept sufficient risk transfer. While the level of interest among those in the computer industry is generally high and the market is developing strongly, the initiative has controversially allowed one company—Electronic Data Systems (EDS)— to become a dominant player in the British government marketplace.

Largely through its government contracts, this US firm has expanded its UK operations to more than 13,000 employees at over 140 locations throughout the country. The company has multiyear, multimillion outsourcing contracts with the Inland Revenue, Employment Service, Health Service, and Prison Service, among others. In September 2000, it was awarded a 10-year, £200 million contract to run the Department of Social Security's entire IT operation, including managing relationships with the department's other IT suppliers. Under the deal, some 1,550 government staff automatically become employees of EDS or one of its consortium partners, IBM and PricewaterhouseCoopers.

A fully outsourced IT environment frequently raises political issues, can be difficult and painful to implement, and doesn't always save government money. While outsourcing should be a flexible concept, there are often problems aligning policies and technology. Confronted with such issues, many government organizations have been slow to take a leap of faith. When the GSA launched a seat-management program in 1998, selecting eight vendors to compete for task orders from individual agencies, officials hoped that the concept would save money, provide more information about an agency's systems, and improve information sharing. All systems were to use standard software, freeing federal IT workers from the mundane and time-consuming task of managing the daily upkeep of networks. Two years on, only 15 percent of US federal government IT managers had plans to outsource their desktops, against 37 percent who had ruled it out; the rest were still undecided. Some managers feared that a single "cookie-cutter" contract would not be able to meet their diverse IT needs, while others did not want to relinquish control of their networks.

Often accused of only wanting to skim the cream, outsourcers are falling out of favor. "Insourcing"—the decision to bring projects back in-house—is increasingly being required to pick up the slack when outsourced IT projects are not completed on time or on budget, and are canceled before being finished. By their nature, outsourcing contracts need to be specific: the vendor needs to be made aware of performance requirements such as how success is measured, timetables, and the consequences of a failed project. In-house projects don't require as many formalities and instructions don't usually have to be written down or explained.

As they get started in e-business, and as they look to build and manage portals and develop online services, government organizations will want to weigh their options in order to maintain the flexibility of in-house projects while achieving the efficiencies that the private sector can deliver. Many governments are looking at ways to rise above the political dogma of the past when the right insisted that the private sector should provide services and the left insisted that this was the responsibility of the state. The governments of New Zealand, Singapore, and Denmark have each established something called a "domain partnership" with IBM, which seeks to establish areas of common knowledge or interest spanning different projects that require the involvement of industry. Integrated public–private project teams deliver the project while central government staff monitor and determine priorities.

The British government is also looking to foster new types of relationships with the private sector by folding its private finance initiative into a wider public private partnership (PPP) program, which includes joint ventures where the costs of a project are not met entirely through charges to the end user but are subsidized from public funds. In many cases the government subsidy is to secure wider social benefits, such as economic regeneration, which are not reflected in project cash flows. The subsidy can take a number of forms, but the government is limited to a contribution toward asset development and operational control rests with the private sector.

As new procurement models continue to emerge, it is clear that the greatest innovations in the e-gov era will come through new kinds of partnership that remove the dividing line between the public and private sectors in a way that outsourcing in the 1980s and 1990s did not. The links between government and business aren't just about the administration buying pencils from business; they are about both parties finding new ways to work together to deliver the e-government vision. While "partnership" is a vague term used to cover all sorts of business relationships, the primary idea is a contractual arrangement where each brings something to the table, where private-sector enterprise and innovation are combined with public-sector experience and values, and where there is a shared approach to the provision of services and to the risks and rewards involved. The experiences of many who have so far embarked on the e-gov journey show that a private-sector partner can help their organization be more flexible and innovative, areas where the public sector is traditionally weak. If a private company working under contract to another private company found a better way to carry out the work, the two firms would simply agree to modify their contract and get on with the job. But in the public sector, companies are traditionally tied to the word and nature of the contract. Partnering can get around this problem.

BREAKING WITH TRADITION, PALATABLY

The states of Pennsylvania and Washington are two of America's e-gov pioneers. Both provide all the online and transactional services one would expect to find on a leading-edge government portal: citizens and businesses can pay taxes online, order birth certificates, renew vehicle licenses, enroll their children in school, locate unclaimed property, reserve campsites, buy fishing licenses, read legislative decisions and state government news, access lottery pages, and so on. Yet in terms of how the two states got to where they are now, each has a different story to tell.

The Pennsylvania government homepage, the URL for which nobody can ever forget because it's stamped on all state license plates, has recorded more than one billion hits since its inception in 1995. Over the years, it has kept on adding new features and expanding what it offers. Pages are continually updated to improve their appearance and user-friendliness, and technologies such as video webcasts and chat rooms have been used to make government events more accessible. In October

2000, to make online services even easier to find and use with the fewest possible mouse clicks, the state launched a new portal called PAPowerPort. This includes a power-search function for users to find information by typing keywords, an online blue-pages listing of all state government officials and a calendar of state government events, and a facility that lets users customize the site to their specific interest areas. PAPowerPort was a new-flavor government portal to replace its previous "plain vanilla" home page. To ensure that the new flavor wasn't rocky road, the state entered into a partnership deal with Microsoft, which provided, at no cost to the government, a minimum of $100,000 worth of consulting services as well as value-added services so that citizens could check the weather, stock quotes and news (via MSNBC), open email accounts (via Microsoft Hotmail), design simple web pages and even manage their finances online. Microsoft hopes to recoup its investment through development work tied to the portal. For example, businesses participating in the portal's PA Small BizNet pay a subscription fee, as do local governments that ask for assistance in developing their websites. (At the time of PAPowerPort's launch, only 148 of Pennsylvania's 2,565 municipalities had a web presence.)

Pennsylvania's philosophy is to spur e-commerce in the state by making basic services freely and widely available. If a business wants to get on the web, the government will help. Yet many Pennsylvania businesses have complained that the state is duplicating services already offered by the private sector and competing against the very people it purports to want to help. Further objections have been raised over what some see as giving away to Microsoft the best consumer marketing platform in the state. The government website receives 95 million hits a month from more than half a million Pennsylvanians; links from such a high-traffic website usually cost a small fortune. "Content is not provided to create marketing opportunities for select big businesses, any more than the state capitol was built to place billboards in downtown Harrisburg, or legislation is printed to include advertising aimed at lobbyists and legislators," says Wayne Kessler, a local internet entrepreneur and adjunct fellow of the Commonwealth Foundation of Pennsylvania, a nonpartisan public-policy thinktank.

Meanwhile, Microsoft's home state of Washington was the first to offer citizens single-site access to every one of its agencies when it launched Access Washington in 1998. This portal focuses entirely on the provision of traditional public services and does not offer added-value features like email or web page design. There are no links to private-sector websites other than to some educational sites for children, lodging associations on the tourism page, and the state's chambers of commerce and trade alliances on the business page. The portal uses the same under-lying technologies as PAPowerPort but was implemented by the govern-ment itself, with the private sector's contribution limited to web design and maintenance. Washington's philosophy is that the people have entrusted the government to deliver certain services and that responsi-bility doesn't go away just because those services are being delivered online. If the government doesn't know how to do something, then it had better figure it out.

The problem that most governments face is a lack of in-house expertise to undertake major e-gov initiatives. Not many jurisdictions have Washington state's luxury of being able to draw on a large, techni-cally skilled workforce. Government e-business requires systems integra-tion skills and people who can develop middleware to link together different legacy systems to the open standards of the internet. Those who are recruited and trained to do this kind of work are quickly snapped up by the higher-paying, higher-flying private sector. Project-management skills are also beyond the level of smaller agencies and local authorities. So as governments come under pressure to meet the digital expectations of their citizens, private high-tech companies will increasingly be called in to implement solutions quickly, regardless of whether they're seen as a necessary evil or a great opportunity.

Not so long ago large corporations, like government today, did all their jobs in-house, with a hierarchy of workers assigned whatever tasks were needed to make the company's product. Now companies enter into joint ventures or subcontract so much of their work that computer hardware manufacturer Dell claims if it did everything in-house it would have to hire 80,000 people to achieve the same productivity it currently gets out of 15,000. "Just as businesses are being forced to rethink traditional practices and assumptions because of e-commerce, governments must do the same," said Pennsylvania Governor Tom Ridge, at his state budget address in February 2000, when he announced PAPowerPort.

Doing e-business puts new and different kinds of strains on government. Public-sector websites are a favorite target for hackers; the infamous Love Bug hit government particularly hard. More innocently, there are power outages that can take down a web server and perhaps a department's website with it, or a transaction might be lost because of a tenuous connection to the back-office platform. Often it's simply easier if all these things are somebody else's problem so public employees can get on with their jobs and the government as a whole won't have to be distracted from its political agenda. The main attraction of partnering with one of the big IT heavyweights—a software giant, a systems integrator, an IT services company, or a big five accountancy-cum-consultancy—is that they all have battalions of technicians and consultants. If something breaks, they'll always have somebody who can fix it. It's difficult to challenge IBM's claim that it is the best company for connecting legacy systems, because it was IBM that developed the legacy systems in the first place. Nobody understands information technology better than those who make and sell it.

Major industry players offer complete packages of consulting, web development, systems integration, systems architecture, code development, business process reengineering, enterprise resource planning—whatever the customer needs and wants. Yet the sheer size of these companies often means that they cannot help but supply government with the same e-business "solution" they originally developed for a large retailer or a bank. That's like selling baseball gloves to a soccer club—government is a whole different ballgame. And when IT companies dispatch their government industry manager (an oxymoron of a job title if ever there was one) to address a public-sector audience, all too often they dig into their bank of PowerPoint slides and simply change the word "company" to "organization" and hope everyone will swallow the glib talk about profit margins and competition.

When doing business overseas, large American IT companies (and most large IT companies are American) often don't appreciate the need to comply with local cultures and many tend to underestimate the market fragmentation on other continents. They are like former US Secretary of State Henry Kissinger, who once infamously asked: "If I want to call Europe, who do I call?" Many US companies decide to enter the "European market" without realizing that each European government is completely different. Besides the question of language, it is not obvious to many, for example, that the French government prefers dealing with companies that have already established themselves in the country and have been endorsed by a leading (usually nationalized) French business. So it is not at all surprising that major software firms report only modest growth in Europe while their sales thrive in North America. Companies that have been able to balance and grow their revenue abroad recognize the need to reshape how they do business and how they build products, for both public-sector and specific national markets. EDS has done well in the UK, for example, because rather than cutting and pasting solutions it had developed stateside, it was able to grasp and embrace the thinking behind the British government's private finance initiative. In this way, EDS is much like McDonald's when it studies local tastes for tomato sauce and tailors the flavor of its ketchup to national palates.

A TWO-WAY STREET

Even when an IT company does make its products and services more palatable, there is still a perception in government that, while the public sector enters into a partnership deal to learn from the partnering company, the private sector sees it as just another form of outsourcing and is out to get the most money possible for the least amount of effort. The private sector doesn't actually believe it could possibly learn anything from the public sector. However, the public sector can be impressively decisive and effective when there's a fire or a plane crash or a natural disaster of some sort. The police, emergency services, health service, military, and even parliament all rally around, take quick action, and coordinate efforts to minimize damage and relieve human suffering. Private companies, on the other hand, usually have difficulty handling an emergency, often can't cope and go bust. Nevertheless, few firms would think of approaching the public sector to learn something about crisis management.

A lack of understanding between what a public-sector organization needs and what a private-sector partner can offer is not uncommon. Many agencies have had experiences similar to the Office of the Inspector General in the US Department of Housing and Urban Development (HUD), which, in October 1999, suspended implementation of an automated workflow application three months into its contract with DynCorp. The technology was relatively simple, an off-the-shelf workflow application and a virtual private network that would permit the department's 700 auditors to file documents and reports from anywhere in the country. But there were communication problems from the outset and the agency wasn't able to develop a sufficient level of trust with its private-sector partner. HUD staff felt they had little input into the system that DynCorp was planning to introduce and the solution was accepted by management with little discussion.

It wasn't until after the implementation was suspended that the department and DynCorp started talking about requirements and how the system related to the department's core business. After both sides brought in their most senior management, including the inspector general of HUD and the president of DynCorp, the two partners were better able to cut through each other's fear and end the bickering. To keep the project alive, the department formed a dedicated team of senior personnel from its IT, operations, security, and telecommunications staffs to meet weekly with DynCorp to check on issues involving the contract. Both sides also worked together on a daily basis to straighten out technical and cultural issues before problems arose. Part of the increased communication included having the DynCorp team listen to suggestions from HUD employees, who, because of their experience, often thought of things the contractor might have missed. In one case, HUD staff members pointed out to DynCorp that some of its housing projects did not have the digital bandwidth connection required to dial into the virtual private network.

DynCorp learned quickly that a successful partnership needs to be a two-way street, otherwise the public-sector partner is put off by the company's arrogance. The HUD managers learned the need to put forward promises to their employees to convince them that their jobs were safe and that, in fact, they would be performing duties more in line with the department's mission. Many government workers take a cynical view of the real motives behind public–private partnerships, and politicians driven by ideology, who partner for partnership's sake or privatize for privatization's sake, tend to damage the morale and ethos of a civil service. They can even shake public confidence in a particular service.

It has to be accepted that some government projects will fail. It's a private-sector adage that if every initiative succeeds, you haven't taken enough risks. So governments can't be expected to take risks if they're pounced on every time something goes wrong. It would be useful if more best-practice case studies of successful public–private partnerships were published, as only the screwups seem to attract attention. But to minimize failures, both government and business must be prepared to admit that it's not always best to work in partnership—sometimes it's better to keep services in-house and sometimes it's better to contract them out entirely. One local council IT manager expressed a wish for some kind of cheap-to-administer pregnancy-testing kit to determine if he had a suitable partnership case, but the best advice is to be pragmatic, not dogmatic, about how public services should be provided. Bill Clinton and Tony Blair call it the third way; most people call it keeping an open mind.

DOT-COM MEETS DOT-GOV

One thing governments might want to keep an open mind about when putting services online is the benefits of partnering with a startup of the kind that fueled the dot-com mania. While the big IT companies were preoccupied with making sure their public-sector customers were Y2K compliant (a huge issue in government), many of the small internet startups were able to use their absence of pre-millennium baggage to steal a march and enter the public-sector market, which might have otherwise been closed to them. These companies tend to be less contemptuous of government and are often led by people who believe strongly in open access to government information or in citizen-centric public services. They might even be patriotic and want to give something back to their country. For example Eric Brewer, a University of California computer scientist and founder of the search engine company Inktomi, offered to build the US federal FirstGov portal free of charge, as "a gift to the American people," without even a link to the Inktomi website.

Those running startups are good at understanding government because it is often where they've cut their teeth, or because they are former public officials themselves. One such person is Stephen Goldsmith, who as mayor of Indianapolis in 1996 set out a vision to allow citizens to do all their business with the city without setting foot in city hall and launched IndyGov, one of the earliest public-sector websites. In December 1999, he resigned from public office and, with a few other former city officials, set up eGov Solutions, a technology and consulting company to help other local, county, and state governments create online services. He says: "A number of folks nationwide began calling and asking for our advice, so we decided to roll the dice."

Goldsmith and his company face increasing competition from other dice rollers who are finding a niche market in government. New York's govWorks has developed a technology platform that lets people pay taxes, fines, and water bills, as well as apply for permits and licenses. It sells these applications directly to local and state governments, collecting either a standard licensing fee, transaction fees, or a percentage of the savings the organization realizes from the system. Other firms such as ezgov.com and the National Information Consortium (NIC) are also developing portals, transaction processing tools, and web interfaces that sit on top of legacy databases and networks. There are even more specialized web companies such as NetClerk, which lets contractors and building professionals apply for government permits online. In Europe, the Swedish portal developer Linq started working for the city of Gothenburg, while Austria's Fabasoft grew up in Vienna's *Rathaus*.

These fast-growing companies are usually able to work more quickly than the large computer blue chips because they don't have to pull together so many disparate pieces, and being plugged into Silicon Valley venture capital means they can approach government with a specific idea and turn it into a fully fledged business. The British e-government strategy proposes that there be no exclusive contracts and that instead any number of private companies and voluntary organizations be given a license to provide an online public service. This flexible approach provides dot-coms and others with a great opportunity. One can almost picture a computer geek and a garage mechanic getting together, backed by venture capital, setting up my-vehicle.com as a one-stop online shop for motorists, offering vehicle registration, license renewal, car insurance, roadside assistance, safety tests, tune-ups, and numerous other car-related services that currently involve separate transactions with different private and public-sector organizations.

Most IT partnerships contain a mixture of equipment and services, and it is often difficult to determine which procurement regulations need to be applied. While the purchase or rental of equipment is generally considered to be a supplies contract, special considerations may apply to IT contracts if services are also included. Contracts for off-the-shelf software may be considered supplies, while a bespoke development is considered services. Governments need to review their procurement rules to allow greater flexibility for partnerships and create a climate where innovation can flourish. Some governments are starting to allow "competitive negotiated" procedures to enter into partnerships and the European Commission is intending to introduce a "competitive dialogue" provision to its procurement rules. Whatever that means exactly, it is a recognition that making companies compete directly for contracts with definitive specifications doesn't always bring out technological innovation.

Thorny issues such as public accountability and transparency need to be addressed, but given the pace of technological change, it's perhaps best for e-gov partnerships to make the rules up as they go along—even the rules themselves can be established in partnership. The services provider govWorks has started an alliance to establish a code of conduct for the e-government industry to ensure public trust and to encourage fair business practices. The code has five main points:

➤ Adopt strict consumer-privacy policies that prohibit the improper use and resale of consumer data to third parties.

➤ Disclose all fees and other costs associated with e-government services.

➤ Accurately represent the number and scope of e-government products and services offered.

➤ Accurately represent corporate structures and affiliate relationships that may affect vendor selection.

➤ Help bridge the digital divide and ensure universal access.

This seems like a more sensible approach than piling on too many complicated, bureaucratic directives that discourage innovation and, in any event, do not necessarily prevent abuse and stop people from messing things up. The majority of people—public and private sector—are responsible and ethical. So rather than laying down rules for a tiny minority of potential troublemakers, a less visible control can be exercised through strong leadership, teamwork, and subtle culture changes such as rewarding innovation. Rather than instilling a fear of punishment in people, it's better to be clear about the expectations of both partners and have mutually derived, understandable, and realistic goals.

Partnerships can help a government get online sooner and cheaper, even at "no cost" if the administration is willing to give the contractor revenue opportunities such as advertising or service subscriptions. Whether such tradeoffs are a better deal for the government or the company is a moot point (they are usually touted as win–win situations), but it's important to note that the success of partnerships must be measured on best value rather than price, with an emphasis on outcomes rather than ownership. Ultimately, both public and private sectors will be judged on the same standards by citizens/consumers who don't care who's providing a service so long as it's good. The two sectors need each other, to ensure that people consistently receive the better-quality and more dependable services they demand.

3 Getting from A to A: Administration to Administration

HORIZONTALLY CHALLENGED

Encouraging the public and private sectors to work together is one thing, but trying to get two government departments to sit down and cooperate is another matter entirely. Interdepartmental politics means that civil servants are employed to protect their minister's (and therefore their own) interests, which often requires running down other departments. Counterproductive disputes between federal and state or central and local levels of government simmer constantly. Government employees work in a culture where information is considered an asset best kept to oneself. Every public-sector organization has its own work methods, business processes, rules, and procedures. Mass-produced, one-size-fits-all public services are delivered uniformly through vertical and rigid "silos" or "stovepipes," provided for the sake of administrative ease rather than public convenience—take as evidence the opening times and locations of public offices, the demands that departments make on citizens, and the help they do and do not provide.

This all too familiar model of government was designed for post-Depression and postwar industrial society when everybody had the same basic requirements for public education, healthcare, housing, social security, power stations, roads, and railways. Vertical departments were created to oversee every task and they each got on with their jobs. There was no need to collaborate. Compared to the overt patronage of earlier times, when all strings were pulled by some cigar-chomping larger-than-life politician, the rise of the professional civil service came as a welcome relief. Every citizen was a number, but at least the system was fair.

Society has changed. Today's communities are multicultural, multiracial, and more conscious of age, religion, gender, and subcultures than ever before. Social problems are complex and cross-cutting and people's needs no longer fit neatly into departmental compartments. But still governments respond to new challenges by putting in more procedures and more stovepipes, to the point where agencies today find themselves floating in a vast sea of public and private, semi-public and semi-private organizations, all with ever-increasing staff levels, duplication, and overlapping responsibilities. As a result, a shopkeeper might have to entertain a dozen public inspectors during the course of a year and fill out two dozen or more forms. An at-risk child from a dysfunctional family might receive "help" from four or five public officials, from the school guidance counselor to the social worker to the parole officer. Well-intended policies have unforeseen consequences: a new performance management regime in schools might lead to a rise in the expulsion of difficult pupils, which in turn sparks an increase in teenage crime and substance abuse. Governments look at each as separate issues, to be dealt with by the appropriate education, criminal justice, social service, or health authority. Incapable of working together to address either the big picture or an individual's specific situation, and working with obsolete systems and methods, civil servants are left exposed to ridicule and accusations of incompetence and inefficiency.

Ultimately, governments will have to obliterate their vertical, industrial-age organizational structures and instead present themselves horizontally, with public services based on citizens' life events, as discussed in Chapter 1. This is already occurring to a limited extent: there might be an office for small business or a social exclusion unit. These are small organizations relative to their importance and the big vertical ministries still call the shots, but efforts to streamline processes and alleviate duplication and inconsistencies will force governments to think beyond internal organizational issues and look at problems from the point of view of overall information flows. The wide availability of online data is pushing government departments to cooperate more along value chains and provide linked service packages. In time, this will encourage them to match their internal procedures, allowing for even greater collaboration and joint ventures between departments, between different levels of government, and between the public and private sectors. In Italy, the Automobile Club collects road taxes and manages the auto registry on behalf of the government and it, in turn, has a joint venture with the Post Office, so motorists can obtain information and pay road tax by accessing the public automobile registry through post office terminals or over the internet. This kind of flexibility and innovation should at least join a few silos together, if it doesn't knock them down.

There are hundreds of reasons for the going having been slow so far. Some bureaucrats don't want to give up their petty kingdoms, others simply fear change. The way government budgets are negotiated department by department means that organizations devote their efforts to maximizing their internal funding rather than considering how they can deliver actual results. The system encourages mediocrity and an aversion to risk, with both government staff and ministers operating in an environment where the rewards for success are limited and the penalties for failure rare but harsh when they are handed out. Citizens can express dissatisfaction through the ballot box, but this is a blunt instrument. Removing a government because you're tired of standing in line doesn't address the underlying reasons for the service being bad.

Computer systems have been part of the problem because they were never built to provide a holistic view of data, knowledge, and resources across an administration. When bureaucracies first started to apply information technology to their work, their stovepipe procedures and processes were simply encoded into the software. Huge, unwieldy mainframes cemented the old ways of working and even added to the bureaucracy, since more people were needed to implement, maintain, and operate the complex systems. Information has become inaccessible, locked away in thousands of disparate departmental systems. Every government agency has its own IT department, with its own policies, strategies, and standard computer configurations. And standards within departments often go unenforced. People left to their own devices follow their individualistic instincts and make unauthorized IT purchases or, to keep staff happy, an IT manager will relax adherence to a standard so long as the extra cost comes from the user's budget. But an employee who uses a spreadsheet, for example, that's different from the department standard will require special training and support. Once a standard is breached, there are on-going and unrecorded expenses. It's as if the national Department of Transport decided to post highway signs in kilometers while the local authority signposted local streets in miles, and other cities and regions in the country used a mixture of other measurements. There'd be chaos on the roads.

Information technology should serve to unify rather than disconnect government's organizational structures. Productivity tools should function with business applications, allowing employees to work in a predictable, consistent manner. People should be able to move smoothly between working on a document, surfing the web, and accessing databases on a variety of back-end machines. If government's stovepipe applications are allowed to permeate the online world, people will need multiple logins and passwords to access transactional services on different websites, none of which will have a common look and feel. And there can be no high-level portals. Take a small country like the Netherlands, with its 36,000 different public-sector databases. If these can't converge and connect, e-government there will be a non-starter.

WEB ENABLE EVERYTHING

Connecting disparate computer systems isn't easy. Normally, an application program interface such as an electronic data interchange (EDI) system is required to access and download data from an incompatible computer. This entails custom programming every time two systems need to connect, which means painstaking mapping of one field on to another and skills that take time to master. Then the interface has to be altered again when data in one system changes. Consequently, programmers spend all their time developing interfaces between applications and ensuring that they function properly rather than working to improve the systems themselves. Or they just chuck the whole thing away, especially if it wasn't Y2K compliant anyway, and buy something new. But ripping and replacing gets expensive.

Take Beaumont Hospital in Dublin, Ireland, which faced a familiar problem: how to connect 15 different systems on a limited budget. The IT department programmed four linkages, but it became clear that it would have to quintuple the number of support staff if the exercise was to be repeated 11 more times.

As countless information-age visionaries have said, the internet changes everything. For IT departments, this means they no longer have to spend all their time and money interfacing and replacing legacy systems. Now aging but still functioning mission-critical applications can be "web enabled." A graphical user interface can be slapped on the front end and be made more widely accessible to government employees over an intranet, to external partners over an extranet, and to citizens over the internet. Governments should web enable and connect everything they have, leaving no computer to stand alone. Even the most technologically advanced program will fail to deliver if it is operating in a vacuum, if the data is isolated and can't be leveraged across a department or across government.

Beaumont Hospital understood this. Its 11 remaining disparate systems—including the hospital information system, renal and diabetic management systems, clinical emergency department system, and a new laboratory information system—were eventually all linked to a single server using an interface engine that allowed the connection of a limitless number of dissimilar hardware and software systems.

To ensure a coordinated approach to system integration, governments need to be "net ready." This involves publishing a comprehensive e-government plan that adopts commercial open internet standards across the board. There should be a manageable schedule and it should have top-down support from ministers and senior management. Unlike in the past when each department would set its own IT priorities, an e-government plan needs to be a corporate strategy, covering all of government's technological infrastructure, all online applications, and all governing policies. Developing and implementing a government-wide strategy will require collaboration among agencies, since they are best placed to determine what is and isn't feasible from a user's perspective, and among the IT industry, since it is best placed to determine what is and isn't feasible from a technical perspective.

Singapore is one of very few national governments to have taken an integrated and coherent approach from day one, with the launch in 1981 of a national IT plan. The Infocomm Development Authority (IDA), responsible for spearheading and managing all government-wide IT initiatives, has been careful to evolve the program and exploit new technologies as they become available. Its Government Information Infrastructure (GovII), which supports the e-Citizen Center portal, is a multilayered IT platform that links every public-sector agency and facilitates communication throughout the civil service with a suite of internet applications including smart cards, email, and a government intranet.

SOUNDS TECHNICAL, AND IT IS

Extensible Markup Language (XML) is emerging as the natural extension of the internet. It is a standard ratified by the World Wide Web Consortium (W3C) to provide a mechanism for representing online text data from otherwise incompatible systems. This web-based authoring language is expected to become the primary data-interchange method for all systems, because it can be applied to just about any application and isn't limited to databases. Users can create and share documents running on any local or wide area network, helping governments to integrate applications on their mix of legacy mainframes, client server, and web-based systems. With XML, whenever a computer application receives a file, it includes codes that describe what the data actually means—whether it's a person's name, an address, a file number, or whatever—and how it can be exchanged between servers and clients via a network. XML together with XSL (Extensible Stylesheet Language), a scripting language used to transform and display XML documents, is much more adaptable than HTML and is considered an interoperability standard because of the language's self-describing nature and platform neutrality.

Sure, it's technical, but any programmer can become proficient in XML in a matter of hours. Where it takes six months to implement an EDI interface at a cost running into six figures, a comparable XML system can be implemented in weeks for a few thousand. It is the key to enabling online transactions and transferring large amounts of information without the laborious task of converting data structures. Microsoft, IBM, Oracle, and a raft of smaller software firms have all moved quickly to incorporate XML support in their products. Public administrations also see XML's potential and are testing the water, perhaps a little too cautiously, by including it in pilot projects and requests for proposals.

The British government dived in at the deep end. Its first-ever corporate IT strategy, the e-Government Interoperability Framework published in August 2000, stated that XML was to be the core standard for data integration for all interactions with different government departments, the wider public sector, foreign governments, businesses, and citizens. A public–private forum called the UK GovTalk Group, led by the Cabinet Office, was set up to drive and coordinate interoperability efforts throughout the public sector. It commissions working groups to develop XML description codes, or "data schemas," for specific government projects such as its UK Online portal. Approved schemas are published on the web for use on other public-sector projects.

UK GovTalk also tracks international XML developments through affiliations with W3C and international organizations such as the United

Nations body for Trade Facilitation and Electronic Business (UN/CEFACT), the Organization for the Advancement of Structured Information Standards (OASIS), and the Electronic Government Framework (EGF). UN/CEFACT and OASIS joined forces in 1999 to establish the Electronic Business XML Working Group to standardize XML business specifications. EGF was initiated by Microsoft in early 2000 to give industry and governments a global forum to share XML schemas and service specifications designed specifically for government. Both EGF and UK GovTalk were inspired by private industry's BizTalk initiative, which has launched XML schemas for a large number of commercial web-based transactions, especially in the area of procurement.

The shift to web-enabled government requires certain enabling technologies such as smart cards, digital signatures and certificates, electronic forms, and so forth. To support these, a reliable transaction infrastructure has to be built using leading-edge (but not bleeding-edge) commercial products. Most recent technology investments have focused on the back office of government, including enterprise resource planning (ERP) systems that group functions into cross-cutting categories like finance, human resources, procurement, and logistics. There are still some serious limitations to these technologies, however, the most obvious being that the vast majority are based on private-sector business processes that are not always applicable to the public sector. Even though the public sector already accounts for up to a quarter of their international customer base, ERP vendors such as SAP and PeopleSoft see e-government more as a future market opportunity since so many agencies still lack widespread desktop internet access. The need for cross-departmental communication and better access to applications and information will drive the more widespread adoption of ERP and, in anticipation, the vendors are starting to ship government-specific web-enabled versions of their software with modules for tax management, public–private partnerships, and so on. Once in place, ERP will provide the foundation for e-government transactions that need to interact with financial and HR systems, such as online permits, licenses, and procurement.

Some government agencies resist ERP because of its monolithic image (for that reason PeopleSoft has taken to calling it "best of breed enterprise applications"), but infrastructure and back-office software will remain a priority for most IT managers, who fear that otherwise they will pay the price later with server crashes and web service interruptions that could ultimately drive citizens offline. Nevertheless, IT departments are under heavy pressure to shift their focus to the front office of government, including citizen relationship management (CRM) applications to provide a single data source to answer all queries in one call to a call center, one visit to a one-stop shop, or one connection to a portal. For politicians and senior managers trying to deliver an e-gov vision, there is a compelling need for quick results, so their emphasis is to get services online where people can see and use them. To them, ERP and XML are four-letter words—they want CRM.

The good news for everybody is that the front office doesn't have to wait until the back office is finished. ERP vendors are adding CRM components to their software so that rather than coming online in a big bang, the development of web-based services can be a work in progress. Simpler applications can be implemented earlier than those that take longer to plan and develop, such as services requiring electronic payments, encryption, and authentication.

The British government is typical of the incremental approach. It has partnered with a number of industry leaders on several demonstrator projects to test new services requiring connections between different departmental systems. The Intelligent Forms (I-Forms) project was piloted in 1999 for the 10,000 people a week in the UK who start their own business. Previously, those registering for self-employment had to contact three different departments and fill in six different forms. This was replaced by a single online transaction, with the information replicated to each of the three departments in question: the Inland Revenue, the Contributions Agency, and Customs and Excise. When the I-Forms model was determined to be applicable to other paper forms and processes, the government looked at integrating services based on other life-event scenarios, including "having a baby," "going away," and "dealing with crime."

A "moving home" pilot demonstrated how citizens could notify government of a change of address. When the trial began, the TV Licensing Authority was the only agency that allowed people to use email or a website to inform it of a change of address. Others required notification in writing or by completing a form, usually a couple of weeks in advance. A mapping exercise of department practice in gathering information showed that there were 56 different statutes and 186 different regulations dealing with the simple matter of changing an address. About 2.5 million Britons move house each year, resulting in more than 20 million change-of-address notifications to government. In other words, people usually have to tell at least eight different agencies that they've moved. This could include contacting the tax office, the benefits agency for child allowance, the motor vehicle agency for their driver's license, and the Post Office to forward the mail.

The municipality is usually the first point of government contact, to sort out local taxes or to inquire about schools in the area, although people's immediate concern is to make utilities and banks aware of their move. It would make sense to have online change-of-address forms linked to and from these organizations because, frankly, many people can't be bothered volunteering any kind of information to government (unless, of course, it's to receive financial benefits). An easy-to-use system that automatically informs a wide range of private and public-sector bodies of a change of address would be useful to everyone and so, by the end of 2001, all Britons will have the opportunity to take this one small step to change their address and make one giant leap for e-government.

COOPERATION NOT CONFRONTATION

Responsibility for an increasing number of costly public functions is today being transferred from central government to local, regional, and state levels, as a result of a general trend toward devolution as well as changes in policies in areas such as welfare reform. While standards are often still set at the center, most countries are finding that the tiers of government closest to the people make the best service providers. Towns and regions have many public access points—schools, libraries, leisure centers, municipal offices—just waiting to be wired up so government can provide effective integrated services.

However, for many local administrations, IT development is a recent phenomenon. In 1996, two-thirds of the 545 local councils in the Atlantic Pyrenees region of France didn't even own a single computer. By the end of 1999, through a program initiated by the central government's regional administration, 400 of these municipalities had connections to an extranet that enabled the introduction of mutual services in such areas as medical assistance, intermunicipality administration, staff recruitment, and intermunicipality technical and IT support. Says Laurent Dourrieu, general secretary of a group of municipalities in the region's Aspe Valley: "These tools represent a good way of making local administrations less intellectually secretive and more informative."

Users of public services tend not to differentiate between levels of government. A single mother on welfare might not know that her social benefits come from central government and her housing allowance comes from local government. Consumers couldn't care less that their sales tax goes to the state government while import duties go to the federal government. The internet can blur these distinctions and enable a cross-jurisdictional approach to service delivery, through combined-access portals. In Germany, the federal government works in partnership with the 16 *Länder* (state) governments to offer citizens a single filing of taxes online to both levels of government, and the federal Ministry of Health has joined the *Länder* and third parties such as health associations and insurance companies to set up a health information network that collects and provides health information to increase public awareness of health issues.

In Canada, the Nova Scotia Business Registry (NSBR) is a joint initiative of the federal government's Customs and Revenue Agency, the province of Nova Scotia's Department of Business and Consumer Services, and the provincial Workers Compensation Board. Accessed over the internet, the registry provides a single place for Nova Scotia businesses to handle registrations, licenses, and permits, and make payments without having to know which forms and procedures come from which level of government. Previously, each agency would assign businesses a different identification number, and often different numbers for different purposes. A company could end up with five or six identification numbers, which, besides being a nuisance for the companies, made it difficult for the agencies to share information. Now, the federal agency assigns each business a single identification number that the two provincial organizations also use. That consolidates processes and simplifies the enforcement of regulations across government.

NSBR has also become the repository for tombstone data such as mailing addresses and phone numbers of all Nova Scotia businesses. If a record is changed with one agency, the update is replicated to all the others. At the same time, sensitive information such as tax data is not shared and remains protected. The registry was established through the integration of existing hardware and software, including the provincial government's accounting systems.

The NSBR is linked to the technology infrastructure of Atlantic Canada On-Line (ACOL), a partnership between the four Canadian provinces of Nova Scotia, New Brunswick, Prince Edward Island, and Newfoundland, and a private-sector consortium led by Unisys. It provides web access and handles online payments for all four governments. Among the services is a personal property registry, which is used to detail property held as collateral in financial arrangements. The website directs citizens and businesses to the institution or individual holding a security document, eliminating the need to maintain paper documents manually within the registry. Previously, property information could only be accessed county by county through a personal visit to a registry office; the new system maintains a database across all four provinces. Such cooperation is unprecedented in Canada's often icy interprovincial politics, but it was done in response to demands expressed by the region's financial and legal communities.

Globalization and new world realities are also putting pressure on governments to create and join more and more supranational bodies, to which they inevitably cede some political or economic control. Franz-Reinhard Habbel, speaker of the Berlin-based German Towns and Municipalities Federation, boldly predicts: "In the virtual world, territorial boundaries will be a thing of the past. Completely new potentials for cooperation are being created that go beyond the boundaries of mere administration and overcome boundaries of responsibility."

The Schengen agreement, which abolished border checks within 13 European countries, is an unprecedented example of how different countries are learning to collaborate. In principle, there is now one uniform customs procedure for checking people and goods crossing in from countries outside the Schengen group. All persons are subject to an identity check with a data search conducted by the Schengen Information System (SIS), a network that gives police and consular agents access to data on specific individuals and lost or stolen vehicles and objects. Each member state supplies data from its national network and these are connected to the central SIS system in Strasbourg.

No two governments work the same way even though they perform largely the same tasks and share common problems. Each has its own culture, its own decision-making processes, its own timeframes, goals, and objectives. Nevertheless, governments today have to operate at many different levels, from local to global, and to do that successfully they must cooperate rather than confront each other. Aligning different traditions and priorities isn't always easy or possible, but once the steering committees are formed and the various parties start working together, they find synergies that, in the end, improve their services. A neutral third party, such as a private-sector partner, can often provide support and help find common ground. Internet technology can also help different governments and different levels of government get over potential antagonisms by giving them an effective means to communicate, share data, and provide integrated services across geographical, jurisdictional, and program boundaries.

THE WAY YOU'VE ALWAYS DONE IT ISN'T ALWAYS THE WAY TO DO IT

So the standards and policies are agreed, the technical infrastructure is in place, systems are connected to enable data sharing with other jurisdictions, internet applications are developed, services are ready to roll out on a new government-wide portal—and then a government employee who is suddenly expected to work with someone from another agency says, "It's not my job."

Cultural resistance is the greatest obstacle to integrated online public services. There will be employees who resent the intrusion of new technology in their daily routine and cling to old, familiar ways no matter how well processes are improved. There are employees who have a natural tendency to hoard information and look suspiciously on and discredit data that others have developed. To many, entering what they know into a computer system and passing it on to someone in another department is not only threatening, it's a pain in the neck. This way of thinking is difficult to overcome but it has to be if bureaucrats are to work for wider government objectives rather than narrower departmental ones. Staff at both the corporate and personal level need to be convinced that cyberspace is more than a new space to work in the same old way, and that the "way we have always done it" is no longer always the best way to do it.

This is a bit like getting all the countries of Europe to use the same currency: it makes economic sense but it will take time, there will be some technical challenges along the way, and many people will resist the change. Like the euro, people will need to see evidence of the merits of e-government and the value it can add to their daily lives. Or as Robert Mallett, US deputy secretary of commerce, says: "We need to show them how the internet can work for them and make their jobs easier, even while they are asleep at night, or asleep on the job."

The internet itself is promoting a new culture, one that thrives on and expects change. Online communication provides a sense of urgency, which should act as a catalyst for civil servants to face citizens' questions directly, provide answers, and treat them more like customers and less like an obligation. In delivering online services, government employees will have to embrace the internet culture or risk becoming irrelevant. Mallett suggests that those who refuse or can't adapt should be removed: not put out of a job, but redeployed to other tasks to make way for those who are willing to work collaboratively. General Sheikh Mohammed bin Rashid Al Maktoum, crown prince of Dubai in the United Arab Emirates, takes this notion a step further: public officials who fail to make the transition to online service delivery within 18 months will be fired.

Governments that can't so easily deploy fear tactics might instead try to appeal to greed, but even here they must proceed with caution. As part of a competition-based reform of every aspect of its operations, San Diego County in California introduced a management bonus scheme to motivate managers to move a reluctant bureaucracy. This provoked strong opposition from union leaders, received negative media coverage, and ended up undermining the morale of nonmanagers. The county's chief administrative officer later told staff that he did a poor job of explaining the program and misjudged the reaction of employees, the press, and the general public. The lesson learned was that what works in the private sector does not always work in the public sector. Government must not focus solely on senior management: it must reach out to all employees to encourage them to be creative and innovative and to think outside their boxes.

Civil servants aren't usually rewarded for considering the big picture; they should be. Performance pay systems should be introduced for both good work and as an incentive to accept change. There should be schemes to reward employees on a sliding-scale percentage for cost savings achieved as a result of their suggestions, and staff who have good ideas for improving services should also be recognized financially. Some administrations are starting to reward group performance and success sharing by using team bonuses or by linking pay, bonuses, and other rewards to performance or efficiency improvements. Some public-sector union leaders will still see these programs as a threat to their organization's survival and seek to undermine them, but it is important that somehow managers and staff begin working as a team.

To pave the way for a more modern workforce, governments also need to change recruitment and hiring practices. Those that are serious about putting the citizen at the center of their thinking will want a civil service more representative of the people they serve, so targets to eliminate the under-representation in government of women, ethnic minorities, and the disabled are required. Administrations need to make greater use of part-time and short-term contracts and more talent has to be brought in from outside the civil service. New search tactics using the internet should be used to solicit candidates and to make it easy for people to find out about and apply for government jobs.

If people can be trained to work in a single-silo way, then they can be trained to work for outcomes in partnership with others outside their own department or professional group. Although behavior cannot be changed overnight, governments can strive to become learning organizations, continually sharing experience and benchmarking themselves against the best in all sectors. Civil servants must be given opportunities to learn new skills throughout their careers. To be a public-sector IT manager today, for example, business acumen and project management and negotiation skills are as important as computing skills. Having an MBA is as important as having technical qualifications.

Some administrations are starting to introduce schemes to allow early promotion for those who show great potential. Some are increasing secondments to and from the private sector, the voluntary sector, other levels of government, and other governments. Those that want their employees to forget about departmental boundaries and bureaucracies are removing barriers to staff transfers between agencies by setting mobility targets for both senior and junior staff. They could also modernize their systems to track government managers and make their names available on the government intranet to agencies seeking to fill key positions. It used to be that people who changed jobs more than once or twice in a decade were derided as job hoppers, but employment mobility in the private sector is now so widespread that anyone who stays in the same job for 10 years is considered suspect. In this respect, most government employees are highly suspect.

Corporate-speak about the need for civil servants to be more professional and embrace greater flexibility in their work worries many who believe that, first and foremost, government employees should be dedicated to public service and public accountability, and that commitment is what motivates civil servants the most. There is no incompatibility here. Democracies still need a permanent, politically impartial civil service that acts with integrity and propriety, and where staff are hired on merit rather than allegiance. Opening up the civil service to new people and new ideas can build on these values. Government workers can be more businesslike without being more like business.

The biggest barriers to cultural change are emotional rather than rational. Fear, mistrust, turf protection, victimization, miscommunication, and preconceived notions can surface at any time and in a variety of ways. People affected by change aren't likely to come right out and say they fear they'll lose control of a project, or they're worried they'll lose their job, as that would be to admit their objections are emotional. So instead, they come forward with technical objections or requests for unnecessary feasibility studies, hoping to delay the project and wear down management's enthusiasm for change. Agencies must recognize from the start that there will be cultural barriers and plan in advance to deal with them.

The Nebraska Commission on Local Government Innovation and Restructuring was formed to act as a liaison between the state government and local authorities under pressure to modernize. The commission is staffed with trained mediators/facilitators who help public-sector employees on change projects communicate their perspectives clearly, identify and clarify issues, and reach agreements if possible. The mediator/facilitator is a neutral third party who controls process, not content, and has no authority to make a judgment or influence any decision.

Employees are more likely to buy into a project if they have an active role in the decision-making process. This requires listening to staff and enabling them to put forward ideas for improvement, and working closely with trade unions to achieve shared goals. While many agencies hold forums where their own staff can air grievances, the British government brings together front-line staff from different organizations to sit with ministers and senior officials in workshops and explore barriers to partnership working in such cross-cutting areas as providing long-term care or meeting the needs of school leavers. As well as being a learning experience for management, front-line staff who perform similar functions but rarely if ever meet are able to share ideas, develop understanding, address common problems, and compare notes. Some governments are following the US experience of "reinvention laboratories" (called "learning labs" in Britain) where staff get together to find ways to get around nonstatutory rules and regulations that stifle innovation.

GIVE ME A COMPUTER, PREFERABLY ONE THAT WORKS

Career advancement, financial incentives, and being treated with respect are all fine and dandy, but if you really want to motivate civil servants and propel them to the cutting edge of the information revolution, give them a proper computer. In the digital age, technology facilitates culture change. Neither businesspeople with their Pentium laptops nor the kids at home downloading their MP3 files would believe it, but many government staff still spend their days fumbling through character-based monochrome computer interfaces connected to dot-matrix printers. Put a web front end on their machine, give them a mouse and let them point, click, and experience dropdown menus like everybody else. The amount of time it will take them to complete a task will decrease, obviously, and there will be no need to waste time teaching the old system to younger employees who have grown up on a healthy diet of Java and Windows.

Serious consideration should also be given to the idea of furnishing every government employee with a computer, preferably a laptop, that they can take home for their own personal use. This would instantly make government a model employer and send out positive vibrations in all directions. It would tell civil servants that they're worthy and can be trusted with a valuable asset, but that also they should spend time on their own development. It would imply that all employees are considered knowledge workers, that they can use a computer to do their work and are being prepared to deliver public services electronically. And as not all government workers are middle- or high-income earners, it would help bridge the IT gap between rich and poor. Funding, technical support, information security, and the question of ownership would have to be addressed, but these details are not insurmountable and similar programs already have a proven track record in the private sector.

The Ford Motor Company provided a package that included a top-range computer, printer, internet service, and user support to 350,000 employees worldwide, at a cost of $800 per employee. Governments could negotiate similar discounts based on high volume of business; the US Congress estimated that a proposal to give a free computer and internet access to every federal employee who had completed at least a year of service (up to 1.8 million people) would cost about $1.4 billion. That sounds like a lot, but the investment would see rapid paybacks if done in conjunction with other initiatives to deliver online services. It must be recognized that it's impossible to have e-government without e-workers.

Rather than sitting at a paper-strewn desk, civil servants of the future will be knowledge workers located in virtual departments with vast amounts of valuable information at their fingertips. They will work for an agency like Europol, the European police organization. The primary function of this modern, supranational public-sector agency based in The Hague, the Netherlands, is to cooperate and share knowledge (with different European police forces). Its employees work in a heavily computerized environment where electronic messaging is used instead of other modes of communication, where there are workflow applications rather than multiple data entry and multiple handling of documents, and where data warehouses exist for storage and retrieval instead of filing cabinets. Nicolas Pougnet, the organization's head of IT, says: "From the driver to the director, everybody logs on to their computer every morning, every day. Everything goes on the network, including meetings and appointments, agendas, holiday and travel requests, as well as business administration."

The government form is here to stay. For collecting data, it's ideal. But automated and secure systems can provide a unified method for working with forms throughout their entire lifecycle without having to change standard workflow procedures to request, verify, approve, reject, disseminate, dispatch, and delegate work. An electronic form can be submitted online to an agency by a citizen or employee and the web server will verify its contents and immediately inform the claimant of any problems, removing the need for clerical assistance over trivial problems like a missing zip code. The server routes the verified form as an email to the relevant processing clerk, who might do a quick manual check for items that can't be processed automatically. The clerk then clicks an icon to send the form to the approval authority who adds a digital signature, preventing crucial fields from being changed. The form is emailed simultaneously to the accounting office and back to the clerk, who executes the required service. Altogether this represents a big saving in time and effort compared to the old way of processing forms using interoffice mail and fax machines.

With the workflow automated, document management and data warehouses can be used to consolidate data and centralize it for easier analysis and reporting. More effective decisions and actions can be taken by using associated data mining techniques to extract hidden patterns in large amounts of data. For example, by recognizing two billing codes for the same procedure, a social welfare agency can uncover the double payment of a benefits claim. Search and analysis techniques can similarly help tax inspectors identify tax fraud. Or an analysis of adoption and fostering records could help governments design better social services, with the social services agency working in collaboration with other organizations like the police, health department, nongovernmental organizations, and the public at large. When government organizations buy document management and workflow solutions, they generally look for products that can provide a repository of data tailored to both the employee and the citizen, so that each can access content specific to their needs.

Internet technologies such as intranets and messaging infrastructures can further augment communication and information sharing and, when these are used together with workflow and document management and data warehouse technologies, governments can create a workplace where data is stored and organized across departmental boundaries and processes are optimized for staff to work on a team-oriented basis. Although agencies shortchange training at their own risk (no automation tool is productive if staff don't know how to work with it), most of these products are surprisingly easy to use, and graphic user interfaces speed the learning curve. When all employees are online, everyone can move naturally back and forth from working within a document to working within a virtual group and be kept up to date no matter how fast a situation changes. They can break away to resolve an immediate problem or contribute to a goal without major interruptions in the flow of their other day-to-day work.

In 1998, the Department of Employment, Training, and Education in the state of South Australia built an online solution to coordinate the rollout of thousands of computers to more than 600 schools spread across a large geographic area. It was the first time the department had ever completed such an operation on time and within budget; previous efforts to get computer equipment delivered and installed and users trained had taken as long as a year. The new collaborative tool let everyone involved in the project—department staff, school administrators, and independent suppliers—enter actions, questions, tasks, contacts, learning experiences, troubleshooting ideas, and solutions to specific problems. Every time a piece of equipment was shipped to a school and installed by a vendor, or local staff encountered an implementation problem, it was logged in the system. Project managers were alerted immediately through integrated journaling and fault reporting. They were able to examine all aspects of the rollout, make decisions, and assign tasks to subordinates. Links to databases, queries, and reports allowed users to view data in different ways, and integration with the internet gave all project participants access to the same information at the same time. Because the system recorded collective learning from every installation and every problem solved, department staff grew wiser with each completed task. Says Karen Dermody, the project manager: "We're not wasting our time solving the same problems over and over."

Government is notoriously bad at learning from past experiences, so the ability to reuse knowledge is vital to ensure consistent performance, especially on large-scale projects. Agencies typically capture huge amounts of data—terabytes are collected on a single project or citizen—and that data has to be stored, organized, analyzed, and shared for it to be transformed into something useful. Facility tracking, trend analysis, response-time analysis, and knowledge sharing will all increasingly become the basis for future decisions in government.

MAKE IT EASY

Front-office public-sector staff working in the online world have to deal with a wider range of subjects than they do offline. They face greater challenges than commercial customer service centers, which normally have a narrowly defined focus and answer questions of a predictable nature. In government, it isn't always possible to predict or control the nature of a query, and staff have to understand that some calls are more important than others. Responding to a query about a tax bill is important, but responding to a call to social services could be a matter of life or death. This has implications for opening hours, staffing levels, training, and procedures. Government call centers and one-stop shops need to assess and categorize the types of query they receive and the responses they must give. Processes and structures must be flexible enough to enable access to a mixture of both generalist and specialist staff, with appropriate procedures in place to ensure employees are fully utilized and citizens are not kept waiting. In many situations, telecommuting and *ad hoc* workgroups become viable options.

Staff at the Newham 2000 call center in London deal with everything from local taxes to the local environment, and from housing benefits to school travel passes. They handle credit- or debit-card payments from citizens and provide switchboard services for the whole council. The call center's computer system requires staff to "close" every query, so in cases where an immediate response is not possible, individual employees take responsibility and follow the matter up until they can call back with a resolution. In this way, call center staff act as advocates for citizens, making sure that other council departments provide the information or action required. Giving employees this kind of responsibility, and the right tools to access the accurate and up-to-date information required to meet a caller's demands, helps ensure a focus on outcomes rather than processes. It also reduces the need for middle management, making it easier for government to flatten organizational structures and remove traditional hierarchical barriers.

People are more likely to look things up if information is easy to access. They are more likely to involve and use the experience of others if those others are easy to contact. They are more likely to follow correct procedures if the procedures are easy to follow. This is the basic premise of "knowledge management." The term has many definitions, but what's important is the concept of making full use of data coupled with employees' skills and ideas. Successful knowledge management harnesses new technology so the right information goes to the right person at the right place at the right time. Although technology facilitates it, knowledge management cannot be sold in a box. Many agencies implement sophisticated intranets, data warehouses, and other systems, but fail to capitalize on their investments by ignoring everything else that needs to be done to make knowledge available, such as embedding information in systems and processes, applying incentives to motivate employees, and creating alliances to infuse the organization with new wisdom. Knowledge management needs to be treated as an investment rather than an expenditure. There are many examples in government of developing costly, ineffective programs and making poor decisions based on faulty knowledge. Agencies also pay dearly when they forget what employees and partners know, or when employees leave and take everything they know with them.

In most organizations it isn't all that clear who owns staff knowledge, whether the information employees have in their heads or on their hard drives is the property of the government or is merely rented. It isn't clear who holds the rights to the knowledge of consultants and outsourced employees. It isn't clear what information can legally and ethically be shared across organizational boundaries, and with private-sector partners and with the public. Andersen Consulting was able to submit a winning bid substantially lower than other shortlisted companies for a contract to run the British national insurance recording system because it developed the original system and retained the intellectual property rights, which were valued at £100 million ($60 million). Any other supplier taking over the system was obliged to license it from Andersen Consulting. A parliamentary committee advised the government to "look again" at its decisions on ownership rights to government computer systems, "particularly where those systems are crucial to public business and will need to continue even where the contractor might change."

In Canada, to deal with this kind of issue, a set of knowledge management guiding principles proposed by the Public Service Commission said that information and data resources should be made available to all employees, other government departments, other levels of government, and other partners, except where there is a demonstrated need for confidentiality or protection of privacy; that information should be easy to access and easy to use, with knowledge systems integrated with business applications; that knowledge, information, and data should be managed to protect intellectual property rights and to preserve an agency's corporate history; and that managers should be accountable for knowledge and information management in their areas and ensure that staff have the training and skills development opportunities to manage information effectively.

BRING ON THE CZAR

The shift to a web-enabled, information-age government can be highly political, or at least it should be. If no politics are involved in an e-gov initiative, this is a good indication that the political leadership either does not perceive or does not understand its value. In organizations that are truly embracing e-government, the lines between the technological and business sides are becoming increasingly fuzzy.

Money is a big factor. Public-sector spending on information technology is now too high for politicians and senior bureaucrats to ignore. In the early 1990s, a major government computing project might run up to $50 million. Today, larger figures are being attached to fewer projects and it's not uncommon to find contracts running into the billions. The US Department of Health and Human Services is spending $15 billion over 10 years for IT integration and outsourcing support services. The Navy and Marine Corps are spending $6.9 billion over five years on an intranet with secure voice, video, and data networking, as well as other services for more than 400,000 computer users. Since both the paybacks and risks of IT failures are now higher than ever, leadership from the top is crucial to improve coordination between departments, change working cultures, and drive e-government forward. If an IT guy's in charge, it won't work.

Politicians and their advisers are supposed to be good at anticipating change but, bizarrely, most have no understanding of the internet or its potential to reach out to citizens in a new way. When British prime minister Tony Blair delivers a speech about technology, he often starts off with a story about an adult computer course he takes where the person sitting next to him in class seems a bit edgy. Seeking to reassure him, Blair says, "I know I'm the prime minister, but don't let that make you nervous." His classmate replies, "It's not because you're prime minister that I'm nervous. It's because I'm passing all my tests and I'm unemployed, while you're failing all yours and you're running the country!" This is a joke but, at the same time, it's no laughing matter. How many people can imagine their prime minister or head of state surfing the web? Most can't. Most politicians still print out their email to read. Government ministers never work with their department's technology experts because while they're struggling to open their email, the IT guy is bombarding them with opaque talk of secure socket layers and RAS server configurations. The two don't speak the same language.

How are leaders supposed to guide society through the information age if they can't live in it themselves? And how are the techies supposed to guide the information age into society if they can't relate to society? The politicians and senior bureaucrats need to learn some basic facts of IT life and the technology experts need to drop the jargon and focus on benefits. Maybe then the two sides will be able to meet somewhere in the middle.

Don't forget senior management. They traditionally understand their agency's mission and the processes and business units that provide individual services to the public, but they don't usually see how each relates to their organization's underlying technology infrastructure, applications, and databases. A new breed of manager must understand the importance of current and future technology platforms to ensure that e-government projects support the mission of the organization and real improvements to services. To keep pace with the ever-changing online environment, agencies have to update their business models continuously and view processes, business cases, and financial analysis as "living" documents. Planning has to be done quickly, focusing on strategic guiding principles rather than in-depth analysis. New staffing issues include the need to react quickly to fill gaps and support new functions. Those managers incapable of seizing the opportunities of the internet risk being swept away by all the changes going on around them.

An extreme example is the mayor of Hirata, Japan, who announced in the summer of 2000 that all draft proposals submitted by city officials were to be written by hand and that there would be a weekly "computer-free day" in all local authority departments. At the city council offices, where there is one computer for every employee and where over 90 percent of draft proposals were until then being submitted electronically, staff claimed that work on computer-free days would simply be left undone and the administration would come to a standstill. But public administration was human-contact work, reasoned the mayor, and "there are a lot of young staff who mistakenly think that they are working by just sitting at their computers."

Some government managers also mistakenly think that by outsourcing a service, they are also outsourcing the responsibility. Experience shows this isn't the case, so managers need to adopt risk-management skills if they are working with a private-sector partner. Large, complex IT projects often suffer from cost overruns and delayed implementations not because of technological problems, but because of weaknesses in the management process.

Computer experts understand what is and isn't possible from a technological standpoint and managers need them to help distinguish achievable goals from industry hype. Some agencies have teams of both operations and IT staff, and many are creating the position of chief information officer (CIO) or naming a senior department official to champion the e-government agenda. However, because governments too often view IT as a support function rather than a strategic asset, their CIOs are treated as support officers rather than decision-making executives. Many public-sector CIOs don't have direct influence over IT procurement, and very few have the same level of authority as their boardroom counterparts in the private sector. CIOs should have an open relationship with their cabinet secretary or minister, giving strategic advice on a daily basis. They should be change agents with the responsibility to apply technology for achieving major improvements in business processes and service operations.

To coordinate integration efforts between departments and gauge government's overall progress in putting services online, it also makes sense for governments to designate some kind of central CIO, or a national information technology czar or computer guru. Call them what you like, they should be working by a president's or prime minister's side helping to set e-government policy. In January 2000, the British government appointed an "e-envoy" who reported directly to the prime minister. This was more or less the right idea, although his responsibilities weren't clearly defined and, instead of focusing solely on e-government initiatives, he also had to bear the brunt of criticism for some misguided internet laws and tax regulations being introduced by the government. He resigned within nine months.

Nevertheless, given a specific task and enough clout, an IT czar should be able to overcome all the major technology challenges facing government today. They should have the power to break down barriers to cross-departmental cooperation and unify diverse policies and services. They should be enforcers, naming and shaming departments that overprotect their turf. They should gauge the progress toward online service delivery, benchmarking department against department, government against government, and government against industry.

Part Two

Living with eGovernment

4 Social Exclusion: Better Ways to Work

WALK IN WITH NEEDS, WALK OUT WITH HOPE

The most vulnerable people in society have long experienced systematic discrimination because modern culture is oriented to serving mainstream needs. The price of the economic liberalization of the 1980s and the globalization of the 1990s was increased social deprivation for many countries. Growing numbers of people suffer from insufficient income and unemployment, together with poor access to education, healthcare, food, and housing. The welfare state is supposed to prevent people from falling into the poverty trap, yet too often government welfare programs are costly without being effective.

Today's social problems are complex, multiple, and overlapping, but governments persist in defining them in simple, singular, and separate terms. A social welfare department is expected to take the lead on the income aspect of poverty, a justice department or interior ministry deals with the crime and disorder that result from deprivation, a health department copes with the health problems caused by poverty, an employment department focuses on helping the out of work find jobs, an education department helps them develop their skills, and an industry department works to create employment through new business and investment opportunities. Local authorities and charities are then left to pick up the pieces of the resulting social exclusion.

The reasons for institutional separation are historical. When social welfare systems were established after the Second World War, governments tended to disregard the need to provide financial assistance to people in residential care, since their needs for shelter, food, and other basics were met by the institution. When the need to get social welfare budgets under control coincided with professional opinions arguing for a move away from institutional care to community-based services, little consideration was given to how disabled and mentally ill people, for example, would support themselves. Social exclusion shouldn't exist in today's rich societies but it does, mainly because a person's particular situation falls between the cracks of different public administrations' responsibilities.

Welfare services rely heavily on information and information systems, and greater integration between these systems is clearly needed to deal more effectively with social problems. A single mother may receive welfare payments from one agency, child benefits from another, housing benefits from a third, job and career counseling from a fourth, and so on. For each benefit, she has to trudge across town to different offices, meet with separate caseworkers, fill in forms and be interviewed at each place—all to get a minimum amount to sustain her family. This lack of integration and information sharing creates a stressful situation for the citizen; the bureaucracy may become so overbearing that some can't cope and end up on the street.

Governments have lost sight of the original vision of social welfare: to provide financial assistance to people and families who need temporary support, to help them through difficult periods, and return them to the community as self-supporting, functioning individuals with a sense of their own worth. Instead, people become trapped on welfare because inflexible stovepipe systems can't enable them but only provide them with financial benefits. While the shift from universal to discretionary block-grant benefits is controversial, focusing on outcomes rather than eligibility can ensure that public money is spent on helping people find work rather than simply sustaining them while they're unemployed.

Without coherent, all-encompassing social welfare strategies, caseworkers don't know where to focus their energies and can't work to clear goals. Without operational systems that allow them to access information on their clients from other programs, they are unable to obtain detailed knowledge of how the benefits system works. Although they may be trained to be knowledge workers acting as the focal point for citizen contact, instead they push paper and write checks and issue food stamps before sending the client out the door. A person who walks into a social welfare agency with needs must be able to walk out not despairing, but hopeful.

CASE MANAGEMENT CULTURE

Most governments' biggest expense is the money they pay out on welfare, pensions, unemployment insurance, child benefit, and support for disabled people. Not all of that money always goes to the right people: an average-sized country loses billions of dollars every year to fraud and error. Some people claim to be unemployed when they are actually in paid work; others use false identities to obtain benefits. Payments may go wrong because of genuine errors: someone doesn't know to declare their savings on a benefit claim, for example. And with double handling of claims by different agencies and millions of changes of circumstance reported each year, mistakes made by government staff are all too frequent.

Employees are under extreme pressure to pay money out quickly rather than wait until people have provided all the facts to justify their claim. It is difficult for staff to ask for evidence when the advice on what they need to support and process a claim is contained in hundreds of separate guidance notes. Delays in transferring information from one part of an organization to another also lead to incorrect payments based on outdated information.

False claimants leave a trail of evidence on different computer systems across government. For example, the social security department might hold details of a welfare claim, while the tax office has a record of the same individual claiming back value-added or sales tax for a private business. Introducing routine cross-checks would immediately highlight such cases, and the knowledge that data matching takes place might discourage fraudulent claims. Although the merging of databases rightfully raises concerns about compromising data protection, governments should at least have a coherent plan to ensure accuracy in their day-to-day business of working out and paying benefit claims. Currently, very few welfare agencies do any systematic checking of claims against information already held in the different parts of the benefit system. Safeguarding social security requires a more intelligent use of information and technology, such as integrated systems that automatically revise payments whenever one point in the system learns of a change in a claimant's circumstances.

Social security in Belgium underwent a profound crisis in the 1980s with people cheating on the system, lengthy delays in benefit payments, an excessive staff workload, and major communication difficulties due to countless incompatible information systems. It was decided at the highest political level to restructure social security completely, doing away with ponderous administrative procedures and deploying network technology to allow the electronic exchange of forms. By statute, all social security agencies are now only allowed to exchange information through an intersection database that passes on requests for information from one agency to another. The system ascertains whether an agency is entitled to the data, thereby keeping the information infrastructure under control and ensuring privacy and data protection. Another regulation states that any piece of information about a person that is already known to one social security agency may not be sought from that person by another. Dr. Johan Verstraeten, administrator-general of the National Office for Family Allowances (NOFA), says: "Now we don't have to disturb unemployed families with any more questions. Instead we ask the institution that is granting them unemployment benefits, and they give us qualified information."

NOFA is Belgium's lead agency for the provision of social benefits to poor families. It was in the classic situation of having one mainframe computer for business-critical data and another for business-critical processes, leaving staff to deal with various islands of office automation. In 1998, the agency implemented a change management program that streamlined 440 mainframe links into 29 processes covering all the procedures of issuing family benefits. These were then grouped into eight clusters. The cost of converting all the business-critical data and mainframe processes to an open system would have been prohibitive, so instead NOFA implemented a middle service layer with production workflow software and a web server using XML (eXtensible Mark-up Language) as a bridge to the mainframe and the open environment of the internet. This provided staff with a common Windows-based front office and kept intact a fully independent mainframe back office. It also allowed for the development of an intranet to manage interactions with the mainframe and workflow engine.

The agency can now ensure automatically that employees follow correct procedures from beginning to end. For example, logical checks built into the system won't allow large benefits to be granted to someone in full employment. With checks and scanning, management can now evaluate staff on final results—or outcomes—rather than the individual actions they take. With processes implemented in a workflow management system, and with all staff receiving the same, qualified information, there is now a consistency in decisions and conformity throughout the agency and between agencies. "We will only have integrity if we are offering the full range of services to families," says Verstraeten. "So often we see a paradox where people who are not skilled and are dependent on social benefits don't even know their entitlement to family allowance. That's what we are fading out."

As welfare reform is being introduced in many countries, human services agencies are increasingly looking to integrate computer systems. To maximize benefit to the citizen, integration needs to run throughout and not simply mask the stovepipe organizational structures that are the root cause of fragmented social services. Web-based collaborative workgroup processes, including data warehousing and data marts, are the best way to place cross-benefit information on caseworkers' desktops, enabling them to assess the type and level of social benefits that best suit a client. Citizens and caseworkers can sit down together and identify all public and private-sector programs that will help the individual or family achieve specific, well-defined outcomes; one that moves them from welfare to work, for example. Caseworkers don't even necessarily have to be government employees; they can be employed by a volunteer or nonprofit organization, or even a private company. The important factor is to have a culture of case management and service delivery backed by technology that supports the integration of data for decision support.

SELF-SERVICE SOCIAL SERVICE

While Belgium fixed its internal processes, other governments concentrated on the front-end integration of social welfare programs. The Australian Centrelink program replaced counters with open-access customer bays in 400 offices countrywide, so that families, students, the elderly, the disabled, farmers, and job seekers could receive more personalized services. It integrated the services of five historically separate departments and categorized them by citizen group rather than bureaucratic organization. The program's goal is not just to provide "one face" but a "whole body" to the citizen.

The state of Arizona's No Wrong Door project similarly transformed more than 150 social welfare programs from five agencies into one integrated service, so that people can receive assistance no matter which agency they approach. Using a web-based architecture, the five departments all worked together to plan, design, and build an integrated front-end screening and referral system that handles eligibility and assessment as well as providing actual service delivery. Web-enabled case management tools allow caseworkers to interact with services as a collection of related programs, rather than having to connect with single systems supporting single programs. Each social welfare program system is a module that plugs into the overall architecture. Says Arizona state CIO John Kelly: "This is a big strategy, not a big project."

When developing a customer-oriented approach to service delivery, government officials are usually encouraged to listen to users of the service. The problem with listening to the users of social services is that they are largely voiceless. They live on the margins of society, out of sight and out of mind, and it is all too easy to forget about them. As a result, those with the most pressing needs often have the most difficulty in accessing services. It's not unusual to hear a social services manager say, "We'd like to carry out more of our business over the internet but the vast majority of our customers don't have access to it."

It is time to demystify the internet. It is time to stop patronizing the socially excluded. Governments can't allow a situation to arise where people who are in gainful employment go online to conduct their government business, such as paying their taxes and registering their vehicles, but those who are unemployed are left offline to conduct their government business, such as finding a job and applying for social benefits. This approach will only condemn those already excluded from the information society to eternal deprivation.

Government must think in terms of providing electronic services through multiple delivery channels such as web-enabled kiosks and PCs located in public libraries and other public spaces. Public web access gives people hands-on exposure to internet applications and builds their confidence in using technology while, for example, they're checking out what jobs are available. Front-end social welfare systems like Australia's Centrelink and Arizona's No Wrong Door could easily double up as self-service websites for job-seekers, whether they're on welfare or not.

Most governments see social services as the last area to automate and provide electronic service delivery for, but the government of Spain is exceptional in seeing it as the place to start. Concerned about social exclusion in the information society, and recognizing that its people were among the world's greatest users of bank machines, the Spanish Ministry of Labor and Social Security had by 1999 issued new social security smart cards to 40 million citizens. These memory-packed cards are used to access welfare benefit payments and a range of other government services and information from kiosk terminals located around the country. Citizens insert their cards in a kiosk and interact through touch images with a narrator providing information about the various functions. Online bulletin boards post information about government agencies, job offers, and training opportunities. As an extra security measure, citizens can choose to imbed biometric fingerprint identification into their card, so they can access more sensitive information and "sign" for benefits, make unemployment claims, or even book a medical appointment.

Spanish citizens today manage their social benefits in much the same way as they manage their bank accounts. They process routine transactions and access their personal records from self-service terminals rather than government offices. This has given government staff more time for other activities, and has made information about government programs and policies far more widely accessible.

Spain piloted the smart cards with the 500,000 citizens of the city of Cordoba and then with seven million users in the Andalucia region before rolling them out nationwide. The pilots helped the government perfect the system for distributing the smart cards and explaining their use, and it was able to improve on the technology to link kiosks to the terminals of the ministry's different agencies. The pilots also showed skeptical decision makers that smart cards would be accepted by the public and beneficial to government processes. With citizens using their social security smart cards, the Spanish government has been able to eliminate routine paperwork by automatically updating clinical histories and electronically monitoring appointments. By improving its information-gathering techniques and exercising greater control over the processing of data, the government can also detect inaccuracies in benefit payments more effectively.

FINDING JOBS ON THE WEB

Governments are also turning to the internet to help reduce the cost and time it takes when people are looking for work. Employment websites are being used at local, regional, national, and even international levels to match job seekers with vacancies and to give employers current information to help them determine job market conditions.

One effective local initiative was in Cambridge, UK, where there was a high level of unemployment among single parents despite increasing job opportunities and prosperity in the area generally. Many found it too difficult to juggle raising their children with having to trudge from one government office to another to look for work, locate training and childcare facilities, and determine how a job would affect their social security benefits. To help single parents access all the information they needed to re-enter the workforce from one point, the Cambridge ChildcareLink project was created in just six months by a partnership of 20 local and national government agencies, volunteer organizations and community groups, and local companies. This portal of services is accessed through the internet or information kiosks located around the city, including all main libraries. The kiosks allow users to store notes in a personalized notebook that can be printed out at the end of the session. Advice and guidance on the content of the system come from the various agencies involved in the project.

At a regional level, the Ohioworks website, created by the Ohio Department of Human Services and local chambers of commerce, is the most comprehensive real-time job market information service in the US. It averages more than 500,000 visits a week from people looking for county-by-county job information. Jobseekers can search which professions are in most demand, which jobs pay the most, or which match certain skills. They can access job search strategies, develop résumés, and match training courses with the skills required for particular vocations. The site also links to job banks, childcare listings, transportation information, and other resources that could be relevant to a person's ability to accept a job.

SkillNet.ca is a collaborative network of the Canadian government, industry, educators, and the voluntary sector, linking employers' needs to jobseekers' skills. Employers can request résumés and jobseekers can access labor market information and training programs. While each recruitment service on the website is managed independently, all are interconnected to create a seamless service.

On a wider scale, while the European single market permits any EU citizen to work in any EU country, free trade hasn't occurred to the same extent in labor as in goods and capital, often because people are simply not aware of job opportunities in other countries. The European Commission's EURES Network now connects all national job vacancy databases, providing European jobseekers not only with employment opportunities but also with information about the requirements for working in other countries.

MORE BRAINS, LESS BRAWN

If anyone out there today who is gainfully employed doesn't know how to use a computer, chances are they won't be in a job for much longer. Computer automation is displacing factory and office work alike, putting millions of people in the unemployment lines. Yet the sad irony is that many countries are enjoying their longest ever period of uninterrupted non-inflationary growth and there's no shortage of work. The new economy is creating many more jobs than the underlying technology is destroying, but positions remain unfilled because people don't possess the right skills to perform the work. Demand far outstrips supply for software developers, programmers, systems integrators, database administrators, web administrators, network specialists, and technical writers. The US has an IT workforce of over 10 million but there are jobs for 850,000 more. In western Europe, where unemployment rates continue to hover around 10 percent or higher, there are 500,000 unfilled IT positions, and there will likely be 1.6 million by 2002. India is short of 145,000 software specialists. Australia needs 31,000 techies right now. Most of the vacancies are in industry sectors other than technology and communications. Small and medium-sized businesses are desperate for IT staff—and so is government.

Businesses have not traditionally invested a great deal in either entry-level training or retraining existing staff because they are unlikely to receive an acceptable return on their investment. But as companies everywhere start to feel impeded by the lack of technical expertise within their organizations, many are becoming more enthusiastic supporters of education. There is a trend toward offering career mentoring, internships, and cooperative work terms, in which university students can earn course credits for their work in private companies. Some firms have even set up their own corporate universities—there are 1,600 such institutions in the US alone. Motorola University has a dedicated campus and a faculty of 400.

A good example of a company doing its bit to close the skills gap is Cisco Systems, which makes most of the routers and other networking equipment that power the internet. In partnership with government, education, business, and community organizations, the Cisco Networking Academy Program was launched in 1997 with a $20 million initial investment by the company. There are 5,391 academies in 86 countries teaching more than 139,000 high school and college students how to design, build, and maintain computer networks. Working with organizations such as the Asia-Pacific Development Information Program based in Kuala Lumpur, academies have been established in countries that traditionally lack specialized training and basic infrastructure. The program involves 280 hours of web-based and hands-on curriculum, teaching internet and technology literacy and specific skills of network principles, building, and maintenance. The curriculum is correlated to national math and science standards and is developed by educational and networking experts. There are internship placements, college scholarships, and corporate sponsorship opportunities.

Organized labor is also becoming more involved in retraining union members whose jobs are threatened or already terminated. Whenever a union runs a computer course, it's always full. In 1997, concerned about the low level of computer skills among its members, the Lands Organisationen (LO), the largest trade union in Sweden representing 2.2 million blue-collar workers (one quarter of the country's population), negotiated a bulk purchase deal with Hewlett-Packard to supply 55,000 computers with full internet access at almost 30 percent below retail price. Dubbed the "people's computer," these were leased to union members for about $50 a month for 36 months. The LO deal accounted for one-third of all home PCs sold in Sweden that year and thrust Hewlett-Packard to second place from sixth the previous year in terms of market share, stretching its assembly plant in France to breaking point.

Around the same time, it was becoming common for Swedish companies to make computer equipment available to employees for self-study at home, perhaps with the help of an interactive training program combined with long-distance instruction. However, under Swedish law, computer equipment placed in an employee's home was considered a fringe benefit liable to taxation. With the country's tax structure potentially impeding training efforts and indirectly contributing to the skills gap, the government introduced legislation in 1998 to exempt company-provided computers from taxation, on condition they were made available to the entire permanent staff. Companies immediately took advantage of the new legislation.

Volvo negotiated a bulk purchase discount with IBM to offer each of its Sweden-based employees a top-end Pentium together with a printer, internet account, software, delivery, and support. Some 31,000 Volvo employees signed up, three-quarters of its Swedish workforce. Since most of the remaining quarter either already owned a PC or had obtained one through the earlier LO offer, more or less every Volvo employee, from administrative staff to assembly-line worker, now has a computer at home that's connected to the internet. Says Hans Kristensson, Volvo's IT manager: "The long-term benefit for us is that every employee will have a basic skill in using a PC."

Government, industry, and organized labor in every country need to knock heads and rub shoulders to come to terms with the demands for new skill requirements and to ensure that training programs are complementary and vocationally relevant. Businesses and unions need to respond not only with resources but with knowhow, supporting education projects that link the expertise of their organizations with the needs of schools. To move the agenda from debate to action, some governments are setting up IT skills taskforces with representation from businesses, unions, government organizations, educational institutions, and training providers. These forums need to consider all options, including accelerated training programs, retraining people already in work, skill migration, and better promotion of technology career opportunities.

There's no one solution to the problem, but governments that do nothing will find that the high-tech jobs sitting unfilled in their jurisdiction will get up and go to another city, state, or country. Waiting for their youngest and brightest talents to graduate from the conventional academies isn't an option; governments must act now to fill jobs and compete in the global economy.

BRAIN DRAIN, BRAIN GAIN

In many developed countries, the immediate short-term response to the market failure to supply skilled IT employees has been to increase immigration by engineers, computer scientists, and other highly skilled workers. This stirs up criticism from advocacy groups, organized labor, and others who accuse technology firms of hiring foreign nationals ahead of their own citizens, resulting in depressed wages and less willingness to train and educate the domestic workforce. While the comparatively higher salaries and demand for IT workers in North America and Europe has led many foreign nationals to relocate there, this approach is not without limitations. There are arguments for and against the benefits to the domestic economy, but there is no dispute that a brain drain does no favors for the country from which the émigré is being poached. Because so many of its talented techies emigrate, computer-savvy India is in danger of remaining a simple provider of software coding and programming services (for which it now has competition from countries like the Philippines) rather than advancing its skilled workforce for continued prosperity. Even Pennsylvania, of all places, is concerned about the quarter of its college graduates who seek employment outside the state. In an initiative to retain its high-tech talent, the state government initiated a SciTech program that awards scholarships and provides internships in technology companies to students who commit to work in Pennsylvania for one year for each year of assistance.

To build a technologically competent workforce quickly, and to move people off welfare and into work at the same time, governments need to encourage the jobless to enroll in short conversion courses such as industry-certified technician-level training schemes. A number of training initiatives are springing up in this area. In the state of Victoria, Australia, the Go For IT program provides 12-month work trainee placements for young unemployed people. The program includes one-to-one matching of skills and employer needs and provides for pre-employment training. In Ireland, to cater for its booming technology sector, the government launched an industry-driven Fast Track to Information Technology program in which 3,500 long-term unemployed receive both technical and personal skills training, after which they are offered full-time employment in the IT industry.

The European Computer Driving License Foundation is another public–private initiative, allowing jobseekers to demonstrate their IT proficiency to companies through the establishment of a standard and recognized accreditation for computer literacy. The computer driving license was conceptualized in Finland by the Finnish Information Technology Development Center (Tieke) and the Ministry of Education in partnership with the Ministry of Labor, adult education centers, universities, vocational colleges, and training companies.

As technology jobs require more brains than brawn, and as the internet allows for greater flexibility in working hours and geographic location, the door to employment should open further to many underserved groups who have traditionally faced barriers on grounds of accessibility and perceived inability to perform certain tasks. If women, minorities, older workers, and the disabled were more proportionally represented in the IT workforce, there would be a more than adequate supply of technical staff and knowledge workers.

A number of public–private–NGO training initiatives, especially in the US, are trying to spur interest in technology careers and training among these social groups. The Pass it On program, operated by Denver Community College with the support of IBM, teaches computer skills to people with disabilities. Green Thumb, a Virginia-based nonprofit organization, has a program funded by Microsoft and the federal government to train people aged 55 and over for helpdesk and network administrator jobs. It includes online training in order to reach older workers in rural areas. The Recruiting for the Information Technology Age (RITA) program, run by a nonprofit organization called Women Works and administered under a federal Department of Labor grant, trains women coming off welfare and housewives returning to the workforce. While none of these programs on their own is going to produce a flood of job-ready high-tech workers, they can make a difference when totaled up. Perhaps more significantly, they demonstrate how everyone can participate equally in an information society.

By being more flexible in their teaching methods, established universities and technical colleges could also more quickly contribute high-level skills and formal qualifications to the workforce. In some instances, there could be less slavish adherence to outmoded academic syllabuses and a greater willingness to recognize training from outside the traditional classroom. For example, most of the students at the Queensland University of Technology in Brisbane, Australia, which calls itself "the University of the Real World," are so-called earner-learners, people who are already employed in demanding full-time jobs and have little time for formal education. One student had a day job implementing a state-of-the-art project management program for a major telecommunications firm and this work was recognized as a component of his university course.

Most IT employees still get their education from four-year degree programs, and this is expected to continue as technology becomes ever more sophisticated. As big corporations and recruitment agencies make their presence felt on university campuses, graduates in advanced computer science and electrical engineering are able to write their own tickets.

Because IT skills are embedded in just about all new jobs, computer literacy should be one of the core subjects that students require to graduate from school and go on to university. It is as important as reading, writing, and arithmetic. Information and knowledge industries such as banking and media are dependent on a fully computer-literate workforce, even in their marketing departments. Other sectors such as retailing and services—and government—are also experiencing rapid technological change in which all employees need new skills just to retain their present positions. While technology replaces low-skilled routine work, it totally complements skilled work by allowing staff to use information more creatively.

Yet schools and universities must not get carried away with technical education. Four or five years from now, when today's freshmen are ready to graduate, the biggest thing in information technology will be something that nobody has yet heard of. Unless they're considering careers deep into hard science, younger students in it for the long haul might be better advised to get a general education and develop their learning capabilities rather than try to target specific IT jobs. Learning languages, economics, and history enables students to compose their thoughts and communicate more effectively. The internet is about creating applications out of real-life situations, so the students with the greatest career prospects are those who take an interest in computers and keep conversant with new technology through school or hobbies, but who are inclined to direct their studies into areas other than IT.

Taking a combination of hard and soft subjects can lead to interesting careers in technology-driven areas such as (in today's terms) computer-aided design, environmental assessment, investment banking, marketing, and the civil service. Even for programmers and systems analysts, employers are looking for people who can do their technical job but who can also work in teams and expound ideas. Employers today want employees to understand technology, but they also want them to understand the business in which they work.

5 Learning: Lifelong and Online

REDEFINING EDUCATION

The concept of what it means to be educated is based on the needs of an era when most of the globe was controlled by European armies whose soldiers were illiterate. The factory workers and miners who provided the industrial society's economic muscle received little, if any, formal schooling. People divided their lives into a period of education or apprenticeship, followed by a period of work and finally retirement. Many people still think that once they have learned a trade or profession, they are set for life. The reality now is usually something rather different.

We need to reassess completely the level of education that citizens require to participate in our much more complex knowledge society. Simply raising existing school standards is not enough—the very meaning of education must be reconsidered and redefined. Governments and educators have to respond with policies to develop a society in which everyone can learn and upgrade skills throughout their lives. While lifelong learning is a broad concept, it basically means getting rid of the notion that education is finished once a student leaves school or university. Education should be standard practice and open to everyone, and it should encompass all activities that improve knowledge, skills, and competence, whether formally in school, higher education, adult education, and vocational training, or informally at work and leisure. On-the-job training should not be simply a fringe benefit for middle management in big companies.

Northland Trucks is a company of 30 employees in rural Saskatchewan, Canada. It sells, leases, and services transport vehicles and other heavy machinery. It is not the sort of business that traditionally provides a high degree of staff training. But the heavy mechanics industry is undergoing a transition from mechanical-based to electronic-based components and onboard computerized systems. Tougher emissions standards, for example, have forced manufacturers to install electronic air-conditioning systems in vehicles. As a result, service technicians working for dealerships such as Northland Trucks must learn how these more complicated components function, and be trained on the equipment and methods used to service them.

There is a further trend among suppliers such as parts manufacturers to replace their customer service personnel with online support and interactive voice response (IVR) systems over the telephone. This has forced dealerships to integrate new technology into their own operations. Northland Trucks has installed a computer network with several systems, including inventory and ordering software, and now must train its service and parts personnel to use these technologies. All of this is quite a tall order for a small business. To compound the problem, there is a lack of qualified service technicians and management finds it difficult to attract young local people to a career in heavy mechanics. Journeyman accreditation requires a five-year training period combining classroom and on-the-job training, but Northland Trucks is located a long way from any training center. Dealer-designed training sessions also tend to be offered only during peak periods or summer holidays, making it difficult and expensive to provide employees with either apprenticeship training or skills acquisition.

Northland spends about $500 per employee annually on training, mostly on airfares, hotels, and meals for staff sent on out-of-town sessions. After a technician receives outside training and the new skill has been mastered, knowledge is spread to other technicians with the support of an in-house library of videos from suppliers and dealers. After the new computer system was installed, the videos were replaced with CD-ROM training and information packages that were loaded on to the network for easy access by all employees. With today's fickle and fluctuating business objectives, it's not unusual for training material to become stale before a course is ever delivered, so updates to CD-ROM courseware can be downloaded from the internet, and content is also now accessible directly from suppliers' websites.

Learning technologies are becoming increasingly important in providing employees of many companies like Northland Trucks with the information and training they need to keep abreast of new products and servicing equipment. The main cost involved in integrating e-learning into an enterprise is acquiring the computer equipment, which most companies will have to purchase in any case for their business operations. Once online, a company can maximize its IT investment by incorporating learning technologies into its training programs, delivering knowledge straight to the desktop.

The lifelong learning agenda requires flexibility, and the most flexible delivery channel available today is the internet. The web provides a forum where a vast array of educational materials and learning resources can be continuously updated and quickly accessed at any time and from any place, nationally or internationally. In a system of lifelong learning, people will accumulate qualifications over the course of their lives from a variety of schools, colleges, universities, libraries, cultural centers, museums, private companies, and so on. Class lectures won't necessarily be the preferred learning style; people will increasingly favor a more direct learning experience with a greater emphasis on the tangible and practical.

UNIVERSITIES OF THE FUTURE

The concept of lifelong learning combined with the possibilities offered by the internet breathe new life into the idea of distance learning. As in earlier incarnations such as correspondence courses, distance learning is being advocated for the flexibility it gives people who have to juggle work schedules with family lives and others who have difficulty getting to a class at a fixed time and location. For people who have been out of school for a long time, it can be a less intimidating way to, for example, brush up on new health and safety regulations or achieve an MBA. And in some far-flung corners of the earth, distance learning is the only formal education available. In Alaska, more than 8,000 people are enrolled in distance education courses even though the University of Alaska, the state's main postsecondary institution, does little to promote them: they are not mentioned in the university's annual catalog and information about them on university websites is difficult to locate.

Online learning is considered more practical than traditional distance learning in which students receive their coursework through the post. In addition to offering greater convenience, the teaching methods of online learning—web-based instructions, researching on the net, email networking, chat rooms—increasingly reflect the way people live and work in today's global economy. Athabasca University in Canada has been one of the early pioneers of networked learning, issuing a strategic plan in 1996 to expand individualized, electronic, learner-driven distance education models. Its business and management programs, including an executive MBA, use online delivery platforms that incorporate individual and group interaction with a virtual faculty of nearly 60 academics across the country. There are online simulations, self-tests, survey tools, internet links, a help hotline, and course materials such as key concepts, reading lists, case studies, popup links, and glossaries. Most importantly, students can interact with each other. The internet makes human interaction possible while at the same time allowing people to remain remote and anonymous if they wish.

For companies with operations and business partners spread throughout a country or around the world, the internet is the most cost-effective way to train staff and ensure consistent standards in all offices. An e-university can also spread its net to pull in people who have never been exposed to formal education and give developing countries a chance to catch up. The Monterrey Institute of Technology and Higher Education, or Monterrey Tech as it's called, operates a virtual university that offers PhDs and master's degrees to 43,000 students at 84 receiving sites in educational institutions and corporate workplaces throughout Mexico and Latin America. It is the largest geographically dispersed educational system in the world. In Egypt, a government-sponsored project has developed an online "utopian school" where students take "the best courses from the best teachers from around the world."

In India, just 6.5 percent of school leavers go on to higher education, compared to about 30 percent in developed countries. Yet with its IT services in high demand by multinational corporations (40 percent of Fortune 500 companies outsource projects to India), the country has become increasingly education conscious. Indian IT professionals cannot be trained fast enough, resulting in a huge "education gap" in the demand and supply of higher learning. India simply does not have enough universities. In response, more than 60 of the country's 200 universities now provide distance learning courses. The Indian government encourages the trend by providing tax breaks to institutions that offer online programs.

With India becoming more connected to the internet, and attracted by the size of its English-speaking population, more and more foreign institutions are also arriving to market their e-learning. Carnegie Mellon University of Pittsburgh, Pennsylvania, in partnership with Sterling Infotech, an India-based technology company, offers Indian students skill-certification computer programming courses identical to those the university teaches to its American students. The classes mirror those taught in Pittsburgh by conventional means, except that the coursework is done over the internet. Indian students do not need to own a computer or have a dedicated internet line, as they are provided access to both through computer centers located around the country.

Touted by many as the university of the future, the global "webucation" market is already estimated to be worth $70 billion. Many established institutions are looking to develop web-based applications and offer accredited online learning programs so that students can earn a full degree without ever physically attending a class on campus. There are also major efforts to make library reference materials available via the web. To reduce the cost of producing high-quality distance learning materials, and to reach the largest market possible, many universities are starting to form global alliances with governments, businesses and, especially, other learning institutions.

No well-established self-respecting bricks-and-mortar higher education institution is missing out on the opportunity. Distance education courses and academic texts are being marketed by a for-profit organization called Fathom, established in partnership by Columbia University, the London School of Economics and Political Science, Cambridge University Press, the British Library, the Smithsonian Institution's Museum of Natural History, and the New York Public Library. Cambridge University and the Massachusetts Institute of Technology (MIT) have struck a deal to develop virtual learning together, while Oxford University has partnered with Ivy Leaguers Yale, Princeton, and Stanford to build an online college for their alumni.

In the UK, lifelong learning is usually associated less with Oxford and Cambridge and more with the Open University, which has been broadcasting course material on BBC television for decades. When the British government first proposed the idea of an "open university to the public" in the 1960s, it was at a time when television sets hadn't yet made it into everyone's living rooms and there was both faith and belief that the new technology could deliver social good. This is uncannily the position in which the internet finds itself today, and so it should come as no surprise that the Open University is now conducting courses over the web.

Academia is being forced to provide scholarly content on the internet largely to ensure that private industry and commercial training enterprises do not take over universities' traditional role of authenticating information and delivering knowledge. In so doing, universities are increasingly working with private-sector partners to deliver e-learning, or adopting business practices and tactics, including aggressive marketing campaigns and going out to attract investment capital. Either way, academia is becoming entrepreneurial and global.

The internet is also changing the blue-collar worker's traditional venue for lifelong learning, the trade union study circle, where groups of like-minded people meet to discuss issues of importance to the world labor movement. The International Federation of Workers' Education Associations (IFWEA) and its European regional body, EuroWEA, which together represent national workers' education councils, trade unions, foundations, democratic socialist political parties, and NGOs from around the world, now run an internet-based education program on issues concerning globalization. The first of these international study circles, on the impact of transnational corporations in local communities, was held in 1998 and involved 170 workers from 12 countries. The course was run in each country by a local trade union and attended by rank-and-file members.

For example, in the UK, the Transport and General Workers' Union conducted the course for workers at a car assembly plant, while in Kenya, the Women Workers' Organization ran the course for plantation workers. In each location, the workers met once or twice a week to discuss how transnational corporations were affecting their community. All participants worked simultaneously to a common curriculum, set of materials, and educational method. Each study circle had a facilitator who took notes and posted them on a website. Between meetings, participants (or anyone else) could read the discussions from other countries, which allowed more ideas to enter their own study circle. This also stimulated discussion and debate between the groups.

After the course, it was felt that if international discussion was to be meaningful, the process of communicating needed to be in the hands of the participants themselves, otherwise it was in effect the facilitators talking to each other. So the second time around, rather than simply posting a summary of discussions, participants wrote and emailed their own reports. This allowed individuals' characters to influence the content of what was being communicated and by experimenting with other techniques, such as online discussion forums, participants obtained a clearer idea of how the internet could be used for information gathering, research, education, and solidarity purposes. In some instances, it resulted in people making more direct use of the technology in their workplaces.

By 1999, international study circles were being held on a regular basis on a range of topics and using a range of internet options to strengthen international communication. The IFWEA website includes educational materials available in several languages, discussions that took place between the groups, and links to other organizations with a similar focus. Each course costs about $20,000 to run, which isn't so expensive considering it's global and there are hundreds of participants, potentially many more. The internet throws the discussion forums wide open, with anybody anywhere in the world taking part. At first, fearing online chaos, IFWEA wanted to maintain a disciplined structure to the discussions rather than having people dip in and out or surf in by accident. But in the end it was decided to keep the website open to the public because of its potential for mass involvement in an educational process.

CLASSROOMS WITHOUT WALLS

Lifelong learning begins in nursery school. Just ask Léo the virtual dog and Max the virtual hedgehog, who in September 1999 left their home computer at Ecole maternelle de la Roue, a preschool in Fontenay-aux-Roses, France, and spent the school year traveling the world and meeting pre-schoolers in far-off lands. Classrooms around the world hosted either Léo or Max (they didn't travel together) for a week or so and then sent them packing to another pre-school with a description of their adventures and the country they had just visited. The animals carried virtual luggage, in the form of attachments of children's drawings. The children back in Fontenay-aux-Roses kept track of their progress throughout the year on their school website. The purpose of the journey was, of course, to bring children together and broaden their horizons through exchanges with e-pals in other countries.

Through Léo and Max, these young pupils created a connected learning community, whose general idea is to use the internet to bring outside organizations and resource material into a classroom to enrich students' learning experience and allow them to communicate and challenge each other with ideas, knowledge, and best practice. There can be networked communities of students, teachers, professional groups, businesspeople, trade unionists, government officials, hobbyists, environmentalists—whoever. For schoolchildren, creating a classroom without walls involves connecting schools with libraries, museums, cultural centers, other schools, homes, and the community at large.

Canada was the first country to start connecting every one of its schools to the internet with the launch in 1993 of its SchoolNet program, devised by a partnership of federal and provincial governments, universities and colleges, educational associations, and the private sector. All schools in the country were online by 1999, and all classrooms were connected by 2001. The network offers students and teachers more than 1,000 learning services and resources, including training and research tools. Students can find reliable facts on just about any topic. They can tour a virtual museum or zoo, sail around the world in a virtual boat, discover their national heritage, talk to an astronaut in space, and communicate globally with other students.

Building on the success of SchoolNet, the Canadian government then spearheaded a Network of Innovative Schools project in which it provides C$10,000 ($6,600) to schools that use information and communications technology in new and creative ways. There is also a public–private partnership called the Grass Roots Project, which provides grants to schools for teachers and students to develop, manage, and market learning projects and post them on the internet. The idea here is that learners not only consume educational materials, they produce them. Says Jean Monty, CEO of Bell Canada, one of the private-sector participants: "These kids are mastering important employability and entrepreneurial skills, applying their creativity and working in teams and, I imagine, having a lot of fun in the process."

Many countries are following Canada's lead. Schools in Israel are connected to a national education network giving teachers and students email and internet access, at school or from home, with 24-hour technical support. The UK's National Grid for Learning similarly provides teachers and students with individual logon accounts so they can use email, the internet, and productivity applications, including online services provided by libraries and museums. Parents have immediate email access to teachers, and adults can also use the Grid to get online training from schools that are open for that purpose in the evenings or on weekends.

Another example of a connected learning community is the Science Learning Network (SLN), which was developed by the US National Science Foundation and Unisys as a web-based education program to pair science museums with schools. Students use the internet to research a subject and engage in email correspondence with educators from one of the museums. They share their experiences with other students and teachers over the network by contributing to an online journal and posting digital photographs. SLN now incorporates a global network of science museums with a website that offers virtual exhibits where teachers and students can conduct exercises ranging from building a wind-powered machine to charting the course of a hurricane.

Networked learning is also about bridging the gap between a student's home and school lives. While parental involvement is widely recognized as having a powerful effect on a child's learning, the sad reality is that many parents have difficulty finding the time to pay much attention to their children's schoolwork or review results with teachers. The internet can make their involvement easier and more convenient by allowing communication to take place outside school hours and classroom walls. Private conversations can be held online between teachers and parents, and tutors can also join in. Parents can access the web to compare their child's progress against defined standards, check their grades and attendance record, and view homework assignments and teacher evaluations.

Students who access projects from home have a better opportunity to take advantage of parental guidance and involvement, and they can research education websites for papers and assignments. When school-children are away on a field trip, they can use mobile communications to post digital photos of their activities on the internet, allowing their parents to check on the school website and feel reassured about their wellbeing.

A growing number of schools have their own websites, displaying picture tours, chat rooms, event calendars, and even the lunch menu. Viewing sites is becoming a popular way for parents to decide whether or not to enroll their child in a particular school. However, when judging a school website, parents ought to be aware that the least professional-looking sites were probably created by the pupils themselves, which suggests a healthy school environment. Slick professional sites, on the other hand, might mean that the students aren't interested in the internet, or that the school feels it needs to promote itself by spending a lot of money on outside help.

Recognizing that a computer is as important a tool in the class-room as a chalkboard, most forward-looking governments are making it official policy to link all primary and secondary school classrooms to the internet by a certain date. While the emphasis at first was to put a couple of computers in each classroom, the trend now is to set up separate suites or labs with 20 or 30 computers, so a whole class can take a technology lesson together. Sometimes there are rooms containing video and virtual reality technology adjacent to the computer suite. Some schools have one or two partner schools in other parts of the world, and many offer after-school computer clubs with a managed system for surfing the internet, filtering out unsuitable material for children. Some open the computer suite as a cybercafé for parents one evening a week.

Pupils typically spend up to half a day each week in computer lessons and, depending on the availability of computers in the school, they also use computers for math, history, geography, science, and language lessons. It is important to accelerate the integration of computers with the school curriculum, as there is little long-term educational value in pupils spending class time simply surfing the web. Malaysia is starting to issue electronic books to schoolchildren, to introduce them to technology at an early age and to reduce the burden of carrying heavy bags full of regular books. IT experts from Universiti Kebangsaan Malaysia are training 1,500 teachers to use the e-books, to which Universiti Utara Malaysia is transferring the information from school textbooks. If a pilot involving 8,000 students in 100 schools proves successful, e-books are expected to be in use in all schools nationwide by 2007.

Parents often complain that their children spend too much time on computers at the expense of the basics, but this should not be an either/or proposition. "Computers are the basics," says Donald Tapscott, author of the bestsellers *The Digital Economy* and *Growing Up Digital.* "It is like saying kids spend too much time on pens and paper."

Just as they have their own pens and paper and their own books, students ought to have their own laptop so they don't have to wait for a shared computer to become available. They should use their computer for all subjects, and it should include wordprocessing, a dictionary and encyclopedia, and spreadsheet software to improve learning in math, perform analysis in science class, and make sense of tables and data in geography. It should have internet access and an email address to research assignments and to participate in connected learning communities. A laptop or notebook is better than a PC so students can take it from class to class and use it to do their homework. Schools that have participated in fundraising schemes to provide laptops for pupils claim that many children are more motivated and creative when using laptops and that they are more likely to spend extra hours on educational activities. And, of course, they can no longer use the old excuse that the dog ate their homework—instead, they can say the computer crashed.

FUNDAMENTAL QUESTIONS ABOUT FUNDING

Some schools put a greater emphasis on technology than others and are prepared to allocate more of their budgets to purchase computer equipment, develop network infrastructures, and provide online learning material and support. This is leading to an uneven level of computer education in many countries and, as the laptop model of teaching takes hold, parents will increasingly shoulder the cost of buying, renting, or leasing computers for their children. Already, the main reason people with school-age children purchase a PC is to support their child's learning, and many will buy laptops for the same purpose. Yet there will always be cases where families can't afford a computer or simply won't buy one.

Governments are starting to consider the risk of some schools becoming more technologically privileged than others, and are looking to create some kind of equal-access baseline to prevent students in disadvantaged areas, with all their other inherent problems, from being left further behind those from better-funded middle-class schools. Clearly, policies are needed to direct funds to less privileged schools as quickly as possible to get them up to a certain level of computerization. But, at the same time, governments face the dilemma of funding disproportionately and discriminating against schools that have already made sacrifices in other areas in order to invest in new technology. Governments would prefer to reward rather than penalize schools that take the self-initiative to arrange financing, insurance, maintenance, and support, and show good practice by establishing computer plans and milestones. Schools that are prepared to grind it out and get parents and the community involved to help raise money for computers have the best chance of attracting private-sector partners to donate time, money, hardware, software, or at least advice.

The Charlotte-Mecklenburg school district, covering 140 schools and more than 100,000 students in North Carolina, regularly seeks contributions for everything from tutors and computers to landscaping services and security cameras. Locating, obtaining, and managing volunteers and donors was becoming a time-consuming and costly endeavor. If a school needed technology tutors, for example, staff members would drive around the neighborhood looking for computer firms that could help out. To cut back on the driving time, the school board approached the IT department of Mecklenburg County to develop an online geographic information system (GIS) known as the School Partnerships Resource Locater. By logging into community and government databases, staff can now instantly identify potential partners and volunteer sources located close to individual schools. They just enter the school's zip code along with resource keywords such as "technology tutor" and all relevant firms located within a chosen radius are listed. Bank of America, a long-time corporate sponsor of the Charlotte-Mecklenburg school system, even agreed to pay the $16,000 it cost to develop the system.

A "catalog of needs" breaks down each school's requirements according to time, talent, and treasure. One school might need six math tutors (time), another wants technology gurus who can motivate students seeking careers in IT (talent), while another needs $10,000 for statistics software (treasure). Integrated with the GIS system, the database lets the school district prioritize the various needs and, when approached by a donor or volunteer, it can search the requirements of all schools. The initiative has been a godsend for the school district's partnership development program, with the number of corporate sponsors jumping from 400 to 650 almost immediately after the School Partnerships Resource Locater went online in 1999.

While some school boards such as Charlotte-Mecklenburg are enjoying tremendous success developing corporate relationships, such initiatives have given rise to a debate about private-sector sponsorship of public education, and whether it commits schools to certain products or locks them into particular technologies. Some people question not whether schools can afford to get into a private-sector scheme, but whether they can afford to get out—a Microsoft-sponsored program that provides students with laptops equipped with Microsoft software has been likened by some to giving children their first pack of cigarettes.

The reality for many public schools is that they simply cannot get by on their tax contributions alone. Governments inevitably will have to find and accept some kind of public–private balance as they seek to ensure access to quality education for all. This is not going to be easy, but neither should it be impossible.

Universities started addressing this kind of issue much earlier than secondary and primary schools, and some are finding independent and innovative ways to provide disadvantaged students with universal computer access. Mayville State and Valley City State universities, located 75 miles apart in North Dakota, were two of the first four colleges in the US to provide all their students and faculty with notebook computers, and students now graduate with an electronic portfolio that documents their best work. Classrooms at both universities have multimedia presentation equipment and power and network outlets at every seat. Residence halls have network clusters on every floor. Shared-use printers are widely available. To reduce costs, the two universities share academic and administrative computing functions and established helpdesks, with more students than staff directly involved in computer support. Students participated actively in the decision to adopt the notebook initiative and serve on the institutional technology planning committees. North Dakota ranks 44th among the 50 US states in per student government funding of higher education, and the extra $4 million per campus required to provide each student with a notebook computer was paid entirely through student fees, grants, and reallocation. Students pay $950 per year for a leased computer, software, and access to networks and the helpdesk. Despite representing an almost 50 percent increase in tuition fees, enrollment on both campuses rose 20 percent in 1998, the year after the program was introduced.

Another fully wired campus is Acadia University, a small institution of about 3,600 full-time students in a town called Wolfville, in the Canadian province of Nova Scotia. After investing in upgraded seats, fiberoptic wiring, and plug-ins for notebooks, the university introduced a program known as Acadia Advantage in which students can choose to lease a notebook computer for $800. In 1996, the first year of the program, 375 students took advantage of the offer and the number has climbed each year. With the widespread use of notebooks on campus, science students no longer take three-hour lab periods, but instead have integrated two-hour sessions in which they move back and forth between the classroom and laboratory, allowing them to relate theory and practice more closely. The university has also closed its language lab where students used to listen to tapes for language practice. A web-based program now allows students to use their notebook computer to practice speaking a foreign language in less public, less embarrassing places.

STUDENT-CENTRIC TEACHING

Children start out keen to learn, but the existing education curriculum is often too placid and alienating for them. Schools would do better to consider their pupils' interests and let them use those interests to learn. Children today are interested in computer games. They program their parents' video recorders, share and download music from the internet, and participate in online chats. Immersed in this digital world, they have developed a different way of thinking and a different way of dealing with people and with information compared to previous generations. They have grown up interacting with media rather than having it broadcast to them. By using the same technology at school, pupils expect a model of teaching that is similarly interactive. They want to learn by doing and exploring.

If a teacher is merely going to stand at the front of the class and spoonfeed mass-produced lessons, education authorities may as well enlist the top teachers in the country to web broadcast their lectures to schools, and perhaps simply place a teacher's assistant in each classroom. Students would learn from the best and governments would make enormous savings on teacher salaries. This is starting to happen in some places by default. The Eden (Electronic Distance Education Network) project in Ontario, Canada, started out as a closed system designed for students who couldn't attend school for various traditional reasons such as being home bound. But what began as a distance education initiative has become an internet-based e-learning system offering full-credit high school courses, including chemistry, math, and English. Launched by the

Simcoe County Board of Education, the courses are now used in seven school districts by about 100 schools serving 11,000 students. The system allows every student who takes chemistry lessons, for example, to be linked electronically with one chemistry teacher and all other chemistry students, regardless of location.

Schemes such as the Eden project are helping to fuel a North American trend for home-based education, where children are not enrolled in any school and their parents take responsibility for their education. Home schooling traditionally occurred because parents wanted to ensure a religious education or because they were dissatisfied with the ability of the public school system to deal with a child's special needs. However, with e-learning and a wealth of online support materials at their disposal, many parents now believe they can give their children a better education than any teacher. Forced to compete with the internet, connected learning communities, parents and, ultimately, the whole world, the traditional school teacher is decreasingly seen as a source of knowledge.

While the internet has empowered children to learn, it has not done much to help teachers teach. Very few teachers are sufficiently prepared to integrate new technologies into their classroom instruction, and many still need a little help from their pupils to get the class computer up and running. When it comes to using new technology, teachers are vastly outdistanced by their students. Governments are making efforts to provide computer training to teachers, develop teaching services and software, and increase networking between teachers. The UK's National Grid for Learning includes a Virtual Teachers' Center on the internet to help improve training and curriculum support.

Half of Sweden's teachers were themselves sent back to the classroom to learn not just how to use technology, but how to teach with technology. Through the Swedish government's In-Service IT training (ITiS) program, teachers receive a computer and an email address and then sit in a classroom, read articles and write reports, usually in teams of five to seven. Then they meet with other teams in seminars where the reports are read out and peer assessed. Says Lena Nydahl, director for ICT in schools at the Swedish Ministry of Education and Science: "The teachers take responsibility for their learning just as we expect pupils to."

Teachers often need to be convinced that there is no reason to be frightened and perplexed by computers, but this will dissipate over time as those currently graduating with education degrees, especially from those universities where computers are used for learning, head into the teaching profession. By then, the integration of technology into the classroom will have forced a radical change in education, from a teacher-centric system to a more student-centric approach. This will include allowing students to learn at their own pace. Traditionally, students' only constant is the time they spend in class, which means the amount of learning they receive is variable. Adept students get bored if they are ahead of the rest of the class and must endure periods when they are not learning. Conversely, slower students get frustrated when they don't have enough class time to complete their work, and end up falling behind the rest. Everyone should be able to keep up if learning is made the constant and time is the variable.

While schools are restricted by class hours and opening and closing times, the strength of the internet is its ability to loosen the bonds of time that affect many students' ability to learn. In the future, students will use the internet to follow individual learning paths, a process that will continue throughout their lives. While some contend that learning through technology is impersonal, a more persuasive argument credits the internet with personalizing education by enabling students to learn in the way that suits them best.

Teachers can still play an important role in creating and structuring a student's learning experience, but they will have to change from being a purveyor of information to being more like a coach, helping students navigate their way through all the online information they've accumulated. The personal relationship between teacher and student, whether online or face to face, should grow stronger as a result. It has been said that teachers in the future will do more caring and less carrying. They will be relaxed in this new role because, having dealt extensively with computers during their own secondary and post-secondary education, they will easily be able to handle technology and they will know that this is how they can best facilitate their students' education. Already, at the Alameda cyberschool in San Diego, California, pupils use computers all the time for all their work and they see teachers, whom they call facilitators, just twice a week to organize their projects. Perhaps in the future, a student might choose a registered teacher over the internet and have a direct link from home to a virtual class via web cameras, freeing up the considerable resources currently invested in bricks-and-mortar schools.

This sort of scenario frightens many people who think that too much would be lost if everyday learning were done individually. Some argue that school is a necessary social activity and that to learn, people need to get together to stimulate one another. Even when lessons are delivered electronically, students may still want to meet as a group once a week or so for live demonstrations or experiments. But a group of people sitting quietly in a room listening to a lecture is not social interaction. If the only purpose of a school building is to nurture personal growth and development, perhaps this could be achieved in a better way some place else. Primary schools may indeed remain much as they are today because of parents' need for childcare, but there are no convincing reasons why secondary and postsecondary education can't be delivered in a cyberschool format. In surveys conducted by the wired-up Mayville State and Valley City State universities, students say that their use of technology increases their critical thinking and makes it easier to work in groups, and that they are communicating more with others. They claim that their computers neither decrease their socializing nor increase their sense of personal isolation. Let's face it, students will always want to party.

While study after study has shown that grades in all subjects improve when computers are used in schools, it has to be accepted, for the time being at least, that some people will want to be taught in a room with others. So initially students will do a combination of online and classroom-based learning, and computers will be used alongside more traditional teaching tools to ensure that the technology does not over-shadow the teaching culture. There will still be schools, there will still be teachers in the schools, and there will still be students learning together. But it's important to appreciate that this is not the only way to learn and that classroom walls are becoming more porous, whether people like it or not. Nothing will stop students from going online and learning from the wider world. In doing so, they will force a greater flexibility and choice in education. By accepting this reality and combining the new approaches with the more traditional forms of education, government and society have an unprecedented opportunity to create a fully integrated system of lifelong learning.

6 Quality of Life: a Greener and Healthier Society

BITS MOVE SO ATOMS CAN STAY AT HOME

In the digital age, it is no longer necessary to communicate by attending physical meetings or by publishing paper documents and having them delivered by post or courier. People can work as a team remotely from various locations and, by telecommuting, they can do their jobs without coming into the office. The internet creates the ability for bits to travel instead of atoms. However, no communications technology has ever resulted in a reduction in travel, and the internet is no exception. Making the world smaller only gives people more reason to get together. Today, hundreds of people travel half way around the world to attend conferences on e-business.

Of all the modes of travel, driving remains the most popular. Car traffic is a complex global problem that isn't going away. As incomes increase and car ownership becomes cheaper, there will be ever more vehicles on the roads. Urban sprawl makes it difficult for many people to get around any other way.

While new technology will not necessarily change driving patterns, it will give policy makers more options for pushing vehicles through the congestion. The Swedish Road Administration has a traffic management system that coordinates traffic flow in the city of Gothenburg. Information integrated from different sources has been linked to forecast models using information from road sensors to build a single database of the road network. Using a geographic information system (GIS), the Best Route Through Gothenburg program makes traffic information available to citizens in real time via the internet.

Similarly, the Minnesota Department of Transportation provides a traffic website for commuters in the Minneapolis/St. Paul area. Detailed, color-coded congestion maps are updated every minute with incident icons and road-construction information indicating trouble spots. The site collects traffic information from 230 closed-circuit TV cameras posted along 210 miles of freeway and 3,700 road-embedded sensors that measure traffic speed, volume, and occupancy rates. The website is viewed 300,000 times a day and the information is shared with local media, traffic information providers, and other websites. More people will have access to the information through the advent of wireless web-enabled devices and digital television (Traffic TV as a local cable channel has great potential to attract a cult following). There are already voice-activated computers built into car dashboards providing traffic information over FM radio, while commuters in Seattle can input details of their car journey into Seiko's website and receive messages about delays on their route through their pager-watch.

Because the addition of just a few extra cars on a road can lead to bottlenecks, the theory behind traffic management systems is that delays could be reduced if only a few motorists checked the web for current traffic flows and advanced or delayed their trips accordingly. Other intelligent transportation systems include the linking of traffic signals so that lights stay green longer on streets with heavy traffic flows. Road sensors and weather sensors connected to a fiberoptic network provide highway motorists with electronic messages indicating a changed speed limit, and warn of crashes, detours, or extreme fog. Use of variable message signs on European highways has reduced rear-end collisions by 30 percent, and by 85 percent in fog. Yet the total money spent by governments on intelligent transport systems is less than it takes to build a few miles of new highway.

With some justification, many transport departments aren't convinced of the benefits of applying new technologies to the highways because smoother traffic flows would only encourage more people on to the roads. So intelligent transport must be used with other approaches, such as road-user charges, and it must accompany an investment in public transport.

Using global satellite positioning, for example, websites can allow people to see the exact location of their bus before they head out into the rain. The city of Turin, Italy, has a system that turns traffic lights green for heavily loaded buses but not for empty ones. Many public transport operators are introducing ticketing systems based on smart cards embedded with microchips, issued and updated at touchscreen kiosks in shops and stations, over the phone or over the web. In Cologne, Germany, a city-issued smart card enables residents to access online public services in the areas of education, culture, and healthcare, and can also be used as a bus ticket.

ALL EYES ON BOGOTÁ

Bogotá is like many cities in developing countries—it is large and growing larger, and it is clogged daily by traffic and deafened by the constant honking of car horns. It takes more than an hour to drive five miles during peak hours, even though the city has a successful even/odd car restraint day. On average, 70 pedestrians and cyclists are stuck by cars every day, three of whom are killed. This is even though only 14 percent of the city's seven million residents own a car; that number is expected to triple over the next decade. Nestled high in the Andes Mountains with a delicate ecosystem, the Colombian capital also suffers some of the worst smog in the world. Residents say you can smoke a couple of dozen cigarettes a day without opening a pack.

To raise public awareness of this "suicidal" prospect, Mayor Enrique Peñalosa banned all private cars from all Bogotá streets for one day, between 6.30 in the morning and 7.30 in the evening, on February 24, 2000, a normal working Thursday. It was the first car-free day to be held in a developing country and the largest to be held anywhere, ever. About 850,000 private cars stayed home and residents took public transit, bicycles, taxis, regional trains, rollerblades, and other modes of transport to reach their destinations. On the day, nitrogen oxides decreased by 8 percent, carbon monoxide by 22 percent, and particulates by 21 percent. It was the first day in four years that no one died in a traffic accident. Hospitals reported a 20 to 30 percent decrease in emergency consultations. Retailers didn't experience any noticeable decrease in sales. Schools and universities across the city had normal attendance levels. And perhaps the most lasting benefit was public sensitization to the impact of the car on the city and to the need for sustainable transportation.

Encouraged by the day's success, the mayor held a citywide referendum in October 2000 to institute an annual car-free day as well as a permanent daily ban on private vehicles during peak-hour work days, to be implemented by 2015 so there was time to develop services such as a new bus network and bicycle paths. Both ballot initiatives were approved by large majorities.

The Bogotá car-free day has nothing to do with the internet—except that it wouldn't have been possible without it. The European car-free day movement published all its experiences and ideas on the web, so Bogotá city officials were able to learn about different initiatives and develop an understanding of the issues. No one in a developing country had ever before seen a car-free day, and the press reacted with skepticism when the mayor proposed the idea. Because the project was associated with both the person of the mayor and his political party, the greatest resistance came from the "country club set," the political and business opposition circles of the Bogotá élite, who also happen to be the city's car owners. If this wasn't enough, the event had to be organized during a civil war in which the mayor and top city officials lived under constant threat of kidnapping and assassination. Faced with these tough barriers and tough people, the mayor did what anyone would do: he set up a website.

Online communication allowed the city to draw on solutions and make European contacts, in particular with Paris-based EcoPlan, an independent forum on environmental management technology issues that's plugged into the European car-free day movement. More than 100 strategists and political figures from around the world channeled their expertise and technical assistance over the internet into preparing for the event. An online international guest book received messages of support from government ministers, secretaries of state, members of parliaments, mayors, European Commissioners, United Nations advisers, OECD officials, academics, transport consultants, environmentalists, authors, journalists, and even the president of the European Cyclists' Federation. This attention generated hundreds of articles in the national and international press, as well as radio and TV coverage. All eyes were on Bogotá, for a change because of something besides the crimes of the drug cartels. It was a big morale boost for the city and the country.

On the car-free day itself, webcams were set up around the city, transmitting "before and after" images to the world. Even the most progressive European capitals watched and learned from the Colombian urban jungle how a car-free day ought to work. Says Eric Britton, managing director of EcoPlan: "It is important to distinguish this kind of car-free day approach from the much milder version that is presently being played with in parts of Europe. We call these 'low perturbance' or 'car-free lite' days, as opposed to the much deeper and more difficult and far-reaching approach that we are seeing in Bogotá."

Soon after the event, the Colombian Ministry of the Environment indicated that it would extend the Bogotá experiment to the country's provincial cities. Other developing countries have been encouraged to look at their own urban transport situations, and a Prague-based organization called Car Busters contacted Bogotá city hall to suggest the formation of a World Car-Free Day Consortium based on the Bogotá organizational model.

WORD OF MOUSE

Maybe the internet can't save the planet, but it is a tool people can use to make it a more habitable place. Anyone can go online and easily disseminate information, attract and rally volunteers, and bombard targeted people and organizations with email messages from around the globe. The Bogotá car-free day demonstrates more than anything the networking power of the web. Increasingly, word-of-mouse campaigns are raising the profile of many social, environmental, and developing-country issues and affecting government policies in the process. This is especially true in the area of sustainable development. The internet gives scientists easier access to environmental data and allows them to work together on research projects. Information about polluters can spread fast and widely on the web, and governments can respond more quickly to environmental emergencies and determine cause and responsibility for environmental damage.

Forcing polluters to clean up their act by publicizing their crimes—the "regulation by revelation" approach—was initiated in the US with right-to-know legislation and pressure from NGOs. The Environmental Protection Agency (EPA) started providing direct public online access to its toxic release inventory database and, by 1998, its online EnviroMapper and Envirofacts warehouse developed into single access points for multiple official databases containing millions of records on not just toxic discharges but also on air, water, chemicals, byproducts, and hazardous waste pollutants, as well as information on facilities, grants, and permits. Web users can retrieve information from several databases at the same time, create reports, and generate maps of environmental information. Such maps can be tailored to include specific information such as waterways, railroads, or an area's poverty levels, racial makeup, and population density. They can also link to detailed information such as the history of a cleanup site, and there is a data dictionary to ensure that the information is understood. Merely by typing in their zip code, people can find out the quality of the drinking water that comes out of their kitchen tap.

This huge online ecosystem of data is used by researchers, environmental consultants, school science classes, and even real-estate agents looking for sensitive areas such as wetlands. It provides evidence for environmental activists or local communities fighting against the emissions of nearby factories. And while industries are the target of most map queries, many companies have reacted favorably to the site, using it as an environmental management tool and to engage their own public debates.

The Envirofacts warehouse is helping the US government develop a more coherent approach to assessing environmental impact, by allowing EPA staff to tap into previously inaccessible or incompatible environmental data. While it is often still difficult for two different agencies to produce data like for like, by integrating the EPA's many stovepipe databases into a single data warehouse, it is now possible to get a more accurate view of the total environmental impact of a particular site or project. EPA officers can look at a factory and analyze the surrounding air, water, waste, pesticides, etc., and begin to understand how a particular type of facility located in a particular land formation or watershed affects the whole environment, taking into account demographics, endangered species, land coverage, etc. Once they have brought all this information together, they will also be able to factor in new sources of data that they hadn't previously considered.

Says Mark Day, the EPA's deputy chief information officer: "It is not unlike Columbus who gets his dollars to go to the East Indies but in fact discovers America. We have some idea of what Envirofacts can do for us, but a reading of history tells me that what it will really help us to do is discover whole new avenues of understanding of the environment that as of yet we don't even envision."

The idea of open data access is quickly moving from concept to reality, and this is leading to new ways of thinking. The web is helping to shift the way government carries out policing and regulation in relation to the environment, leading to more of a partnership-based approach that it is hoped will create a greener and more sustainable society. There is at least growing recognition that no one government agency, industry, or volunteer organization can singlehandedly protect the environment. Coordination of shared responsibilities is needed to ensure opportunities for innovation and that all relevant expertise and viewpoints are taken into account in the establishment of common environmental policy objectives.

However, most countries lack common reporting procedures and performance indicators to measure the progress of greening operations. Environmental programs are usually derived from various pieces of environmental legislation, for which data is collected separately from other programs. Often, there is no government organization taking a lead in establishing consistent standards and a systematic approach to environmental protection. Many governments don't even follow the standards themselves, nor do they have complete and accurate data on the environmental impact of their own vast operations. They don't know the annual cost of running all their buildings, how much energy and water they consume, or how much waste and pollution they create. Government cannot lead by example if it doesn't keep its own backyard clean.

WEB DOCTOR MAKES A HOUSE CALL

In much the same way as it allows access to environmental data, the internet is putting health information into the hands of the public and creating intelligent patients. The web has already replaced the family doctor as the first place people turn to for medical advice. Lifestyle and health form the second most popular subject on the web (you can guess the first), with health categories registering about one-third of all hits on consumer search engines and portals. Searching for the word "cancer" in AltaVista gets three million results; narrowing it to "breast cancer" still draws 350,000. Whereas previously the opportunity for the average person to understand medicine and health issues was limited in the extreme, the problem for people today is too much, often conflicting, information.

Charities, self-help and pressure groups all use the web to provide information about specific diseases and syndromes and campaigns for medical research. Children's trusts have sites about pregnancy, childbirth, and parenthood, often offering pre-natal classes that can be booked online, and some even have online shops selling baby carriers, toys, and clothes. By far the majority of online sources of health information are commercial operations. These typically provide information about medical conditions and drugs, provide self-assessment tests, explain the meaning of a diagnosis, give a possible prognosis, and say what treatments are available. There's always a bulletin board for users to swap medical experiences. Even in Europe, where most healthcare is publicly financed and most medical facilities are state owned, there are dozens of "web doctors." Those operating in different countries sometimes (but not always) alter their presentations of controversial topics such as abortion according to local sensitivities and local medical practice.

There are also online pharmacies. In addition to the usual startups, many bricks-and-mortar drugstore chains, especially in the US, are looking to the internet as a new channel to sell pharmaceuticals. Typically, it takes three to five days to turn around an online prescription, but many are starting to offer overnight delivery. While that rules out emergency prescriptions, online pharmacies offer lower prices for regular refills for chronic ailments, which account for two-thirds of all prescriptions. Many countries don't allow prescriptions to be sent electronically, but that is changing with the legal recognition of digital signatures, and over-the-counter drugs are open season. Some online pharmacies offer consultation with an online physician and most offer advice on medical and drug issues, although these can often act more as marketing tools.

Potentially, online pharmacies could be more successful than online music and book stores, because it's not all fun and games going out shopping when you're sick and, unlike other items, drugs are often bought for embarrassing reasons. Among the products most commonly purchased over the web are lifestyle drugs such as Viagra, antibaldness pills, and Xenical, which is intended for obesity but is often used for slimming. There's no shortage of horror stories about people buying drugs over the internet without a prescription or proper checks, and surveys often cite web doctors and online pharmacies among the least-trusted businesses on the web. When President Thabo Mbeki of South Africa spoke out against the side effects of AZT, the anti-AIDS drug, he said he got his information from the internet and encouraged fellow parliamentarians to go online to find out more about the drug's dangers, so they could discuss the issue "from the same knowledge base." (AZT does have side effects, but many websites on the subject are alarmist and don't include objective, peer-reviewed scientific analysis.)

To ensure accurate descriptions of their products, a consortium of pharmaceutical companies, including GlaxoSmithKline and Novartis, established the Pharmaceutical Information Network, which lists hundreds of commonly used drugs, their brand names, availability, manufacturer, what they're for, how they work, and results from clinical trials. People can search by disease, by brand name, or by generic name, and there are links to external sites. However, even this kind of site has been criticized for not keeping their news sections up to date, especially when the US Food and Drug Administration (FDA) issues warnings about side effects of certain drugs. Bayer's website once had a request for lung cancer patients to participate in a trial on one page and a notice that the trial had been suspended on another.

Another issue is that many US health sites contain consumer advertising for prescription drugs, which isn't allowed in many countries, including the entire European Union, out of fear that it will increase unjustified patient demand and put greater pressure on already straining national healthcare budgets. Companies such as Roche attempt to respect these rules with banners indicating "for US audiences only" on potentially culprit web pages and then block entry to computers connecting from non-American servers. But this is rare and, in any event, easy for the determined surfer to get around.

In November 2000, the Internet Corporation for Assigned Names and Numbers (ICANN), the organization that oversees the web's addressing systems, added .biz, .info, and others to the familiar .com, .net, and .org, but rejected a proposal from the World Health Organization (WHO) to establish a new ".health" top-level domain to help people verify the accuracy and reliability of online health information. ICANN was concerned about the vagueness of the WHO's quality standards, and whether or not it aimed to monitor the content of .health sites on an on-going basis or if it would simply assess applicants during the initial application process. The pharmaceutical industry raised further objections to the appropriateness of a single quasi-governmental organization being given a monopoly to decide the accuracy of health information.

Not surprisingly, it is falling on national governments to inject some quality control into the complex and quirky world of online medicine. Some agencies are establishing portals to gatekeep and filter information overload by linking only to those sites deemed reliable and trustworthy. These portals are quickly emerging as the best starting point for online health information. The British National Health Service's NHS Direct website checks the quality of its links, but doesn't exclude connections to organizations that might disagree with government health policy. For example, it links to the Multiple Sclerosis Society website, which believes that beta interferon should be more widely available despite the government view that it shouldn't. The British site also has a clinical section that advises people whether to self-treat a condition, visit a pharmacist, see a doctor, go to an accident and emergency department, or call the emergency number 999.

In the US, the FDA's website is the place to go to find reports of side effects and whether a new drug has received marketing approved. The site is one of the top 250 visited sites on the internet and features an illustrated medical encyclopedia, medical dictionaries, and pages on major drug phenomena such as Viagra. It also links to US patient organizations' directories, online leaflets, the National Institute of Health's database of clinical trials, and an online version of the US National Library for Medicine.

Healthfinder, developed by the US Department of Health and Human Services in collaboration with other federal agencies, is another popular site, visited by 450,000 people a month. It links to selected online publications, databases, websites, support and self-help groups, government agencies, and not-for-profit organizations that produce reliable health information. The department claims it does not duplicate the efforts of other information sources and its indexed resources are located almost entirely on other web servers. It concentrates on adding value through easy, one-stop searching and consistent cataloging. It also provides a quick, nine-point checklist to help determine if a site is trustworthy and reliable.

People are supposed to ask themselves, does a website:

1 clearly state its purpose and sponsors?
2 separate advertising and sales from health information?
3 get its information from reliable sources?
4 keep information up to date?
5 tell you how it chooses to link to other websites?
6 offer a way to contact the people who run the site?
7 tell you the information it collects about you and how it will be protected?
8 make outrageous claims?
9 offer prescriptions or medical advice without licensed healthcare providers?

Users should be able to answer "yes" to the first seven question and "no" to the last two, otherwise they are advised to try another site.

By providing these portals, governments are in effect encouraging citizens to go online to become better informed about their options and choices in healthcare. Many are realizing that the internet, used properly, can reduce patient demand, which is beneficial in a time of overstretched healthcare budgets. Nevertheless, the Healthfinder website maintains that it's "always a good idea" for people to discuss online advice with their health provider, and anecdotes abound about patients arriving at clinics with print-outs from the internet, knowing more about their condition than the doctor does. This is especially true for patients with long-term conditions, who are more often determined to learn everything there is to know about their ailments. Such patients have long claimed that doctors fail to hear them and they complain about the way they are treated. However, a doctor can no longer simply scratch out a prescription, say "Take one of these after each meal," and not feel obliged to provide any further explanation. With the web becoming the most convenient, and credible, source of health information, the doctor–patient relationship needs to change radically from the traditional hierarchical approach to more of a partnership.

Ideally, a patient and a physician should sit down together, browse internet sites, and access health networks that provide technical information on clinical decisions, reach some conclusions on the patient's condition, and make a mutual, educated decision on possible remedies. To do this, doctors' offices must be web enabled. While most general medical practices already have computers, they're used only as administrative tools and to store patient notes; they're not connected to the internet. Therefore general practitioners cannot access information on other computers, nor can they disseminate the information held on theirs. This perpetuates the state of affairs where it is the physician who owns patients' medical records and decides who may or may not see them, including the patients themselves. As a result, in this increasingly mobile society, people's records aren't transferred when they move house or change family doctors, and treatment received abroad isn't registered back home. People have bits and pieces of personal health data scattered all over the place, and most don't even know where, how, or even if this information is stored.

As people seek the information they need to take responsibility for their own health, they will want to own, or at least have access to, all pertinent information about their allergies, medications, immunizations, medical insurance, and even specific doctors. The web gives people the opportunity to replace the family doctor's office as the place where their health records are accurately and completely stored. Private-sector dotcoms like Medicalrecord.com and WebMD allow people to store their medical records online, making them available any time and from anywhere.

The first European-based online health account service was launched in July 2000 by DrGlobe.com, a Geneva-based application services provider that describes its service as being "just like a bank account." For an annual fee of 15 euros, people can deposit all their health data into a secure online vault. Subscribers of the service can log on and print out health reports to share with a new doctor, pharmacist, school nurse, fitness trainer, or whoever; global, 24-hour access to medical records is especially useful for travelers. With everybody working from the same data, doctors and nurses can ensure that tests are not unnecessarily duplicated, that new prescriptions don't conflict with existing medication, and that immunization schedules are up to date. While encouraged to give access rights to their doctors so that they can enter information regarding their patients' health, account holders retain direct control of their records and ultimately decide who can access information and what should remain confidential. They can also monitor when their information has been accessed and for what purpose. In case of a medical emergency, people can carry a wallet card or bracelet containing their logon password to let health professionals access information such as special conditions and allergies, and contacts such as their primary care physician and insurance company. So rather than just hoping for the best when walking into a hospital emergency ward, a citizen can expect any healthcare provider to access their up-to-date record online. But yet again, to achieve this, hospitals and clinics have to be connected to the web.

If there is greater access to information about facilities and doctors elsewhere, an intelligent patient will be able to choose to travel across state or national boundaries to seek the best-quality and most patient-centric care. This will change the shape of healthcare delivery across continents and around the world, with healthcare professionals becoming more like intermediaries, needing to add value to remain relevant. Every medical profession will be affected. If a patient can speak with a doctor on equal terms and keep their own medical records, then the general practitioner's role will have to change. If drugs can be ordered online and sent to a patient directly, then the pharmacist's role will have to change. And if appointments can be booked online, then even the medical secretary's role will have to change.

SEAMLESS CHAIN OF CARE

Medicine generally strives to be at the forefront of technology, always willing to try new procedures and spend time and money on research to the benefit of humankind. New pharmaceuticals and surgical advances have made it possible to prolong and improve the quality of life for almost everyone. Yet, healthcare professionals see information technology as an administrative burden rather than a strategic aid to improve the quality of care. Healthcare agencies spend about $500 per employee per year on IT, compared to $700 in education, $1,430 in government as a whole, and $6,000 in the financial sector. Hospital administrators and health ministry managers think they have bigger problems than worrying about IT, so the government industry manager of any given computer company can't even get a foot in the door to see them. Instead, the company rep trots down to the tax office or the defense ministry, deciding it's not worth the bother to address the healthcare market. Says Ilias Iakovidis, an officer in the Information Society Directorate General at the European Commission: "If you think of a huge line of people queuing up for the healthcare budget, the telematics people are always the last in line. And when they get to the table there's no money left."

Healthcare providers do, of course, have big problems. Developed countries have aging populations and developing countries have increasing populations; both face the twin challenge of improving the quality and accessibility of healthcare while keeping a tight rein on costs. Healthcare organizations talk about a chain of care, where patients move from a doctor's referral to a secondary care institution such as a specialized hospital, and back to primary or community care in their own home. It can take six months from the time a GP writes an admission note to when a patient actually meets a hospital specialist. In larger countries, more than one billion messages are exchanged each year by the different parts of the healthcare system: family doctors, nurses, dieticians, physiotherapists, other hospital staff, and people working for ambulance services, insurance companies, pharmacies, laboratories, blood banks, government departments, and so on. Most requests for appointments, orders for drugs, blood, and other supplies, invoices for services, prescriptions, and so on are handled on paper. Besides being slow, the process is inefficient and ties up staff who could be better employed looking after patients. When inefficiencies lead to errors, in blood orders for example, patients can suffer directly. With overcrowded hospitals, long waiting lists, and a shortage of trained medical staff, governments would like to see patients move along the chain of care more quickly.

Conducting medical transactions online would speed up the process. A shared database of information about patients should be the nucleus of an electronic medical record, accessible everywhere it is needed and used as the basis for all clinical decisions. Healthcare systems should be integrated and web enabled to provide seamless care, giving doctors and hospital workers access to all the information they need to provide effective advice and treatment, and offering patients trustworthy information sources to assist them in looking after their own health.

The Navarra region of Spain faced the usual problems of long waiting lists and inaccurate information exchange between family doctors and specialists. Therefore the regional government integrated all healthcare functions, cutting across the structured departmental hierarchy. Now medical appointments are booked electronically, lab tests and analyses are sent and returned to doctors electronically, patients' files are sent to specialists electronically, and so on. Patient information is accessible from any healthcare center, so any citizen can walk into any hospital or clinic and the doctor can pull up their full medical history on the computer.

In a joint venture between the healthcare organizations and municipalities on the west coast of Sweden, the Coastlink Telemedicine project aims to do "the right thing at the right time in the right place to the right patient." Instead of sending an admission note by regular mail to deliver patients to a hospital, a general practitioner "keeps" the patient and uses email, picture-email, and videoconferencing to seek advice from a hospital specialist. Since most of the time it's not necessary for a specialist to see a patient in person, hospital beds remain free for the more complicated cases. Quick and informal email communication is generating unprecedented dialogue between the general practitioner and the specialist, creating a form of education and cooperation that never previously existed. The internet is also used to communicate at the primary care level, between a GP and nurses working in a patient's home or at an old people's home. And there is communication directly with home-bound patients, especially those with chronic diseases living in remote areas far from medical care.

Also in Sweden, the Council of Uppsala contracted a private company called Consultus to develop a health-profile system providing tailored advice from healthcare professionals and connections to existing databases such as medical records and booking systems. Citizens are given a health account that includes all their medical records, which they can access through a commercial portal using either a web browser or a WAP mobile phone. For the council, the joint initiative is seen as an opportunity to limit its future health-benefits costs, eliminate embedded infrastructure costs, and move away from the thankless role of being the intermediary between patients and healthcare providers. For the private e-health firm, working with the public sector ensures a sufficient source of income, particularly in Europe with its strict regulations and patients who receive medicines free at the point of service. As web doctors fall out of favor with investors, they could win a lot of state-funded business if they're able to demonstrate credibility and the potential for government to save money.

Achieving seamless care requires partnership working across the entire medical community: the healthcare professionals who will use the systems; the IT industry because it will have to design and develop the systems; the administrators who make the decisions and control the purse strings; and the patients who will be at the receiving end. The European Commission's eEurope initiative, launched in December 1999 to take Europe into the digital age, aims to identify healthcare best practices in networking, health monitoring, and surveillance of communicable diseases, and to develop links between healthcare organizations. The initiative proposes, by the end of 2004, to establish online medical libraries and healthcare expertise centers, and to link all healthcare professionals and managers to a telematics infrastructure for prevention, diagnosis, and treatment. While this does not mean harmonizing the healthcare systems of different countries, it does require cooperation so that research can be conducted and standards and product specifications established.

The Commission's 2.4 million euro fifth framework research and development program to foster the creation of next-generation public services has a specific action line for health. Under the program, which runs until 2002, projects are funded to develop computerized clinical systems, advanced telemedicine services, and health network applications, as well as intelligent systems allowing citizens to assume greater participation in and responsibility for their own health. Voice technology, mobile devices, and wireless networks are also all becoming increasingly inexpensive technologies for hospitals where, for example, running new wiring can be difficult, and where medical staff need to walk around with a clipboard or digitizing tablet in hand. Other priorities include electronic ordering of tests and appointments, electronic prescribing and communication with suppliers, and electronic invoicing between healthcare organizations and those who pay the bill, whether public or private. All these innovations require integrated healthcare systems using internet technology.

Europe is also leading the development of smart cards as an authentication and access device for obtaining medical records. The Commission proposes that every EU citizen should have a patient smart card by the end of 2003. France has already introduced smart cards to replace its archaic process in which patients, after paying their doctor for a consultation, are issued a paper claim form that they complete and send off to the Caisse Nationale d'Assurance Maladie (CNAM), the national health insurance agency, to claim a reimbursement. If a prescription is required, the patient takes their claim form to a pharmacist, who stamps the form and applies a small sticker to prove that the patient received and paid for the drug. Then the patient mails that off as well to be reimbursed.

In order to cut the cost of processing an annual one billion paper claim forms, CNAM issued "Vitale" chip cards to 50 million citizens. Some 30,000 doctors, pharmacists, nurses, physiotherapists, and ambulance workers also received a healthcare professional's smart card. At the end of a consultation, the doctor's computer system reads both cards and all data relating to actions carried out during the day is transmitted overnight to a central CNAM computer system via a social health network, which connects all health professionals by email. To fill a prescription, the pharmacist takes a reading of the patient's card and the details are entered into the system. The card eliminates the need for the paper forms and the pharmacist's little stickers, and patients don't have to complete and send in forms by post; their reimbursements are registered and sent out automatically. From 2000, all health insurance information in France was to be exchanged electronically.

Because they make it easy for healthcare professionals to share information, patient cards are especially useful in countries like France, where there is a sharp divide between primary and secondary care, with a mixture of public and private healthcare providers. The cards also encourage the use of computers in doctors' surgeries—or at least they should. Many French doctors have welcomed the new process, realizing that it can reduce bureaucracy, duplication, and delays. However, those doctors who don't already have a computer often react with fear and irritation whenever a patient hands them their Vitale card. While pharmacies are computerized, many resent having to purchase smart-card readers (even though they've always had the on-going expense of purchasing the paper forms).

To turn a vision of a connected healthcare community into a reality, healthcare providers must have faith in the technology, and they must have the technology. Those who don't have the right tools should be given them if necessary, together with training and support. If healthcare professionals still have difficulty coming to terms with new processes and associated technology, even after they're fully equipped and trained, they should be forced to adapt. If a doctor doesn't accept a patient's smart card or won't refer to an online medical record, the government should simply ban paper forms and paper records.

7 Crime: Connecting Cops and Courts

TAKING THE GUESSWORK OUT OF POLICE WORK

The internet is benefiting and improving the efficiency of many in society, including hardened criminals. With an estimated $1,000 billion in illicit annual profits worldwide, the crime "industry" is today all-encompassing. New forms of crime have emerged, such as online harassment, cyberstalking, web hacking, and cyberterrorism. And new technology is being used to perpetuate conventional crimes such as money laundering, credit-card and corporate fraud, possession of child pornography, terrorism, and the trafficking of just about everything—drugs, stolen vehicles, stolen art and antiques, arms and weapons of mass destruction, body parts and human beings. The ability to send encrypted messages over the internet gives criminals a ready-made medium for secure worldwide communication. In 1997, in a hangar west of Bogotá, police in Columbia discovered an ultramodern telecommunications center containing $10 million worth of high-tech equipment. Through a system of timesharing, this had allowed drug cartels to keep permanent online contact with representatives and fleets of ships and aircraft around the world.

The internet is allowing previously unconnected criminal gangs to create alliances, transcending national boundaries, ethnic affiliations, and traditional hierarchical structures. Crime syndicates are building organizational structures to resemble multinational corporations. Online banking and the deregulation of the international financial industry make it easy for them to launder money and even to set up their own banks to control their vast financial empires. Criminal interference in this sector can pose a threat to the financial systems and economic stability of some states. African and former Soviet bloc countries are particularly fertile ground for criminal activity due to their large-scale privatizations and chaotic political and regulatory transitions. In these regions it is often difficult to distinguish between the good guys and the bad guys, and there is a real danger that the normalization of violence and corruption will undermine civil society, political systems, and the sovereignty of states.

Technological advancement has always helped the crook before it helped the cop and, for police detectives, the internet is certainly a double-edged sword. Crime traditionally involves an offender being in a specific place at a specific time and police investigations aim at establishing the facts of the scene. The internet means that a crime doesn't necessarily have to occur at a certain hour or location. An offense can be committed in a split second and computer clocks can be manipulated to make it seem that a crime occurred at an altogether different time. The victim of a crime may be a continent away from the offender and law enforcement agencies no longer enjoy the advantage over criminals of geographic containment. These new global realities render traditional policing obsolete. Law enforcement agencies require new skills and new tools, with greater professionalism and innovation. You can't fight twenty-first-century crime with nineteenth-century methods.

Police detective work tends to focus on the collection of information through street investigations, informants, undercover operations, and interviewing suspects and witnesses. Fingerprints, DNA profiling, and facial recognition are used to build evidence to convict a suspect who has already been identified and arrested. New technological developments are now allowing those aids to conviction to be used as aids to detection; fingerprints and DNA tests can be used to catch criminals, not just convict them. In the US, after he had been tracked unsuccessfully for 15 years, the so-called Unabomber was indicted because of a DNA sample taken from the back of a postage stamp he had licked. Similarly, using facial-recognition technology, police can identify bank robbers caught on video cameras with an 80 percent accuracy rate—more reliable than the naked eye.

Police forces have access to all types of forensic evidence: fingerprints, DNA profiles, mug shots, handwriting, and so on. They also have vast databases of suspects' names, vehicles, locations, property, incidents, intelligence, summonses, charges, bail, and previous convictions. The United Nations Drug Control Program (UNDCP), Europol, and the Egmont Group have all established separate money-laundering information libraries and databases of suspicious financial transactions. The UNDCP, the World Customs Organization, and Interpol have together created a consolidated drug seizure database, bringing together police and customs seizure data that helps to provide a more accurate picture of the illicit drug trade, improved analysis, and a greater ability to predict trafficking trends. Europol has a database that classifies 484 different logos to help officers recognize Ecstasy tablets. Yet, if all these systems are to unveil patterns in a crime and provide real benefits to an investigating officer, they all have to be connected together.

The lack of technological integration is particularly troublesome for sector policing, where a geographic area is split into different operational command units. There might be several cars stolen from different sides of a sector's boundary, resulting in three or four units investigating the same car thief without knowing that other police stations are on the same hunt. Or a serial burglar might leave a fingerprint at the scene of one break-in and some blood at another, and an investigating officer would have to research several databases and produce mounds of paper to find out that there was a connection between the two. An officer should be able to put information into a computer and let it scan all the databases to highlight patterns in the crime.

A detective inspector in the Vancouver Police Department in Canada has pioneered geographic profiling to help establish where an unknown criminal may live, in a way that psychological profiling identifies a criminal's personality traits. Just as people go about their everyday business close to where they live or work, serial criminals tend to commit crimes in familiar areas. While criminals have a buffer zone around their home where they generally won't commit crime for fear of recognition, immediately beyond that is the area in which they are most likely to offend. So for the police, a crime becomes a wheredunnit rather than a whodunnit. The coordinates of each location of a repeated offense are fed into a computer and an algorithm works out the probability of an offender's place of residence, pinpointed on a map using a geographic information system (GIS). In one case, a geographic profile was taken for seven arsons committed in a Vancouver neighborhood full of pathways and small alleys that are difficult for strangers to the area to navigate. While all seven crime locations could easily have been highlighted by sticking pins in a map, and at a fraction of the cost, a digital profile was able to highlight anomalies that couldn't have been seen merely by looking at a map. Performing more than 300,000 calculations to complete a profile in 30 seconds (each calculation would take a human using brain power alone several hours), the computer drew officers' attention to a cul-de-sac in which no crime had been committed even though it was a high-probability area. That was where the arsonist lived.

Much of the legwork and guesswork can be taken out of criminal investigations by integrating profiling and forensic science techniques with technology, and making the tools available to officers on their desktops over a secure intranet. Detectives will be able to jump ahead of the investigative process if they don't have to hunt through thousands of dusty fingerprint records or try to "think laterally" about a link between different crimes. Computers don't solve crimes; they are designed to produce scientific fact, not determine innocence or guilt. Integrated technology can accumulate links in a crime, but it's still up to the investigating officer to decide to make an arrest, bring a suspect in for questioning, watch for developments, or whatever.

Detectives won't be made redundant by technology, but they will have to learn to use the tools. They will have to change their "policeman's hunch" mentality and accept that technology rather than intuition is now their best friend. Technology allows police to investigate a raft of cases at the same time because they no longer have dozens of unsolved cases, they have dozens of pieces of strategic data. Some police chiefs believe it will soon be possible to do away with case-by-case investigations altogether.

TAKING THE PAPERWORK OUT OF POLICE WORK

Police officers carry an overwhelming administrative burden and tend to work without timely and accurate information because of multiple independent computer systems, typewritten forms used for batch data entry, and delayed and inaccurate crime reports. Rarely does one police officer work on a case from start to finish, meaning that the cost of police administration is higher than almost any other public-sector agency. After one officer initiates a case, the next officer on duty often has to fill in another batch of forms and frequently enters the same data and particulars all over again. For a car crash alone, there can be 20 written documents in a case file, starting with the notes taken by the officer at the scene of the accident, which have to be transcribed on to forms back at the station. The elimination of non-value-added tasks through technology can help police officers get on with detecting and preventing crimes, as well as improve morale and public perceptions of the police.

The Mecklenburg-Vorpommern police force in Germany replaced its paper and typewriters with an online "menu policing" system, which gave officers a PC desktop divided into three parts: procedures, measures, and forms. On the lefthand side of the computer screen, the officer can see everything about a case that's already in the system. On the right, there is a menu of suggestions for additional measures, such as questioning a witness, expert inquiries, or an alcohol test. By clicking on either menu, officers can call up all relevant electronic forms appearing in the middle of the screen—the actual work surface. Data on individuals or vehicles involved in a road accident, for example, is input only once and saved centrally on a server, giving officers working on the same case direct and immediate access to all data already on record. An electronic form can be called up from any desk at any police station, and an authorized officer can simply add in new details of a case. Police stations in the area are located far apart and were linked by a courier service serving stations every two days at most. The electronic exchange of data between stations eliminates such time-wasting procedures.

With the introduction of wireless communication, electronic data can also be input remotely from the scene of a traffic accident via a laptop in the patrol car, so officers don't have to transcribe handwritten notes on to a PC back at the station. It also allows for more effective policing. For example, if motorists in Mecklenburg-Vorpommern are found to be driving without their license, a police officer gives a warning and allows them to carry on. If it happens again, their vehicle is supposed to be impounded—except that this never happened because the information on the first incident was not readily available to the officer dealing with the second. Now an officer can tell from information on their laptop if a driver has already been warned.

Good information is the lifeblood of policing and data has to be made available to law enforcement officers on the front line as quickly as possible. In most police forces, officers run warrant checks by radioing to headquarters and then waiting for an answer, which often comes too late to catch a culprit. Computer-aided dispatch systems integrated with mobile computing solutions improve police response procedures, but quick access to computer data about people and cars also depends on officers having access to information held on different databases: stolen vehicle registries, driver's license records, transport department records to identify unregistered and unroadworthy vehicles, and car insurance registries holding information about uninsured vehicles and those that are subject to insurance writeoffs. If all these systems are linked to a central police computer, police officers can confirm immediately whether a driver is bona fide, and a car thief can be identified even before the owner has reported the car missing. This could also eliminate the need to produce driving documents at a police station within seven days, as is the practice in the some countries. In the UK, for example, police can check information from the national driver's license register to see if a car has been reported stolen, but any other checks on driver information must be made in writing and can take up to a week.

An Garda Síochána, the Irish police, faced similar problems before it introduced a change management program and new technology to improve access to information by its front-line officers. A central database now supports links between 17 different types of records and allows them to be displayed on a single summary screen of a laptop computer. If an officer spots a suspicious vehicle and wants to do a warrant check before stopping the driver, one query of the database shows who owns the car, if it has been stolen, if it has been reported at a recent crime scene, if a police warning is attached to it, and if the owner is wanted by the police or is a known criminal. Previously, all this information was held in separate databases or in paper files and was not readily available to police officers.

Police officers cannot, of course, carry computers around with then on motorcycles and horses, or when they're undercover or walking around a neighborhood on a beat. The SWAT team isn't going to bust into a drug house packing laptops. But they could be given shock-resistant handheld wireless devices. Beat officers with the Highland Park Police Department in Texas carry a so-called PocketCop that they use to tap into state and federal databases and query vehicles, people, stolen articles, and guns. The system gives them the same inquiry capabilities as a patrol officer and also allows for instant messaging and email access.

Real-time online information has major implications for officer and citizen safety, because a mobile patrol force can be warned immediately about potential dangers and can make better-informed decisions on how to handle particular situations. Handheld devices could have helped avoid tragedies such as the one in Fort Worth, Texas where, because of incompatible information and communication systems, a unit within the police department couldn't pass on new intelligence to a vice squad that a house it was about to raid was in fact inhabited not by a dangerous drug trafficker as originally thought, but by a crippled 77-year-old with memory loss. The police broke in and killed the innocent man.

PUTTING THE COMMUNITY INTO POLICE WORK

Besides helping officers at an operational level, the internet can help police forces gather intelligence and improve community relations through direct contact with informers, the public, and the media. While many law enforcement agencies have websites, most contain only static information about the history and current structure of the force, along with perhaps some crime prevention tips. There isn't anything approaching a proactive virtual police station that responds to citizens' inquiries, complaints, and emergencies. At best, a site will have the facility to email the police force, and a small number have comment forms and discussion groups concerning local policing.

Italian police forces often put photographs of confiscated objects online to facilitate the restitution of stolen goods, while members of the public can consult the Interpol website to see images of stolen works of art, as well as cultural objects that have been recovered by police during inquiries and for which the rightful owners have not been identified. In the belief that millions of pairs of eyes are better than a few, the FBI publishes its Most Wanted list on its website, Argentine police put out details of missing persons, and the Toronto city police publishes details of cold cases in the hope that somebody will come forward with further clues. In response to attempts by local colleges to email police with information about curb crawling and stalking around their campuses, the force in Bradford, UK, set up a secure website for informants and the general public to report crimes and suspects. Says Detective Chief Superintendent Stuart Hyde: "We know that the site will get rubbish on it but I'm hoping for the little gems of information that will get through."

The Chicago Police Department has a public website that allows people to see the number of reported crimes in and around their neighborhoods. Residents can search for all crimes or certain types of crime at specific locations, intersecting streets, and police beats. The time, date, and block number of a crime are given, but not a specific address. This information has always been available, but only through police meetings or written requests for paper documents. Via the website, the police force hopes to strengthen its ties with the public and engage more people in community monitoring and reporting of crimes. It is also helping to dispel many misconceptions about the safety of some Chicago neighborhoods.

Sometimes a website can draw more information out of a person than a police officer can obtain from a personal interview because, simply, people don't like talking to cops. They don't want a patrol car pulling up in front of their house, and they don't want to be seen standing on their porch pointing out the local drug dealer on the corner. But they don't mind snitching over the web if they don't have to identify themselves.

While the internet can be an enabler for an interactive dialogue between citizens and police, too often it is left to members of the public to initiate communication. CrimeNet in Australia bills itself as the world's first private website that provides a combined information service on "criminal records, stolen property, missing persons, wanted persons, con artists, and unsolved crimes." With the aim of providing people with the information they need for "protecting yourself, your loved ones and your property from crime," the dot-com lists the names of convicted criminals and people wanted by police, together with their criminal records and sometimes their photographs. People pay a fee to access information about criminals and must agree to a series of conditions, including guaranteeing that they are not jurors.

While privacy advocates worry that rehabilitated criminals face persecution from neighbors and potential employers, CrimeNet maintains that it can't be compared to a British tabloid newspaper that created controversy by publishing the names and photographs of convicted pedophiles. Nonetheless, in May 2000, a state of Victoria Supreme Court judge aborted a murder trial because he feared the jury might be prejudiced by information about the accused that had been posted on CrimeNet. The state's attorney-general then called for the closure of the site, claiming that there was potential for outdated and inaccurate information to appear on the site and that it posed a threat to the legal system's ability to provide fair trials. While details of people's past convictions were already accessible from university and legal sites, and CrimeNet's own details of the murder case in question were in fact gleaned from a Melbourne newspaper, none of these were approached to shut down their websites or purge their records. And if the government moved to shut down the West Australia-based site, it could always move overseas where it wouldn't have to maintain any safeguards and Victorian residents could still access it.

It would probably be fair dinkum more productive if dot-coms and governments learned to live with and work with each other. CrimeNet should be more willing to refrain from publishing explicit details of past convictions of people facing trial, while the government should be helpful by providing the website with accurate information on retrials, appeals, and convictions that have been purged from legal records after a period of good behavior. In a democracy, court documents are part of the public record and the onus should be on government to ensure that the public record is accurate. Furthermore, the police should regard the site as a tool to help them solve crimes and reach out to the community. Police forces need to develop relationships with all sorts of external organizations, especially those providing services to the public, and web providers are no different in this respect. Fear and apprehension of technology too often prevent agencies from using the internet for the betterment of law enforcement and the benefit of the public they serve.

GETTING THE DONUT SHOP ONLINE

Exchanging and sharing information with peers is necessary to achieve professionalism in policing, and small and remote police forces in particular have little or no opportunity to make direct contact or compare and contrast practices and procedures with other law enforcement practitioners outside their local area. The internet can make it easy for police officers to consult with their opposite numbers from around the world on emerging crime problems, effective policing techniques, the best equipment, up-to-date training, and thorny management issues. Even informal use of the internet will provide the impetus to break down the traditional isolationism and bureaucracy that too often prevent communication between police officers.

The John Jay College of Criminal Justice and the University Computer Center of the City University of New York sponsor an email-based discussion list called POLICE-L, in which sworn law enforcement officers can exchange messages with each other. Responses to messages are distributed to everyone on the list, stimulating further discussions. All postings are archived, enabling list members to search for and retrieve any prior message. There is no explicit requirement that discussions be police related, although members usually stick to law enforcement themes. Topics have ranged from sharing of personal techniques to discussions of legislation and their impact on the criminal justice system.

In addition to fostering routine conversation, POLICE-L serves as a clearing-house for information requests. List members seek help or guidance with local issues that might have already been addressed by others. For example, an officer from a small police department in the southern US was looking for an evaluation form to assess supervisors' performance, while a subscriber from a European police association sought details of legislation in other countries addressing the crime of stalking. An officer in the US Midwest wanted advice on how to start a bicycle patrol, while the chief of an east coast agency sought help to decide if he should arm his plainclothes officers with nonlethal weapons. An officer scheduled to testify before a disciplinary hearing wanted to know what to expect. Members also routinely announce training courses and professional conferences, and police union and association representatives occasionally use the list to notify officers of pending legislation. Even an occasional job announcement makes its way on to the list.

After a series of email exchanges, the POLICE-L list owner got together in 1994 with other police officers from the US and Canada who were running similar online law enforcement resources and together started CopNet, first as a gopher site and then as a website. The site provides resources for the nonofficial use of police officers worldwide, and assists in establishing core services for the official use of the police community. It includes a closed police newsgroup called the "international donut shop," which is open to all cops 24 hours a day, providing an off-the-record forum where members have open and frank discussions about policing issues. As an independent and unofficial police site, CopNet is driven largely by volunteers in the international police community, although a number of Canadian law enforcement organizations provide financial, logistical, and resource support.

Both CopNet and POLICE-L have a geographically dispersed membership of all sorts of law enforcement officers, including security service agents, military police officers, former officers now serving academia and the private sector, reserve and auxiliary officers. The diversity allows for contacts that otherwise would not be made and lets officers learn from a variety of perspectives and experiences. With all police ranks represented, line officers and upper-level managers are able to exchange views on equal terms. Participants usually work in different agencies and there is relative anonymity, which eliminates the political considerations that discourage such communication within a workplace. As a result, officers are exposed to some of the motives and rationales behind managerial decision-making, and police chiefs are reminded of the environment in which their officers work.

The internet allows police officers from around the world to develop a sense of community in which they freely exchange information that would be impossible or too time consuming to obtain through conventional channels. It is hoped that this emerging informal electronic community will make law enforcement agencies understand the need to implement collaborative technologies and cooperate on a more formal basis.

CROSS-BORDER CRIME REQUIRES CROSS-BORDER COOPERATION

The free flow of goods, services, and people within regional economic trading zones such as the European Union and NAFTA has made it easier than ever for criminals and stolen and illicit objects to slip in and out of countries unnoticed. Increasing freedom from border controls, along with more efficient communications and transportation systems and political instability in some parts of the world, have contributed to an increasing supply of standard criminal commodities such as illicit drugs and contraband. They have also given rise to such phenomena as the trafficking in human beings, stolen art, and football hooliganism.

Trafficking in human beings includes pedophile and prostitution rings, sweatshops, forced labor and domestic work, illegal adoption of children, forced marriages and mail-order brides, unethical organ transplants, involvement in drug trafficking, and other exploitative forms of work. In the burgeoning international trade in prostitutes, for example, criminal gangs use the internet to market and sell Asian and East European women wholesale to buyers in the West, where they are put to work on the streets, and in massage parlors and brothels. Women are also kidnapped and sold to men as internet brides. Like any other commodity on the web, pimps log on to so-called virtual phoneboxes, which provide details of women for sale, and select and order the ones who best suit their market.

Law enforcement agencies are starting to fight technology with technology. In Italy, police set up a phony pedophile website set called *amantideibambini* ("lovers-of-children") that registered 1,032 subscribers despite giving clear warnings of the content. As a result, 831 Italians were arrested in October 2000 for downloading child pornography, and extradition requests or international arrest warrants were issued for 660 foreign nationals residing mainly in Russia, France, and Malaysia for trading in child pornography. The operation focused on a Russian pedophile ring that kidnapped children from orphanages, circuses, and public parks. The children were then filmed being raped and, in some cases, tortured to death.

The theft of cultural property affects both developed and developing nations, with paintings, sculpture, coins, jewelry, and antiques taken from churches in Italy, chateaux in France, and temples in Asia, and artifacts looted from archeological sites in Africa and Latin America. The internet can help law enforcement agencies, customs agencies, heritage organizations, the art trade, and the insurance industry work together on a global basis to combat this illicit trade. To that end, the International Council of Museums has agreements with Interpol and the World Customs Organization to exchange information and establish operational channels of cooperation. Joint projects include the preparation of tools for raising awareness and the online distribution to customs and police departments of information on illicit traffic, including the One Hundred Missing Objects collection and the Red List of African archeological objects particularly at risk from looting.

To deal with the threat of football violence at the Euro 2000 championships, the two host countries of the Netherlands and Belgium used internet technology to create the Football Intelligence Message Exchange System (FIMES). A central computer at the Netherlands national police agency headquarters in Dribergen, near Utrecht, accessed data on all known and suspected hooligans from the 16 countries taking part in the competition, and compiled a risk assessment of all fans who had pre-booked accommodation. People were categorized according to whether they a) avoided violence, b) took part in violence, or c) started and organized violence. A number of English fans were turned back at border controls when scans of their passports revealed that they were on a UK government list of known hooligans. The 35,000 Dutch and 25,000 Belgian police officers on duty during the event itself supplied the system with up-to-date information and names, and foreign police forces provided new intelligence throughout the tournament. The system continually fed local police with the names of hooligans and gave them the ability to run checks on people in their own countries. When trouble flared, the central computer diverted police resources to where they were most needed.

Addressing each of these various crime scenarios requires the speedy exchange of intelligence and analysis between police forces in different countries. Cooperative police investigations require online interoperability of IT systems. But just as police officers cannot cross a national, state, or even municipal boundary line to pursue a criminal, neither can they very often cross technological boundaries to gain access to information from other jurisdictions. Says Nicolas Pougnet, head of IT for Europol: "You can make a request to a foreign police force but you're lucky if you get it in a month's time."

Fingerprinting has long been considered the most reliable method of establishing identification, yet there are barriers to exchanging fingerprint data electronically because different police organizations use different automated fingerprint identification systems (AFIS). Traditional AFIS solutions have been expensive standalone systems accessible solely to experts in a police force's fingerprint bureau. The advent of powerful low-cost PC workstations has changed the cost base of AFIS technology, and access is becoming available to custody units and other points where timely identification is critical. Internet technology means that all the different AFIS systems can now be linked, and access to all fingerprint databases becomes technically possible for any national or supranational authority. The AFIS systems of Norway, Sweden, Finland, Denmark, Germany, and the Netherlands are connected together using fingerprint image-transmission technology developed by Bull and the Norwegian National Bureau of Crime Investigation. It takes 25 seconds on a 64Mb line to transmit a file containing 500dpi resolution fingerprint images, alphanumeric data, and receiver and transmitter addresses. The solution supports workflow processes by automatically sending a case search reply from the country performing the AFIS search to the country that sent the request, and from there to the correct remote user.

In the US, most law enforcement agencies snailmail paper fingerprint cards to the FBI for processing. The FBI receives about 50,000 sets of fingerprints each business day; half are criminal checks and half are civil submissions for asylum seekers and certain job applicants (teachers, childcare providers, security guards, and other positions of trust) for which fingerprint checks are required by law. Until recently, each set of prints was classified and a semiautomated system searched for matches among the 34 million cards the FBI holds in its fingerprint repository. (If all these paper cards were stacked on top of each other, the pile would be 18 times higher than the Empire State Building.) Criminal checks took weeks to process, which delayed court dates and gave fugitives plenty of time to flee because their criminal history was not available prior to a bail hearing. Responses to civil fingerprint submissions exceeded 100 days, during which time people had to wait before they could start a new job or be accepted for asylum. To address this absurd situation, the FBI inaugurated an integrated AFIS in August 1999 and soon afterward 15 states and several federal agencies were submitting fingerprint images electronically. The FBI can now respond to a criminal fingerprint submission within two hours, and with a complete criminal history of a suspect. It makes a positive identification by matching fingerprints even if the fingerprinted person provides false identification. For civil submissions, responses are provided within 24 hours.

To cater to those states that still submit fingerprints by post, the FBI scans the paper cards and inserts them into the system. While this allows for a faster turnaround time than previously, it still takes about eight days to process. These states may well find themselves becoming a less welcoming environment for teachers and a more attractive place for criminals to come to apply their respective trades. The days are gone when law enforcement agencies can be satisfied with response times of days and weeks; the time limit for cases involving the investigation of a person in custody is more like a couple of hours. The message is clear enough—get online.

INTEGRATED JUSTICE, EUROPEAN STYLE

The gradual harmonization of criminal justice systems throughout Europe has been compared in scope and importance to the establishment in 1992 of the European common market. The Treaty of Amsterdam, which came into force in 1999, aims to create within five years an "area of freedom, security and justice" throughout the European Union. This gives people the right to move freely within the EU while guaranteeing public security by combating all forms of organized crime. External border controls, asylum, immigration, and judicial cooperation in civil matters become subject to directives, regulations, decisions, recommendations, and opinions from Brussels, regardless of differences in the laws of individual member states.

The Schengen agreement (named after a Luxembourg border town) was originally a separate interstate agreement, but is now incorporated into the EU's legal and institutional framework. It brings into the fold the Schengen Information System (SIS), a network giving police and consular agents from Schengen countries (all EU countries except the UK, Ireland, and Denmark) access to data on specific individuals and lost or stolen vehicles and objects. Member states supply the network through their own national networks, which are connected to a central system in Strasbourg. Besides abolishing internal border checks, the Schengen countries have introduced a uniform procedure for checking people and goods entering at the external frontiers. In principle, everyone who passes an external border is subject to an identity check with a data search conducted by the SIS. This makes it possible to identify, report, and extradite wanted people.

In criminal matters, the Treaty of Amsterdam replaces previous joint bilateral arrangements between nations with defined procedures and penalties, minimum common rules concerning criminal acts, and strengthened coordination of prosecution. While not seeking to create a European penal code, there are proposals to harmonize a range of serious offenses, including the sexual exploitation of children, drug and arms trafficking, terrorism, and money laundering. The treaty also establishes a European research, documentation, and statistical network on cross-border crime and, most importantly, greater cooperation between member states' national and local law enforcement agencies through the European Police Office, or Europol, which began operating in July 1999.

Replacing the European Drugs Unit set up on a temporary basis in 1995, Europol now has wider responsibility to exchange and share relevant intelligence information on all cross-border criminal activities, and is evolving into the chief instrument for coordination between European police forces. Information exchanges include descriptions of criminal organizations' *modus operandi* and the application of risk-analysis techniques. EU member states provide information from their national registers to Europol, which compiles and processes the data and where necessary supplements it with information from elsewhere. After analysis, the intelligence is returned to the police authorities for use in their investigations. Identifying interconnections between criminal actions requires the handling of not just structured data but also multimedia voice and imaging data, as well as the integration of multimedia translation, intelligence content analysis, and data mining, combined with voice recognition, language identification, automatic document indexing and scanning, and linguistic formatting tools. Europol provides natural linguistic support in 11 languages, with free text, block, and word-by-word translations. This makes it easier for police officers of different nationalities to exchange intelligence, not only in their own European tongues but also in reconnaissance languages of countries where organized crime originates.

In an operation conducted in five different languages, Italian authorities found a store of cocaine and synthetic drugs that had been smuggled in from the Netherlands. Three suspects from Italy, Germany, and Yugoslavia were placed under observation and a considerable amount of intelligence amassed. On the basis of this intelligence, Italian officers contacted counterparts in Austria, Belgium, Germany, Netherlands, and the UK. Their exchange of information showed that police in different EU countries were already investigating members of the same criminal organization. Because of the size and complexity of the case, Europol's assistance was requested to facilitate the investigation and process the intelligence that had been collected. "Operation Primo" unveiled a Europe-wide criminal network, pivoting around a German national living in Amsterdam. Crimes involved trafficking cocaine, Ecstasy, and cannabis, as well as associated money laundering. Twenty individuals of various nationalities were arrested and significant amounts of illicit drugs and money seized. A clandestine laboratory was also discovered. A single country's police force working on its own and in isolation would never have achieved such results. Coordinated transnational investigations and intelligence sharing are the future of modern policing—or at least they should be.

As useful as the Europol and Schengen systems are to European law enforcement agencies, the two don't interoperate with each other and neither links in with the Interpol Criminal Information System—not due to any technical reason but because the politicians haven't allowed it. Europol was created partially in response to the past inefficiencies of Interpol, when paper files would go missing between floors of its headquarters building. The Europol Convention, one-third of which deals specifically with IT, states that the organization's system of collected information "must under no circumstances be linked to other automated processing systems," except for those of the EU national units. Similarly, the Schengen Convention precludes the possibility of connecting Interpol to SIS data.

Inconsistent information about the same cases could be circulating simultaneously on three different systems, each of which was set up to improve law enforcement cooperation. High-speed secure internet technology can assist police in cross-border operations, but the obstacles to police cooperation and information sharing must be removed, and the biggest obstacles are political not technical.

COMPUTERS IN THE COURTROOM

Lawyers and judges dressed in their black gowns and wigs are rarely regarded as modern purveyors of the technological age. Yet there's no reason that a legal professional working late into the night to put the finishing touches to a claim form shouldn't be able to file the document to the court with one last click of the mouse before turning out the lights and going home.

In 2000, the state of Colorado became the first in the US to implement a statewide court e-filing system. Initiated and operated by CourtLink, a private online legal services provider, the system allows the electronic delivery of documents through a secure website. Copies are stored electronically, providing instant access for all case parties as well as judges and clerks. The e-filing system is integrated with the state court case management information system so that judges can also send orders and render decisions directly on their computers. The system was set up at no cost to the government and required no legislation. CourtLink makes its money by charging law firms 10 cents per page to file; other electronically filed documents related to the case can be viewed for free. The system is optional, and while some lawyers balk at the fee and some traditionalists simply don't like the idea of changing their book-bound legal culture, court officials expect even the most skeptical lawyers eventually to embrace the technology. Russell Murray III, an attorney practicing in the Denver suburb of Aurora, said that the experience of being the first Colorado e-filer was "like making the first-ever telephone call."

CourtLink also provided an e-filing service for the Microsoft antitrust class action filed in the San Francisco Superior Court, after Judge Stuart Pollak ordered the electronic filing of all documents in order to keep his courtroom clear of case paper and better manage the volume of filings resulting from a lawsuit of such magnitude.

The courtroom of the future will carry a range of technology solutions to current business problems. Staff will use in-court workstations to capture hearing information in real time. Both prosecution and defense lawyers will use computer support for court presentations, saving them time in preparing for court and saving the judge time in summing up. Computers in the courtroom can improve the ability to present evidence clearly since electronic files can contain multimedia images—a court record of a police interview, for example, can contain text, audio, and video. The electronic presentation of evidence will make it easier for a jury to follow a case, especially a complex matter such as fraud. Technology has the potential to make unmanageable trials manageable.

In countries where law is established by precedence, not all court rulings are reported and judges often produce conflicting decisions through ignorance of previous cases. In future, all judges will have their own laptops, which they will use to search online for precedents and to input judgments that will be electronically transmitted on to the record. The internet also makes it possible to communicate with outside agencies from a courtroom, so the results of a hearing can be transmitted directly to the police, prison service, another court, and other agencies.

Shared online case data and direct access to criminal records can save all criminal justice agencies time and effort, eliminate multiple data entry and the wasteful trail of paper, and make the cumbersome legal system more convenient. Immediate access to case data and court records such as opinions, calendars, docket sheets, and pleadings can reduce the number of adjournments granted by judges and magistrates because the prosecution is unable to proceed or because documents had not been made available to the defense in time. The use of videoconferencing for pre-trial hearings can reduce the number of journeys made by remand prisoners, and prison services will be able to provide faster risk assessment and categorization by accessing police systems.

TRAILBLAZERS STEP ON LANDMINES

People talk about the criminal justice system as if it's one seamless institution, when in reality it's a myriad of independent, inward-looking public agencies and external organizations that sometimes try to cooperate, but at a grindingly slow pace. From the moment an arrest is made and a case file initiated, a lengthy administrative process begins that will eventually distract and engulf the police, prosecutor, defense counsel, lower and higher courts, prison service, probation service, maybe other prosecuting authorities like customs or the tax department, and government departments like interior and justice ministries. Local administrations, social services, health authorities, legal aid, and volunteer groups also often play important criminal justice roles. Case files cross and recross all these organizational boundaries, as they are read, passed on, reread, added to, and amended. Administrative procedures and practices are carried out in an *ad hoc* fashion and, with no serious attempt to manage the system as a whole, each agency ends up pursuing completely different agendas.

Most information exchanged between criminal justice agencies remains paper based because the number of different systems in use within the legal world are not designed to communicate with one another, even within the same organization. Within a corrections service, for example, there will be no integration of technology between different prisons, and frequently not even between prisons and the agency headquarters. Within headquarters there will be separate, incompatible systems for personnel, finance, and prison administration, so it's impossible to calculate a relatively simple matter such as how many more guards would be required for a certain increase in prison population. The information has to be taken from a number of different sources and put on to a spreadsheet, dealing along the way with all the probabilities of error that arise from information being transcribed manually from one system to another.

When it comes to linking externally, criminal justice agencies are often protective of their authority to build their own technology platforms and applications, and they will struggle against anyone who tries to dictate how their systems should operate. Different agencies will argue about who will benefit the most from an integrated solution and therefore who should pay the lion's share of the investment. Integration projects involve both the executive and judicial branches of government and the constitutional importance in many countries of maintaining an arm's length between the two can be an issue. All these obstacles too often serve to ensure that nothing happens, and the ability to track an offender from first dealings with the police right through to probation services remains rudimentary at best.

Creating a holistic criminal justice system is inevitably a long, drawn-out process and many early attempts to link agencies failed. In Canada in the mid-1990s, an ambitious integrated justice project involving a public–private partnership between the province of New Brunswick and Andersen Consulting sought to connect courts, prisons, police, social welfare agencies, and the community at large. There was a planned four-year implementation, but development costs escalated out of control and the project was abandoned after two years. Part of the problem was a lack of precedence anywhere in the world of governments attempting such large-scale interagency cooperation. "As trailblazers, we would often be the first people to step on a landmine," says Frank McKenna, the premier of New Brunswick at the time. "I think we lacked the project management skills to manage some of these very large and complicated projects and, if I had to do it over again, I think we would try to purchase sophisticated project management skills from outside."

There is also a school of thought that criminal justice integration is simply too complex and too complicated for anyone—public, private, or partnership—to project manage, and that it's better to take a piecemeal approach than trying to create a holistic system all at once. When they all move together in convoy, each agency can only progress at the pace of the slowest organization. But in breaking the work up, governments need to ensure that all the pieces will eventually arrive at their final destination where they will all fit together. For that, there needs to be a clear strategic framework and development plan, with demanding but realistic timetables.

AVOIDING TURF BATTLES

Recognizing that new IT implementations cannot be considered in isolation, the UK government formed an Integrating Business and Information Systems (IBIS) board comprised of senior officials from all government departments and agencies involved in criminal justice. The board oversees the integration of existing computer systems and ensures that future developments take place within a clear and agreed strategic "whole system" framework.

One development is the Libra project, which replaces three incompatible computer systems dating from the 1970s. With implementation between 2001 and 2004, Libra will standardize computer services across criminal and magistrates' courts in England and Wales, allowing for the online completion, distribution, and maintenance of court lists. The national police computer and the criminal records database will be notified immediately and automatically of the results of court hearings, and the system will also interface with the Driver and Vehicle Licensing Authority, Prison Service, and Crown Prosecution Service. It will provide public access over the internet to basic information such as schedules of cases being heard in court, and the public and press will be able to request details about individual cases. In time, the public should be able to access court records to view the state of play in any given case. Secure systems could also enable the public to carry out transactions with the courts, such as the electronic payment of fines and fees.

In the US, the federal Department of Justice has set up a National Integration Resource Center to persuade state and local agencies to collaborate on integrated solutions. A dynamic website provides online collaborative capabilities such as conferencing and newsgroups, and integration helpdesk services. It also offers analytical and up-to-date information on new policies, technology developments, integration profiles for states, funding approaches of various states, lessons learned, system descriptions and overviews, telecommunications approaches, mobile data terminal and wireless initiatives, model integrated systems, and best practices.

Pennsylvania is one of the success stories. Its web-based Justice Network (JNET) received strong commitment at the executive level when the independence of each of the 15 agencies involved was assured as one of the project's guiding principles. Agencies did not have to rewrite software or buy new hardware because it was agreed to communicate using open internet standards such as XML, allowing even agencies with aging legacy systems to participate. To avoid turf battles over who owned the information on the network, the agencies themselves were allowed to decide the data they wanted to share. Tight security also helped keep agencies relaxed about publishing data. No specific information is given until a user logs on to the system with a digital certificate, and each user has a level of access based on what data they need to do their job. The thought of putting criminal information and legal documents on the internet alarms many attorneys and judges, but the way to ensure security and privacy is to protect the message, not the medium, using public-key cryptography, an encryption technique based on the concept of key pairs.

The first phase of the JNET project focused on infrastructure and functions such as notification and inmate lookup systems. Criminal justice workers can have JNET notify them by email whenever there is a change in the file of a particular inmate or suspect so that they can easily track the progress of a case. A probation officer, for example, can find out immediately if a parolee has been arrested. While in the past police might have searched for a suspect and not realized he was already in jail doing time for another crime, they are now kept informed by JNET. And while previously police officers, prosecutors, and judges often had no idea where a suspect or convict in state custody was being held, they can now locate an inmate just by typing in a name or identification number.

Subsequent project phases have focused on increasing the system's coverage and expanding its reach to field officers and to municipal and county agencies. The idea is to develop JNET as a criminal justice portal, or a one-stop shop for all criminal justice workers in Pennsylvania. The project is also trying to integrate data from across the state line, such as accessing the FBI's national database.

Beyond police and customs initiatives such as the Europol and Schengen systems, very few governments have faced up to the challenges of integrating wider criminal justice systems with other jurisdictions and other countries. But the police are not the only ones who could benefit from the sharing of information and intelligence. As more criminals move across borders to commit their crimes, more are ending up in foreign jail cells. This is creating unrest in courts and prisons as an inmate's language, values, and culture may clash with those of the detaining country. Extradition hearings and transferring prisoners between national jurisdictions remain time-consuming and logistically difficult processes because information cannot be exchanged quickly and electronically. A bigger problem is that a country too often will not recognize another country's judicial decisions because its laws, criminal code, and legal traditions are different. A judge may only grant a request from another country to seize assets, for example, if the two nations have identical laws, almost to the letter. And even if offenses were somehow aligned, as is proposed for the EU, they will be difficult to enforce if there are no electronic links between foreign criminal justice agencies.

The legal systems of most countries date back centuries and often form the core of national sovereignty, making it extremely difficult for different jurisdictions to cooperate on criminal justice matters. Nevertheless, to create a more secure global society, national traditions and rivalries are going to have to be reconsidered and agreements reached. Strategic planning by criminal justice agencies, governments, and international bodies must take into account the new reality of transnational crime and, in some cases, more penetrating legislation will be required.

While safeguards to protect the privacy and freedom of individuals are important, many of the bureaucratic restrictions on the sharing of information and intelligence only make it easier for criminals to commit crimes and evade justice. Governments have a moral obligation to equip their police forces, courts, and prison services with the tools to ensure that information is made available to those in other countries struggling against criminal elements that could easily spread to other parts of the world. Says Detective Jaun Kotze of the Interpol National Central Bureau in South Africa: "One of the greatest problems encountered in addressing transnational organized crime groups effectively is the reluctance or hesitation of government or its officials to recognize their very existence."

The fight against crime requires huge efforts at local, regional, national, and international levels, with different agencies and different governments all working together, and with businesses, nongovernmental organizations, and individual citizens also pitching in to do their bit. Whether dealing with organized cross-border crimes like drug trafficking or high-volume local offenses like burglary, new technologies and the fast transmission of up-to-date information offer the best hope of developing whole-system thinking and mobilizing those on the right side of the law.

8 War: Establishing Information Superiority

COMMON DIRECTION AND PURPOSE

During the Cold War, the possibility of invasion from another country or bloc of countries posed the most serious threat to a nation's security. Large, standing armies were in a constant high state of alert and their capabilities were oriented toward fending off opposing forces from the other side of the Iron Curtain. It was East vs. West all the way. With the end of this bipolarization, the world has entered a new security era where all-out war engulfing an entire continent is unlikely. Yet, threats to global security have not diminished. If anything, they have broadened and become more complex.

The dark side of globalization is social unrest, nationalism and ethnic conflicts, terrorism, environmental degradation, and resource wars. The preservation of a country's freedom and independence is still the steadfast objective for most armed forces and isolationists believe that should remain the only objective. But a country's security isn't only a matter of military might; defense is deeply intertwined with economics and politics. Armed forces today must play a global role because their countries have global interests. Oil is the obvious example, and it's a big reason for conflicts occurring in the Middle East with such regularity. There are also fears that a country's own peace and stability could be jeopardized by crises spilling over from outside its borders. And finally, in the age of globalization with a free flow of information and modern media communications, conscience does not allow the West to stand by while terror and conflict are being carried out unchecked elsewhere. For these reasons, the prevention or reduction of external conflicts before they spread is now seen by many governments as a legitimate reason to send in the troops.

The term "peace enforcement" wasn't in anybody's vocabulary until very recently. No military mind would have contemplated using troops to enable nongovernmental organizations (NGOs) to deliver aid to warring factions and to those caught in between. No commander would have thought of going into battle with orders to keep the loss of human lives at an absolute minimum, even at zero. And no one would have contemplated conducting a military operation with the support of private-sector partners in the operational theater. But while nationalized infrastructure and telecommunications networks were, in the good old days, easy to define and easy to defend, today's information infrastructures and utilities are global operations not confined to one country and largely owned and operated by private companies. Since armed forces' own communications systems are often dependent on these companies, military establishments can no longer defend their countries without the involvement of industry.

Despite all the dramatic geopolitical and technological changes since the fall of the Berlin Wall, most countries' armed forces still look much the same as they did in the 1980s. In their innate conservatism, military planners remain committed to Cold War priorities of big numbers and large-scale deployments, and political leaders have been reluctant to second-guess the uniformed experts. In the meantime, an increasing number of military operations, from Somalia to the Balkans to East Timor, have called for more agile, expeditionary forces working in coalition with other nations. These peace support operations are forcing defense agencies to review their roles and relationships in order to accommodate the new world realities.

What is emerging is a trend toward powerful, strategically mobile military units that can be deployed as various types of taskforces at short notice anywhere in the world to carry out a range of international peace-keeping missions. The North Atlantic Treaty Organization (NATO) uses multinational and multiservice forces requiring multinational command

and control, or a combined joint taskforce (CJTF) in military jargon. Unlike NATO's reaction forces, the CJTF is not a standing force but rather is organized and formed for contingency operations, drawing on units of contributing nations as required.

The challenges of global crisis management require an unprecedented degree of military, political, and private-sector cooperation. No one government and no one country possesses all the might and means, not even the US of A. The old saying that NATO exists to keep the Russians out, the Americans in, and the Germans down no longer rings true (for two of the three at least). Countries are embracing former enemies and institutions such as NATO are opening up to new members. Even long-time neutral countries are finding that, in nearly every aspect of international security, they are bound together with other nations as never before. A Swedish government working document published in 1998 stated that its armed forces should be "designed to meet the increasing demand for international crisis control," and the country has since developed a military structure with fewer command levels and units and a headquarters organized so that it can command forces outside its borders.

Further reflecting this new ethos of adaptation and partnership, 27 countries with different military traditions and policies cooperate on joint maneuvers in the NATO-sponsored Partnership for Peace (PfP) program, which in turn provides an incentive for nations to resolve bilateral disputes with their neighbors. As more and more democracies display a similar sense of direction and purpose, a common security space from Vancouver to Vladivostok no longer seems the unrealistic goal it was during the Cold War.

INTEROPERABILITY DEFINED

At NATO's 50th anniversary summit in Washington DC in April 1999, the alliance's heads of government approved the Defense Capabilities Initiative (DCI), moving away from previous priorities of consultation and deterrence toward building security across Europe through partnership and cooperative crisis management. The strategic concept focuses on improving the effectiveness of armed forces through harmonization of defense planning, addressing five key areas: deployability and mobility; sustainability and logistics; effective engagement; survivability of forces and infrastructure; and command-and-control and information systems. It aims to ensure that NATO forces can move to where they are needed quickly, be supplied and reinforced for an extended period, and cooperate with each other and non-NATO forces. Says Lord Robertson, NATO secretary general: "It will promote greater interoperability between the forces of allies and will also play a major role in accelerating the development of interoperability between partner forces and those of the alliance."

Military planners and thinkers throw around the word "interoperability" all the time, but most NATO countries don't actually have an official definition of the term. Generally, they see it as being able to use other forces' systems and equipment as if they were part of their own. NATO itself defines interoperability as: "The ability of systems, units, or forces to provide services to, and accept services from, other systems, units, or forces and to use the services so exchanged to operate effectively together."

Whatever. The point is that technology should play a leading role in enabling a common doctrine, but more often it's an obstacle to cooperation because systems at all levels of command don't work together effectively. During the Cold War, the thought of having an outside force link into your information and communication systems was a commander's worst nightmare. So vertical legacy systems were built like fortresses, and today they are proving more difficult to knock down than the Berlin Wall.

The first impediment to interoperability is the deeply rooted culture of rivalry between different military services. The army, navy, and air force of any given nation often have their own intelligence officers, quartermasters, doctors, and radio operators. Even after many attempts and often legislation for increased joint operations among services, there is still costly redundancy and compartmentalization. Services can't even agree on a single military meaning for words such as "tank." To the air force, a tank is something that contains fuel. To the navy, it's something that contains oxygen. To the army, it's an armored vehicle with a big gun. Simple disagreements over taxonomy can undercut a defense department's ability to integrate information technology into its overall planning and operations.

"This parochialism is driven not by military requirements but by the bureaucratic imperative to maintain one's relative institutional status," says Admiral William Owens, former vice-chairman of the joint chiefs of staff in the US. "With traditional service commitments to the planes, tanks, and ships that once defined our military prowess—and each service branch's own war specialty—we are inserting the new technology in uncoordinated and competing ways into our standing force structures."

Before computer systems can start talking to each other, the admirals and generals have to start talking to each other. True operational command resides at the three-star level and this is where decisions need to be made to ensure technical interoperability. In the UK, talking led to the decision in 1998 to form the Defence Communication Services Agency (DCSA) to take over responsibility for all fixed military telecommunications within the UK, which are now owned and managed on behalf of DCSA by BT. Previously each of the three services owned and operated their own networks and the Ministry of Defence created a fourth in order to interact with them all.

While there was reluctance to give up control over such core assets, initial fears have not materialized, largely because the DCSA has rationalized the disparate telecommunications services and increased awareness of the scope of information available. Importantly, it has focused on providing end-to-end information services to each force rather than simply supplying a specified number of boxes. The agency offers coherence and interoperability through a Defence Information Infrastructure, bringing together the former single service systems and providing the basis for a defense-wide intranet. Military personnel can access common applications relevant to their business by selecting icons on the desktop, without being concerned about the number or variety of systems that make up that end-to-end connectivity.

Says the DCSA's Major General Tony Raper: "We must embrace proven commercial policies such as service provision, facilities management, and customer relationship management. It is only by using these tools, which have generated considerable benefits for customers and companies alike, that we will be able to move away from the stovepipe legacy systems that have bedeviled interoperability in the past."

As a country's own forces are learning to trust each other and exchange information, many admirals, generals, and defense ministers are looking to create synergies with forces from other nations through joint military exercises. In combined operations, participating nations want to deploy their own information systems even if they don't interoperate with the systems of the other participating nations. If it's a NATO exercise, there could also be problems linking into NATO static and operational systems.

Rear Admiral Willie Williamson, a retired US Navy aircraft carrier commander and now a senior business strategist for Microsoft, recalls an exercise in the Mediterranean in which it took several hours for the two flagships to communicate vital information to each other, even though they were positioned just one and half miles apart. One ship was French and had to link back to a shore installation in southern France, while the other ship, commanded by Williamson, was American and its systems were directed back to the US. "I could get my binoculars out and literally see him up on his flag bridge," says Williamson. "I would have done better by semaphore."

A modern military cannot develop interoperability capabilities with only its traditional fighting partners, because nowadays it is impossible for any force to predict which country it will have to work alongside and share information with on a peace support mission. The Gulf War

175

brought together a coalition of countries that had rarely, if ever, operated together; even though it is renowned as the war where technology triumphed, helicopters still had to fly out to ships to drop off floppy disks containing the program code for launching a cruise missile.

In Bosnia-Herzegovina and Kosovo, even though NATO provided the technical backbone, troops came from well beyond NATO or even PfP countries. Command and control for these operations was run predominantly at NATO secret level, which excluded the possibility of an integrated exchange of information with units from non-NATO countries. As a result there was a heavy reliance on liaison officers, which simply didn't provide fast enough communication for many commanders. It also contributed to a feeling among the non-NATO units that they were simply an appendage glued to the NATO option rather than equal contributing participants.

Since a coalition is only as strong as its weakest member, the success of a combined joint taskforce depends on all partners possessing similar skills, tools, and authority to access information equally. There is also a need to place greater importance on civil–military cooperation, and armed forces must improve their capability to communicate with the commercial technologies used by the United Nations, the Organization for Security and Cooperation in Europe (OSCE), the press, humanitarian aid organizations, and other NGOs.

Neither the unwillingness to share information nor outdated military security regulations reflects modern realities. Commanders need to learn to manage the risk of exchanging information in the same way they manage other risks in battle. The greatest risk of interoperability is human error. Soldiers will forget to follow basic information security rules and, for example, send classified information over a public network. Or they won't think to extend to the web old virtues such as the need-to-know principle and the use of discretion when speaking on the phone. Neither of these is technology's fault.

Many technology concerns such as security of data are not unique to the military and are being resolved by industry. The survival of financial institutions, telecom operators, and logistics companies, to name but a few, depends on their ability to transmit electronic data reliably and securely. Many companies and sectors operate in a warfare-like business environment, where they have to protect their interests and defend their positions against competitors they consider enemies, and in response they are addressing their vulnerabilities and developing countermeasures to potential threats. Military organizations ought to exploit the commonalities.

BUYING OFF THE SHELF

Peace support operations are unpredictable in nature and armed forces must be able to establish themselves quickly in unfamiliar territory. This requires flexible technology solutions, not the onerous systems that military organizations buy to meet pre-planned or anticipated events. In the operational theater there is no time to a build complex information and communications system, and IT specialists are a scarce resource even in the largest militaries. Most organizations retain only a small pool of trained operations and maintenance personnel who cannot be stationed in the field indefinitely to support a never-ending peace support operation. It is therefore important to deploy proven technologies that regular military staff can administer with little training. The front end needs to be kept simple with a familiar user interface so that soldiers will use the tool to maximum effect.

Defense agencies tend to use the same procurement processes to acquire information systems as they use to buy hand grenades and missiles, or tanks and ships. The emphasis is almost entirely on the product purchase price, with little consideration given to the total cost of ownership in relation to linking together concept, design, manufacture, testing and evaluation, maintenance, repair, and environmental impact. It can take a decade or longer to develop some of the more sophisticated military machinery, by which time, for information systems, the technology is obsolete and the world has changed beyond recognition. Says Colonel

H.J. Boogaard of the Royal Netherlands Army: " If it takes more than two years, you end up with a solution that is solving problems that are no longer valid, or problems that have already been solved by industry."

It used to be that the military led the way in advancing technology, including the first electronic computers, global positioning satellites, and the internet itself. Technologies developed for military purposes would then be applied in the civilian market. With military procurement now incapable of keeping pace with fast-changing sectors such as information technology and telecommunications, the economy is being driven by the research and development efforts of the civilian sector, not defense contractors. The combined market values of the aerospace and defense operations of Boeing, Raytheon, Lockheed Martin, Hughes, TRW, General Dynamics, Litton, Loral, and Northrop-Grumman doesn't even equal the net worth of one Cisco.

This economic shift is having a profound effect on defense, because it means that a country's military strength now depends on the prosperity of the private sector from which it buys its products. Gone are the days when an army general wrote a blank check to develop a bespoke stovepipe legacy system that couldn't interoperate and couldn't be upgraded to a more powerful version later on. Like everyone else, defense organizations are migrating toward commercial off-the-shelf (COTS) products as the only option for reliable, cost-effective, and easy-to-integrate technology solutions. The emphasis is on developing systems based on Asynchronous Transfer Mode (ATM) and internet standards with a web-style graphical user interface for digital, satellite, cellular, and wireless LAN communications, with functionality sustained by databases and geographic information systems. Agencies are also starting to embrace private service providers in order to harness civilian best practice so they can do away with their legacy systems and break down other vertical barriers that prevent interoperability. Commanders want to be provided with an end-to-end technology service and they are not concerned about either how that end-to-end connectivity is achieved or who provides it.

The US military has taken to buying off the shelf in a big way. The CVN 77, the transition to the Navy's next-generation class of nuclear-powered aircraft carrier, will have an integrated warfare system built on openly available software so that it can increase its operational capability and facilitate affordable upgrades over its 50-year service life. Lockheed Martin is the warfare systems integrator and is responsible for inter-operability among sensors, advanced communications systems, high-performance ship network connectivity, aircraft control systems, and other electronics on the ship. And the landmark $6.9 billion performance-based contract awarded to EDS in October 2000 to develop the Navy Marine Corps intranet, the largest US federal information technology contract in history, signals a major shift in the way the Navy and Marine Corps view technology, away from in-house projects toward large-scale outsourcing.

Public–private partnerships will likely become the norm in non-hostile environments because they are cheaper and more effective, and because it means that armed forces don't have to keep old equipment on hand for years on end without it ever being used. They also give forces greater flexibility, because highly trained military IT specialists don't have to be posted permanently to a particular operation and can instead be free to provide technical support in the more difficult, war zone conditions. Private contractors can move in to take over once a conflict area has stabilized.

WHO'S IN COMMAND AND CONTROL AROUND HERE?

While the Balkan conflicts demonstrated the risks of the new world order, they also brought home the reality that deterrence and territorial defense are no longer enough, and that a coherent, cooperative international approach to crisis management is needed. Says Lord Robertson: "If Bosnia-Herzegovina showed us the general direction that adaptation needed to take, the Kosovo crisis shone a powerful light on NATO's military strengths and efficiencies—and the gaps in them—showing us just how much more work we have to do. Put simply, it is a lot."

For many years, military organizations around the world developed costly command-and-control (C2) systems that lacked proper security and failed to meet user requirements. Many armies don't even have computerized systems and still use a paper map on the wall, covered with pins or layers of plastic to show the location of army units, political boundaries, minefields, refugee movements, and so on, to the point where there are so many pins or overlays that it's no longer possible to see the map. With joint combined operations involving such a mixed bag of countries, command and control assumes a broader significance than its traditional combat support role. Therefore, C2 systems have to become more efficient, and they have to interoperate with other countries' systems. Pins and plastic overlays can't be transmitted electronically.

Recognizing the problems, the US Department of Defense now mandates that all proposed C2 systems be based on architectural frameworks using current and emerging standards. The US Air Force's Integrated Space Command and Control (ISC2) project, for example, uses commercial technologies to modernize the battle management and command-and-control systems at the North American Aerospace Defense Command (NORAD) facility at Cheyenne Mountain, Colorado.

Forces that train and fight together have to build their military capabilities together, but American interoperability initiatives so far outstrip the efforts of many of its allies. This threatens to marginalize coalition partners in future operations. The US military isn't at all confident about the ability or determination of other countries to make better use of their resources and integrate their technologies into the battlefield. The Pentagon wants its allies to follow its lead and insist on interoperability standards before granting funding approval. This will be necessary in order for Europe, for example, to shoulder a greater share of the burden of its own security, a need that was demonstrated by the peace enforcement efforts in the Balkans.

Yet, while the US has long pressed its NATO allies to improve their defense capabilities, the American export control system has at the same time worked to discourage this. The US took almost three months before approving an export license to the Netherlands for digital maps of Bosnia, even with a high-level request from the Dutch for an expedited review. The approval came too late for the maps to be of any use. It took about the same length of time for the US to approve the sale of flares to the Italian Coast Guard to use in case it had to rescue downed Allied pilots, including American ones, during the air campaign over Kosovo. In its first review of export controls since the Cold War, the US launched a Defense Trade Security Initiative in May 2000 to increase the sharing of technology, and the Pentagon is encouraging its allies to do the same.

While many European countries are committed to strengthening and modernizing their armed forces to revitalize NATO's European pillar, some are concerned that America's idea of interoperability is to force US standards on them, thereby ensuring that the American defense industry is the greatest beneficiary of greater European military spending. NATO already requires all systems used for classified information to meet the US government's computer security evaluation criteria and, in reality, no NATO country will touch any commercial military software that hasn't received US approval up to the secret level.

As part of its common foreign and security policy, the European Union aims to provide its own defense decision making and strategic direction setting by 2003. EU nations should be able to deploy up to 60,000 trained military personnel to tackle any major crisis on the continent. This force could form part of a NATO-led operation or a crisis management mission led by the EU itself. This may well give the European defense industry a boost and help drive acceptance of European standards, but the best way to close the technical gap between NATO members is through greater transatlantic industrial cooperation. There need to be more links between more defense contractors on both sides of the Atlantic, and more competition in both markets.

Because of certain nations' desires to share the spoils of industrial benefit, the concept of sole-source procurement remains taboo within NATO, even though the procurement of identical equipment would be the easiest way to achieve interoperability. Until governments are prepared to give up their buy-local policies, NATO troops will probably have to cope with incompatible equipment, or at best equipment that can be made compatible but only with different configurations and training. This enables interoperability to be achieved for short periods, but sustaining it through a long joint-command campaign such as those in Bosnia and Kosovo demands a level of standardization that must be maintained and adhered to between incremental procurements. The confusion of battle is not the time or place to start introducing and integrating new systems.

To save time in the development and production phases of new systems, agencies are increasingly looking to simulation and modeling techniques to help test and evaluate new products and processes before they are deployed in the battlespace. Agencies must be willing to refresh technologies, accepting that some will succeed and others will fail, but each individual element of a computerized weaponry has to be tried and tested to ensure that it can be incorporated into one system, which in turn has to work within a family of other systems. So as defense agencies take advantage of the rapid implementations and reduced costs of commercial products and services, their most difficult technological challenge will be to achieve a high level of testing and evaluation.

Military forces will have to expand joint experimentation efforts such as NATO's Joint Warfighter Interoperability Demonstrations, which provides a high payoff by giving forces the opportunity to try before they buy new C2 and communications technologies. Combined Endeavor is another exercise carried out each year to establish the current state of technical interoperability between NATO and PfP nations. It provides a guide for military planners of multinational peace support operations who need to know which products in their existing inventories are capable of integrating in a combined network. Each successive exercise builds on the documentation and lessons learned from the previous year, so if there were a software upgrade or a new microchip installed in a telephone, for example, they could be tested to see if they still interoperate—or more likely, to see that they now interoperate.

Combined Endeavor 2000 focused on the integration of all types of equipment and the management of a multinational, distributed network that mirrored a real-world command center and capabilities for a peace support or disaster relief operation. Combined Endeavor has grown from 10 participating countries in the first exercise in 1995 to the involvement of 35 nations in 2000. Normally held in different locations each year, it is one of the most popular and most important NATO activities—there ought to be more like it.

C2 TO C2

With interoperability a major goal of NATO's Defense Capabilities Initiative, the use of selected interoperability standards and products is now mandated for all new or substantially modified NATO-funded or partially funded systems. New versions of the NATO Common Operating Environment (NCOE) contain criteria required for software to be included in an approved "basket of products." National military systems are encouraged, but not obliged, to adopt the NATO interoperability framework. If enough countries are to adopt NATO standards, this should put the onus on the others to follow suit.

Real interoperability is happening today among smaller nations that don't have the baggage of a significant domestic defense industry. These countries often work in collaboration to develop pragmatic, web-based, COTS-based systems in command, control, and communications that can be applied equally to a national exercise or a multinational intervention, be it NATO led, EU led, or UN led. And the standards they are using have been developed or approved by NATO rather than by any individual country.

Denmark is one of those small NATO countries whose command and control has traditionally involved the use of paper maps with plastic overlays and other manual routines. Communication was by telephone, fax, and radio. In any potential attack against Danish forces, three telephones, one fax, and one VHF radio would have been expected to handle up to 175 incoming phone calls and paper reports an hour to the division level, and another 125 messages an hour to the brigade level. This, of course, wouldn't have been possible, and most calls would have been left unanswered. Information would be lost and the commander wouldn't know if it was something important or just a call from the mess saying dinner was ready.

In 1994, Denmark became an active participant in NATO's Army Tactical Command and Control Information Systems (ATCCIS) project to research and develop highly flexible and interoperable command-and-control systems. In 1995, the Royal Netherlands Army hosted an ATCCIS interoperability demonstration that saw the first ever high-security database-to-database connection between national C2 systems. As a result, the armies of several NATO countries, including Denmark and the Netherlands, decided to develop information infrastructures based on the ATCCIS data model. The Danish Army Command and Control Information System (DACCIS) was implemented in 2000, supporting the planning and control of army operations from brigade level and up, and the exchange of information among national and allied command posts. It includes 85 military applications that interact with each other on many levels, allowing field personnel to orchestrate troop movements and resource allocations.

Since almost every decision an operational commander makes is spatially related, the ability to exchange digital geographic information is fundamental to interoperability. Most armed forces continue to use paper maps to understand terrain, but these can't be shared. So as digital maps become more common, armies will need geographic information systems (GIS) integrated with their C2 systems to show the location of units with standard military symbols, with battles lines continually being updated with connected online data. A user can click on a symbol of a unit to display all known information about that unit. The DACCIS system produces electronic overlays to show friend and foe situations, relative battle power, and so on. It has the appearance of a traditional paper map, except that up to 64 different overlays can automatically be turned on and off without obscuring the map itself.

C2 operation officers typically spend two-thirds of their time gathering information and one-third giving advice to the command. Internet technology can reverse this, so they spend most of their time analyzing data and making recommendations to improve situational awareness, knowing precisely the answer to the questions: Where am I? Where are my buddies? Where is the enemy?

The Danish army's use of the ATCCIS replication mechanism enables users to operate with real-time information sharing so an officer can receive updates without delay. Whenever a moving headquarters occupies a new position and re-establishes communication, DACCIS automatically ensures that any missing information is replicated and that the new land picture is recognized. The commanding officer can react to any new situation quickly and there are no delays between issuing orders and executing them. DACCIS also includes an automated military message-handling system that distributes electronic messages and email to the relevant staff function or role, stating the priority of the message from routine to urgent. The system allows users to set national and NATO levels of classifications, from unclassified to top secret.

A complete command-and-control information system must communicate with a range of military systems, including peacetime administrative systems like those for logistics as well as battlefield systems like those for artillery. Therefore all new projects in the Danish army, such as the development of new unmanned armed vehicles, are required to incorporate the ATCCIS model into their databases so they can connect directly to command and control. Says Major Erling Rasmussen, commander of C2 information systems at Danish Division Headquarters: "DACCIS is the project with the highest priority in the Army; all other projects are based on it. If the command and control does not work, then nothing else will. There's no point having a big rocket launcher if you don't know where to aim it."

Denmark has been conducting tests to ensure compatibility with other countries that have adopted the ATCCIS data model, including the Netherlands, Spain, and Canada. It is part of a multinational corps with Germany and Poland, so interoperability with their command-and-control systems is essential. Since joining NATO in 1999, Poland has made it a priority to modernize its communication and information systems according to NATO standards, but Germany uses an old legacy C2 system, called HEROS, based on formatted messages, so DACCIS has to convert and transfer the German data through a gateway. The Danish army also needs gateways to exchange information with other countries whose systems are not ATCCIS compliant, as well as its own navy and air force. However, the highly flexible and open architecture of DACCIS makes this possible.

DOT-COM THE BATTLEFIELD

The inside of a tank is a dark, cramped, and confusing place. The driver peers through a small portal in one direction while the turret may be pointed in another. He is most likely wearing chemical-protection gear so he's also looking through small eyeglasses. The whole inefficient setup is an accident waiting to happen, and in combat many do. Tankers frequently target what they think is an opponent vehicle only to find out they've hit one of their own.

Tanks are not the sort of place where one would expect to log on and surf the web, but this might just be the best thing to overcome all of their inadequacies. With a computer terminal on the dashboard, an armored combat vehicle can signal its position to give commanders a real-time electronic picture of the battlefield, which is shared among all the other tanks in the battalion. Without ever setting eyes on each other, tankers can see where they are, where their fellow tankers are, and where their opponents are. They don't have to approach too close to one another and risk misfiring before engaging an enemy tank.

This is the sort of web-based technology that is being developed today. Nothing like it existed in December 1995 when NATO was charged with implementing and enforcing the Dayton Peace Accords. All of the alliance's command data was carried on a torn paper tape relay system and exchanging urgent messages took a full day or more, by which time the commander-in-chief had already seen it on CNN. There was a desperate need to exchange information and tactical and military data electronically among the peacekeeping forces, intermediate commands, the Supreme Headquarters Allied Powers Europe (SHAPE) in Brussels, and national sites in 17 countries throughout Europe and the US. Using commercially available software, a system called Cronos was developed, configured, and deployed in less than three months. Servers were located throughout Bosnia, and also later in Kosovo, in secure vans and buildings, and connected using internet protocols encrypted with high-grade cryptography.

The system was originally intended only to provide office automation functions for NATO staff and allow them to forward information up the chain from Bosnia to Brussels, so commanders could have a clear picture of what was going on in the field. However, soon after its implementation, Cronos expanded to become the primary communications network throughout NATO, providing 5,000 users with email and shared data, military maps in digital form, document search and retrieval capabilities, and the "Cronos Wide Web," a World Wide Web lookalike. Significantly, Cronos carries two-way messages, so a commander in Brussels can send an email containing classified information and commands to Sarajevo or Pristina. For Bosnia alone, traffic on the network is the equivalent of 250 typists outputting 100 words a minute around the clock.

Commanders are becoming accustomed to fast, reliable online access to air, ground, and maritime operational information, weather information, target, equipment, personnel, weapon, and logistics data. Internet technology allows C2 systems to include instant messaging and embedded real-time collaboration and support tools, so that military planners in forward-deployed commands can reach back into a national or NATO infrastructure to assess alternative courses of action and make immediate decisions. Commanders like the idea that an officer in a place like Sarajevo or Pristina can remotely connect, click an icon on his laptop, and access support functions and databases held at headquarters. With the internet, the physical location of both the person and the database becomes irrelevant; the user could be sitting behind a desk or inside a tank, the server could be in a building in Brussels or a secure van in the Balkans. It's now entirely possible to dot-com the battlefield.

Online video-teleconferencing has also developed from something exceptional to a normal part of battlefield operations. NATO used real-time media technologies regularly during the Kosovo campaign to run conferences and coordination meetings at short notice, over long distances and without the need for travel, reducing the risks associated with moving commanders during wartime. There were also video-teleconferences for the press. The experience suggested that future operations will require higher bandwidth and crypto equipment running at a higher speed. The lack of infrastructure in the Balkans as a result of both NATO bombing and the existing political situation often meant that use of technology depended on satellite communication. Only a few nations and NATO itself can afford the expense of installing satellite ground stations in a theater of operations, but as commercial satellite technology becomes more widespread and as radio communications and third-generation mobile devices are developed with higher bandwidth, command and control will be able to move more easily from a message-based medium to playing an interactive role.

The emergence of internet standards such as XML will give defense organizations further interoperability options. While not likely to replace existing military messaging standards such as ADatP-3 just yet, XML will provide a common framework on top of which other more complex standards can be constructed. Work is underway to do that in the NATO Message Text Format Working Group (MTFWG), while the XML-MTF Development Team, based in the US with participation from the UK and Denmark, has developed specifications to map formatted messages to XML. The idea is to glue command-and-control systems to XML-enabled commercial products, allowing their integration with web technology.

Branching out from NATO, the PfP Information Management System (PIMS) was initiated with US funding to provide an internet-based host infrastructure and broadband satellite-based network access to each Partnership for Peace nation. The various countries are linked with each other and with NATO and the US. As part of the program, every PfP nation is also partnered and connected with a US National Guard unit located in one of the US states. All these online connections provide coordination and exchange of information from a variety of applications resident on PIMS host servers, including planning data for specific peace support operations.

When military personnel pass information, including voice and video, over the internet using laptops, handhelds, and wireless and universal plug-and-play equipment, then armed forces can truly achieve all the characteristics of what is becoming a mantra in defense circles: deployability, sustainability, flexibility, mobility, survivability, interoperability. The internet will become an operational requirement for all global peace support operations because of its ability to collect, process, and disseminate battle-relevant information from all available sources and rapidly distribute it to those who need it.

In addition to its command and control and other operational advantages, the web benefits soldiers' morale (they can keep in touch with families back home), military healthcare information services, press relations and coordination with NGOs and civilian counterparts such as private companies for contractor logistic support. Says Brigadier General Hans Schulz, deputy controller of the NATO CIS Operating and Support Agency (NACOSA): "Voice, secure and unsecure, is still playing a major role, however if staffs are excluded from sending emails or using the internet, we the service providers are really in trouble."

VIVE LA REVOLUTION IN MILITARY AFFAIRS

As depicted in Shakespeare's *Henry V*, the Battle of Agincourt fought in France in 1415 saw about 6,000 English common soldiers weakened by disease and hunger defeat a French army of 25,000 heavily armored noble knights and infantry. Under the command of King Henry, the English enticed the French forces into a narrow valley so that the slow-moving knights, who occupied frontal positions, became mired in mud and were easily cut down by English longbow archers on their flanks. By the time the depleted and demoralized foot soldiers reached the English lines, they were easy victims to yeoman wielding hatchets, billhooks, and swords. The French troops lost the battle because of their heavy armor, the rainy weather, the muddiness and narrowness of the battleground, and their tactic of using massed formations against a mobile enemy. Henry's victory was the beginning of the end of the age of feudal military strategy based on the use of heavily armored troops and cavalry. It marked the start of a revolutionary change in the way all future armies would fight, maneuver, and organize themselves.

Some of today's military strategists believe that the application of digital technology to traditional land warfare is heralding another revolutionary change. This time, rather than longbows, it's microchips and internet routers that are enhancing the ability to attack enemy targets with great precision from long distances, thereby requiring fewer troops and munitions, and reducing casualties and collateral damage. This revolution in military affairs, or RMA as it's wont to be called, supports the idea that the biggest change in the conduct of military operations is coming not from weapons but from the application of new technology to achieve an integrated, secure, and "smart" command, control, communications, computer, intelligence, surveillance, and reconnaissance (C4ISR) infrastructure that encompasses both strategic and tactical needs. In this revolution, soldiers carry satellite navigation sets on their backs and have M-16s equipped with thermal sensors, laser rangefinders, and image intensifiers. They drive Humvees with computer screens bolted to their dashboards showing troop locations across the entire operational theater. And everyone is linked to their commanders and war planners through the internet, giving them a clear, common, real-time picture of the battlespace.

While it is debatable whether all this amounts to a revolution, RMA does provide a useful explanation and doctrinal platform for the real changes in how wars are now being conducted: the shift from massed to mobile warfare and from overwhelming firepower to smart firepower. Precision-guided missiles taking out pinpoint targets in Serbia made this apparent for all to see. The accidental bombing of the Chinese embassy in Belgrade made it equally obvious that the revolution still has a long way to go.

Kosovo and Kuwait may have been won using long-range precision weapons, advanced sensors, and intelligent processors, but Kosovo was mostly fought in a rural, mountainous region and the Gulf War was conducted on an open, empty desert. By 2020, about 70 percent of the world's population will live in cities, mostly on coastlines. There will be urban combat. There will be cyberterrorism and electronic attacks against information systems (for more on this see Chapter 9). There are already about two dozen countries and counting that have either developed or are in the process of developing weapons of mass destruction: nuclear weapons, low-cost ballistic missiles, and chemical and biological agents. To illustrate this point, William Cohen, the US defense secretary in the Clinton administration, went on television holding up a 5lb bag of sugar, saying that if it was filled with anthrax instead of sugar and if someone spread it over a city the size of Washington DC, with the right wind and temperature, it would wipe out 70 percent of the population. That's just 5lb—there are tons of anthrax in existence.

The widening gap in high-tech military capability between rich and poor countries could lead the West's potential adversaries to unleash alternative weapons and unconventional strategies. Indeed, one of the West's greatest strengths, its technological and information superiority, could also pose one of its greatest security challenges. This irony wasn't lost on William Cohen, who invited Clayton Christensen, a professor at the Harvard Business School and author of *The Innovator's Dilemma: When New Technologies Cause Great Firms to Fail*, to come to the Pentagon and sit down with the joint chiefs of staff, service secretaries, and other military policy people. Christensen's book is about major corporations that were doing everything right—top personnel, leadership, good flow of revenue, investment in research and development, anticipation of customer needs—yet failed because "disruptive technology" had come in, not at the top end, but at the low end of the marketplace. Christensen spent almost four hours with Pentagon planners, looking into the future and assessing the potential disruptive technologies that could come in at the low end and take on the United States.

The revolution in military affairs is about reforming traditional forces to make them more agile in order to face up to a new generation of threats and an uncertain future. Today's military forces never know when or where the next major theater of war will occur, what demands will be placed on them, how the enemy will fight, and who will join them in a coalition. The technologies, weapons, and doctrines that look right for today will be overtaken and obsolete in 10 or 15 years. So rather than committing too far too soon, forces need the flexibility to switch course depending on how the future unfolds.

As Henry V, Clayton Christensen, and many in between have shown, the most profound military innovation isn't technology itself but an understanding of what can be done with technology. A high-tech, information-based type of warfare will require well-educated service personnel who are as comfortable with a keyboard as they are with a gun. It will require soldiers who can think critically, because in a multipolar world with complex missions, there could be lethal situations in which skills and knowledge of history, geography, languages, diplomacy, and economics might be needed. Access to education and lifelong learning will have to become one of the main attractions to get skilled people to enlist.

PROTECTED UNDER AN INFORMATION UMBRELLA

Critics of RMA claim that the concept is simply a way for militaries to keep their budgets as high as possible against the wishes of politicians and public opinion. In a time of relative peace and with no significant military rivals, the US Department of Defense managed to increase its annual budget from $250 billion in 1995 to $296 billion in 2000. Yet, to pay more effectively for the revolution in military affairs, the Pentagon aims to engage simultaneously in a revolution in business affairs (RBA). This means shifting the major share of defense spending from infrastructure and support to modernization and technology. It further means learning the business lessons that have driven American industry during the past decade. Says Jacques Gansler, US under-secretary of defense for acquisition and technology: "I see a Department of Defense not exclusively restructured on the private-sector model, but one that at least concentrates its mission much more on its core, inherently governmental, capabilities: warfighting, policy, management, and oversight. For all other activities, it will utilize competitive sourcing to achieve the best performance at the lowest cost."

RMA is inevitably being led by the US. Some NATO allies, particularly Britain, are looking to tap into developments in order to create more effective coalition operations and to work more as equals with US forces. Others aren't so sure, not so much because they disagree with the doctrine but because they disagree with the pace of change. The US has greater global interests and responsibilities and is more concerned about reducing its own vulnerabilities than most European countries, so this helps to ensure a higher level of motivation. American military planners reject the idea of slowing the pace of RMA to allow their European allies to catch up, stressing that the next generation of threats to democracy and peace will not wait for them. The prospect of yet another round of transatlantic rivalries is cause for concern to many of the fledging democracies that have come to trust and depend on the NATO alliance. Says Major Vasile Paun, section chief within the Defense Intelligence

General Directorate of the Romanian Ministry of Defense: "If Romania wants a revolution in military affairs within its armed forces in the years to come, then it will have to be motivated by a global vision, which has to be common with the Euro-Atlantic one."

If a compromise between Europe and the US can't be reached then, at worst, different countries will move toward RMA at different speeds. Technological progress is rarely picked up everywhere instantaneously and, for most agencies, a period of incubation will be required after which there will be a big technological leap forward. While the US may already be leaping, much of the rest of the world is still incubating. America won't become more isolationist as a result, because its own interests would be severely damaged if it allowed its democratic allies to descend into war or chaos. Investments in interoperability will continue apace to ensure that technologies complement each other, and in time this will have a spinoff effect in encouraging a global movement toward RMA.

During the Cold War, when nuclear deterrence was the cornerstone of US security policy, many countries were able to shelter under the American nuclear umbrella to escape the threat of a Soviet nuclear attack. By doing so they didn't have to develop their own nuclear arsenals, which would have been far too costly or controversial, for various reasons. Sometimes these countries felt that their safety was being compromised either by American weakness (under Jimmy Carter) or American aggression (under Ronald Reagan), but generally a world without the US protective shield seemed a riskier place. As the nuclear umbrella loses its effect, the US is seeking to offer its allies extended deterrence by opening an information umbrella. However, to achieve information superiority, the allies must help out this time, since the only way to accumulate advantages in battlespace information is through the global sharing of knowledge.

In a multipolar world, every country can contribute to the deterrent without stirring street demonstrations at home or posing a threat to others. More friendly nations sharing more data means fewer rogue nations sharing less data. So the greater the flow of information, the greater the deterrent to wage war. Once a country joins the world economy, it cannot so easily be excluded from the protection of the information umbrella. Too many other countries will want its business, and business exchange leads to information exchange. Political upheaval in China or a war over Taiwan would be deeply destabilizing, but as Chinese trade with the rest of the world increases, so too will its need to participate in the global information society. The elections held after the death of Franjo Tudjman, a man not much more loved than Slobodan Milosevic, further illustrates the point. The people of Croatia brought to power a new government proclaiming the merits of sweeping economic reforms, peace with its neighbors, and NATO membership.

Globalization does have its dark sides and these present new threats to peace and security. Nevertheless, there is also the hope that a mutually dependent world will inspire cooperation and prevent war. President John F. Kennedy once said: "Geography has made us neighbors. History has made us friends. Economics has made us partners. And necessity has made us allies." He was referring to US relations with Canada, but today he could have applied the statement to most of the world—and he might well have added that the internet will make us peaceful.

Part Three

The Emerging Challenges

9 Public Policy: Taming the Wild Web

NERD WORLD WAR

As the Middle East descended into bloodshed with street clashes between Palestinians and Israelis in the autumn of 2000, a parallel battle was taking place in cyberspace. The home page of Jerusalembooks.com, one of the largest Jewish booksellers on the web, was hacked into and replaced with the word "Palestine" in flaming letters, and with text asking Israelis if the *torah* teaches them to kill innocent children and rape women. Taking credit for the attack was GForce Pakistan, a well-known Muslim "hacktivist" group that joined forces with Palestinians and other Arab hackers to launch a "cyber-jihad" against Israeli interests.

A highly skilled Arab hacker with the online pseudonym of dodi attacked NetVision, an Israeli internet service provider that hosts 70 percent of the country's internet traffic, including the Israel Defense Force and other Israeli government websites. The websites of the Israeli Knesset, the Prime Minister's Office, the Army, the Foreign Ministry, the Bank of Israel, and the Tel Aviv Stock Exchange also all suffered from virus implants or a distributed denial of service (DDOS) attack, a technique that involves flooding a target website with requests until it crashes. Messages are generated by computers that have themselves been hacked into to serve as a launch pad for the electronic bombardment.

Actions such as this forced many Israeli organizations to hire specialist American firms to upgrade their online security, and sites were also moved on to servers in the US to handle a greater number of users in the face of jamming and DDOS attacks. This prompted the hacktivists to extend their electronic holy war to include US sites such as AT&T and

Quest. The FBI's National Infrastructure Protection Center issued a warning: "Due to the credible threat of terrorist acts in the Middle East region, and the conduct of these web attacks, recipients should exercise increased vigilance to the possibility that US government and private-sector websites may become potential targets."

Meanwhile, websites operated by the Palestinian Resistance Movement (Hamas) and the Lebanese Hezbollah movement were targeted by Israeli hackers. Chain letters were sent online calling on people to join efforts to crash Hezbollah's site and briefing them on how to over-load the site and flood its servers with false alarms. Hezbollah tried creating new sites at new addresses, but they too were discovered and attacked. The site of the Palestinian National Authority was constantly defaced with displays of pornography, Jewish slogans, the Israeli flag, and the Israeli national anthem. The attacks originated from computers located at the Bar Ilan University near Tel Aviv. In a twist of irony, the Palestinian National Authority site was hosted by NetVision, for which the company faced a boycott from many Israelis.

The first known terrorist act against a country's computer systems was in 1998 when an offshoot of the Tamil Tigers bombarded Sri Lankan embassies with 800 emails a day over a two-week period. The messages read: "We are the Internet Black Tigers and we're doing this to disrupt your communications." During the Kosovo conflict in 1999, NATO computers were hit with email bombs, macro viruses, and denial of service attacks by Serbian hackers and other groups protesting the bombings. Hackers from Albania and NATO countries spammed Serbian computers in return. The US government is hit by between 7,000 and 8,000 hacking attempts every day.

After the NATO bombing of the Chinese Embassy in Belgrade, Chinese hacktivists successfully broke into the Department of Interior website and littered it with pictures of a Chinese flag, crowds in Beijing protesting the attack, and the three journalists killed by the bomb. China frequently exchanges cyberattacks with Taiwan, each planting their flags on the other's sites. Chinese dissidents also hack into government computers that are used to censor websites in China, while it's claimed that the Chinese government attacks dissidents' sites, including those devoted to the Falun Gong sect. Pakistan and India trade website attacks, and there was one incident where the content of the Indian army site was replaced with stories of torture of Kashmiri separatists.

The flooding of email boxes at government offices, denial of service attacks, and web page hijacking are relatively primitive techniques of information warfare, achieving a low level of disruption but a high level of publicity. In the context of the Middle East, they are the virtual equivalent to the unorganized stone throwing on the streets. But as the climate of hostility and mistrust leads to guerilla attacks and organized violence in the real world, so too is there a greater likelihood of more sophisticated cyberattacks. Hezbollah has reportedly been trying to recruit professional hackers to conduct more sophisticated electronic terrorist attacks against Israel, and the Israeli secret service could certainly penetrate firewalls and launch application-level assaults without too much difficulty.

Intelligence reports suggest that about 35 countries are developing cyberwar capabilities, in both the developed and emerging worlds. The most technologically advanced nations are also the most technologically vulnerable, and fears run high in the US of the potential of a rogue nation carrying out an "electronic Pearl Harbor." If a dozen laptops can do as much damage as hundreds of tanks, planes, and bombs, then an enemy nation lacking the military muscle to launch a conventional attack against the US may decide to take it on in a cyberwar instead. The US and its NATO allies have traditionally focused on protecting their citizens and industries from weapons of mass destruction, but antimissile defenses are useless against logic bombs, Trojan horses, worms, viruses, and denial of service attacks. The need today is for protection against weapons of mass *disruption.*

"We are at the beginning of a deadly serious, high-stakes game, and we must devote the same resources to it that we did to winning the Cold War," says Sam Nunn, a former US senator who co-chaired the advisory committee to the President's Commission on Critical Infrastructure

Protection. "Our first challenge should be to prepare and train for cyber-attack and its consequences, just as we've done for conventional or nuclear warfare."

One school of thought suggests that cyberwar would be more humane than conventional warfare because it would not inflict loss of life and severe economic hardship. It isn't really that simple. Chaos would ensue if terrorists broke into computer systems *Mission Impossible*-style to disrupt railways and air traffic control, overload telephone lines, change the pressure in gas pipelines, shut down the electricity grid, sabotage stock exchanges and banking systems, block communications used by emergency services, alter hospital patient records such as blood types, and reprogram robots used in telesurgery. There are also worries that military systems could be open to sabotage and espionage through the internet. Taiwan believes that China is conducting military exercises to see how computer viruses could cripple its command and control.

Although computers can be protected, it is difficult to ensure total security because systems are often wrongly configured or inadvertently used in a way that makes them vulnerable to attack. There is also the possibility of insiders and contractors acting alone or in concert with other terrorists. It might just be a disgruntled former employee disabling the company computers after losing his job, or something more serious. A Portuguese bank lost millions of dollars when one of its own systems administrators allegedly added a few lines of code to the bank's software, so that every time he withdrew cash from an automatic teller machine the money would be credited to his account rather than deducted.

Meanwhile, police in Japan discovered that a software system they had bought to track 150 police vehicles, including unmarked cars, had been developed by the Aum Shinryko cult, the group behind the 1995 Tokyo subway gas attack in which 12 people were killed and thousands injured. When police made the discovery, the cult had already received classified tracking data on 115 vehicles, and had further worked as subcontractors developing software for 10 other government agencies and at least 80 private firms.

To terrorists, cyberattacks have advantages over traditional acts of violence in that they can be carried out anonymously and remotely, without the need to handle explosives or send somebody on a suicide mission. While most terrorist groups currently lack the knowledge and skills to pull off a successful cyberattack (they're still more proficient at making carbombs than cyberbombs), the potential will increase as the next generation of terrorists grows up in a more pervasively digital world.

There are already instances of curious cyberkids being approached by seemingly legitimate businesspeople with requests to test the security of a private network, and many never realize they've been duped into working for a mafia-like organization. The Provisional Irish Republican Army once contracted hackers to access the home addresses of British law enforcement and intelligence officers, with the intent of killing them all in a "night of the long knives" if the UK government didn't meet its demands. The attempt was foiled and, with some luck, authorities will be in a similarly good position to respond to cyberterrorism by applying the experience they are now gaining from trying to contain more prevalent cybercrime.

BLACK HATS VS. WHITE HATS

During the tumultuous Seattle summit of 1999, electrohippies staged web sit-ins in which thousands of protestors logged on to the World Trade Organization website at a designated time and flooded it with rapid and repeated download requests using specialized software. Similar software has also been used by animal rights groups against organizations said to abuse animals. Sit-ins and email bombardments require mass participation to have much effect, so they are more suited to activists and acts of civil disobedience than to terrorists bent on violence. "This is an important distinction," says Dorothy Denning, professor of computer science at Georgetown University. "Most activists, whether participating in the Million Mom March or a web sit-in, are not terrorists."

Most hackers don't aim to commit either acts of terrorism or civil disobedience. They break into computer systems as a sort of intellectual exercise, rather than for any political or ideological reason. Most virus writers don't release their work into the "wild" but instead share their code with other virus writers so their ability is recognized by their peers. Software programs that enable hackers to break into private networks can be easily downloaded from the internet and in some countries, such as Russia, they are sold openly at outdoor markets.

At the annual DefCon hackers' convention in Las Vegas in 1999, the Cult of the Dead Cow, one of the first computer underground groups, publicly launched its BackOrifice 2000 (a pun on Microsoft's BackOffice) software, which allows hackers to infiltrate and seize control of computers running the Windows operating systems. The cult's minister of propaganda, who is known as Death Veggie, claimed that the bug was designed to force Microsoft to improve the security of Windows. Several computer security firms attended the BackOrifice launch with the hope of acquiring early versions in order to produce software vaccines. The FBI also reportedly sent undercover agents to discover the identity of the Cult of the Dead Cow members, although several agents were publicly unmasked during a "Spot the Fed" competition.

Hacking into computers to steal information is theft, and the defacing of websites is vandalism. The hacking itself is not a crime. To technology purists, the purpose of hacking is to disassemble a system to understand how it works and then suggest improvements. Hacking tools serve a dual purpose, one for "black hats" (hackers) to find a system's vulnerability to launch a computer attack, and one for "white hats" (network administrators and computer security experts who design antivirus programs) to find a system's vulnerability to protect it from a computer attack. The distinction is lost on many governments, which want to make it illegal to hack and to write or possess hacking software. When governments outlaw an activity in which many people want to partake, then the law is usually ignored and organized crime is enfranchised. Hacking is no exception. Banning it would almost certainly have an inverse effect on internet security, because network administrators need hackers to determine if their systems are safe from attack.

Many organizations, even government agencies, invite and contract hackers to expose weaknesses in their networks so that administrators can plug the holes. In a test commissioned by the state of California to assess the security of online voting, one of the project partners, Safevote, invited hackers from around the world to attempt to break through the system's defenses. The company even provided details of network configuration, encryption keys, and a range of IP addresses to help hackers get closer to the system's inner circle. The results were intended to help the government determine the risk of vote tampering before moving from paper to electronic ballots.

Hackers get their bad name from bored adolescents breaking into systems or releasing viruses to cause mischief, boost their ego, or impress their girlfriend. So-called packet kiddies or script kiddies, such as Mafiaboy, the Canadian teenager who crashed CNN and other sites with a torrent of electronic missives, see the internet as a game and often have no idea exactly what they are unleashing. The creator of the Melissa virus, which in 1999 resulted in more than $80 million in losses, admitted on his conviction: "I did not expect or anticipate the amount of damage that took place."

Private-sector websites are not any more or less at risk than government systems, and hackers (the unethical type) have managed to turn dot-coms into not-coms overnight, wiping millions off share prices in the process. Yahoo!, Amazon, eBay, and E*Trade have all been paralyzed by DDOS attacks. There is also a high risk of industrial espionage from spies planting a worm inside a computer network to download internal documents, often without a firm ever noticing. Microsoft was hacked into in October 2000 when an intruder planted a worm on a Microsoft employee's home PC that the employee used to log on to the company intranet, from where the worm created new user accounts to go deeper into the network and gain access and download portions of the Windows source code.

Government agencies were particularly caught napping when the Love Bug attacked in May 2000, affecting at least 45 million computers and causing worldwide damage estimated by some experts at $10 billion. Really another worm rather than a virus, the Love Bug started in the Philippines and worked its way west, bombarding systems in more than 20 countries with emails with the subject line "I LOVE YOU." When opened, the worm destroyed user files, stole passwords, and replicated itself through computer address books, spreading around the world like an electronic chain letter. Civil servants and politicians—perhaps desperately in need of being told they were loved—opened the message in droves, especially in Europe where the virus was first detected.

Even though it reached the US a couple hours later, the federal Department of Health and Human Services was still swamped with three million I LOVE YOU messages, resulting in email disruptions lasting up to six days. Social Security needed five days to remove the virus from its computers and become fully functional again. The Pentagon pulled military personnel away from other work to deal with the attack. In a review of how the federal government responded to the virus, the General Accounting Office (GAO) said that there was a lack of coordination among departments and that it was fortunate the bug didn't cause greater destruction. Members of the Senate banking subcommittee claimed that the incident demonstrated the government's inability to respond to a cybercrisis.

Should the Love Bug have even reached crisis point? Computer viruses have been around for a long time now and between 300 and 500 new ones are created every month. Yet, people are still taken by surprise when they strike. This suggests that organizations don't invest as heavily in internet security as they probably should, and perhaps computer users' demands for simplicity are leading to security compromises, such as fewer passwords. Computer users must learn to spot suspicious emails and avoid communication with unknown sources, otherwise it's like leaving their front door unlocked while they go away for a week. It is to be hoped that greater vigilance will come as people become more comfortable with computers and familiar with cyberspace.

CALL IN THE CYBERCOPS

As the online population grows, so does the opportunity to commit cybercrime, not just hacking and virus creation but also cyberstalking, online harassment, hate messages, pornography, threats to children, consumer fraud, and the sale of illegal goods. In addition to taking on board privacy and security issues, governments are expected to enforce online intellectual property rights, since web content can be so easily copied and unauthorized links to other sites may violate copyrights or trademarks. Courts have not ruled consistently on whether the speculative registration of domain names, or cybersquatting, constitutes trademark infringement, and difficulties arise when there are two or more unconnected businesses that both have a legitimate claim to an internet address.

While there have been some high-profile cases, the risks of getting caught and prosecuted for a cybercrime are low. Some police forces have created special computer crime units, but the technology changes so fast that they must attract and retain top experts and train continually. Cybercrime investigations take a long time and often require the involvement of multiple jurisdictions, which don't always cooperate.

Even when police do catch a hacker or virus writer, prosecutors often will not take the case on because the evidence is too technical to determine a defendant's guilt or to explain to a jury. The length of a prison sentence is usually dictated by the amount of damage and loss, but it is difficult to measure how much a company suffers financially if it goes without email for a day. Prosecutors also push cases aside because they know judges don't treat cyberoffenses as serious crimes, and their sentencing guidelines will give a hacker nothing more than a probation sentence. Furthermore, because the internet is a new phenomenon, different countries have different legal frameworks covering cybercrime and very few have dedicated internet laws.

The Love Bug triggered an international manhunt and its perpetrator was traced within 12 hours to a dilapidated apartment in a suburb of Manila. Assisted by Interpol and FBI agents, the Philippines National Bureau of Investigation quickly collected evidence from local internet service providers, but could not find a judge who would sign a warrant to search the apartment because the dissemination of a computer virus wasn't a crime under any Philippine law. Eventually, a search warrant was issued when detectives proposed that the suspect may have broken a credit-card law governing the use of passwords. When finally police were able to raid the apartment they found nobody at home and no computer—not surprising, considering the world's press had been camped outside the building for several days.

After the culprit had eventually been caught, investigators spent more than a month looking for applicable laws before filing charges, only for prosecutors to dismiss them all because they did not apply to computer hacking and there was insufficient evidence to support charges of theft. Extradition also was not possible since the Philippines' treaty with the US, for example, could not be applied where a law allegedly broken in America had no equivalent in the Philippines. Legislation was enacted in June 2000 to bring Philippine law up to date with advances in information technology, but it couldn't be applied retroactively.

The progenitor of the Love Bug was a former technology student who failed to graduate after the school rejected his thesis for a program designed to steal computer passwords. After being let free, he reportedly returned to his studies and pledged to design a more socially responsible computer program.

At the same time as law enforcement agencies were tracking him down, government and business leaders from the G8 industrialized nations were meeting in Paris to discuss how they could join together to face the mounting threat of cybercrime. It was the first time that thought leaders from both the public and private sectors had got together to work through the issues on an international basis. Because private industry has such a high stake in its own security, many in government believe that business ought to assume more responsibility for the protection of information systems. Routine cyberattacks cannot become the subject of serious police investigations just because companies don't secure their websites properly. Commercial software developers and vendors should also be held to account because, in order to rush their products to market, they too often place a low priority on security features.

The IT industry should therefore be conducting the cutting-edge research that's needed to shield systems, including government systems, from future attacks. In response, some businesses suspect that law enforcement agencies are simply expecting industry to do their work for them, pointing out that if the defenses of Microsoft, the world's largest software company, can be breached by a lowly worm, there isn't much hope for lower-tech organizations ensuring that their sites are fail-safe.

While some fear that over-regulation of the internet will stifle innovation, there is greater consensus, between public and private sectors and between different countries, that e-business and consumer trust in e-commerce will be undermined if cybercrime isn't stemmed. Says Sam Nunn: "Like the Wild West of the last century, our new frontier of information is exciting and we must retain the freedom to roam and grow. But if the bad guys shoot up the town every weekend and drunken cowboys ride their horses into the saloon, don't be surprised when the public calls for law and order."

However, there is little agreement on who should get the sheriff's badge. Existing bodies such as Interpol, the Organization for Economic Co-operation and Development (OECD), the World Intellectual Property Organization, or the World Trade Organization could play international coordinating roles. The OECD has offered to oversee national government policies on digital certificates, but will not rule on security disputes between nations.

Within their own countries, many governments have set up dedicated cyberpolice forces, such the FBI's National Infrastructure Protection Center, which receives visitors from foreign law enforcement agencies every week and regularly sends agents to train cybercops at international police academies. Some officials, especially in North America, have called for the establishment of a similar supranational organization to crack down quickly on cybercrime, claiming that traditional agencies are too slow and bureaucratic to respond to viruses and hackers. "We don't need Interpol, we need Cyberpol," says Gaylen Duncan, who attended the G8 meeting in Paris in his capacity as president of the Information Technology Association of Canada. "What we need is an international network of cybergeeks who happen to have powers to investigate and arrest, not police who took some computer training."

While recognizing that it's necessary to cooperate with other countries and with the private sector, most governments are adamant that sovereign states retain primary responsibility for fighting cybercrime. Where they are prepared to make strides internationally is in establishing a common legislative approach to cybercrime so that criminals can be convicted wherever they are caught. As a start, the 41-nation Council of Europe drafted a far-reaching treaty to bring the computer crime laws in different European countries into line by as early as September 2001. Given the importance of the subject, non-European countries including the US, Canada, Japan, and South Africa have also participated in the negotiations. This controversial convention not only defines specific cyberoffenses, but includes extradition agreements and proposals to facilitate cross-border criminal investigations into hackers, illegal interception of data, computer fraud, and child pornography. There are also requirements for internet service providers and network administrators to help police by maintaining detailed logs of network activity.

Before governments get too carried away trying to align cyberlaws, maybe they should first agree on how much regulation of the internet is justified. Common standards have to take into account cultural differences between countries. Those with strong free-speech laws might prevent the abolition of certain types of website that other countries would like to ban. Or it could work the other way, where a country perceives its freedom of expression rights are threatened by another country's laws against pornography or racism.

In November 2000, a French court upheld an earlier landmark ruling that US-based Yahoo! must prevent internet users in France from participating in auctions for Nazi memorabilia such as films, swastikas, uniforms, daggers, photos, and medals, which the judge ruled were "an offense to the collective memory of the country." While the French subsidiary of Yahoo! banned access, the court ruled that the US site, which is in the English language and not specifically targeted at French users, also had to comply with French law because it is available in France. Yahoo! argued that it was not technically feasible to prevent French users from accessing the site because there was no foolproof way of establishing an individual's identity or location. The judge gave the company three months to find a way or face fines of FF100,000 ($13,000) a day. Yahoo! shares fell sharply on the news, but the race was on in the IT industry to quickly develop software that could more accurately identify users' locations.

Net filtering to block access to inappropriate content has also become a hot topic as governments and parents consider ways to protect children from harmful material on the web. Some civil liberties groups see net filter technology as a threat to free speech, and argue that government should not determine what people do or don't have access to online. The European Internet Service Providers' Association believes that the Yahoo! case sets a dangerous precedent in this respect. It notes that many European websites are in breach of legal, religious, and moral rules of foreign countries, especially those of undemocratic regimes.

The Yahoo! ruling does raise many questions relating to free speech and the primacy of national law in one country over a company based in another but operating in a global medium. While the Yahoo! auction site is illegal in France under a section of the penal code that prohibits the exhibition or sale of goods inciting violence or racism, it is legal in the US, where Yahoo! could risk contravening the First Amendment guaranteeing freedom of speech if it attempted to close the offending sites. In May 2000, the US Supreme Court appeared to have affirmed that internet service providers were protected against libelous and abusive messages, when it ruled against a man who sued Prodigy after an imposter used his name to send threatening email messages to his neighbors. The ISP was presumed to be as responsible as a telecommunications company was for the conversations people had over the telephone. That is, internet service providers are not purveyors of information but simply carriers.

KEEPING SECRETS IN CYBERSPACE

The French government has also found an interesting, if somewhat Stalinist, way to deal with the purveyors of online material. The Liberty of Communication Act, which inched its way through parliament during the course of 2000, stipulates that any French resident who posts information on the internet, even the most humble family home page, has to register as a publisher with the appropriate authorities. Tabled in the fall-out of the anonymous posting of nude celebrity photos on the web, the intent of the bill is to make people legally liable for their online information. The French government equates internet publishing to a newspaper where the names of the publisher and editor are plain for everyone to see, and where there is a principle that public order imposes certain responsibilities on whoever operates in the public space, one of those responsibilities being to identify yourself.

Critics claim that the law goes too far in removing personal privacy. While its full impact remains unclear, it could conceivably stifle online publishing in France and it might force some web-hosting companies to relocate offshore. If a company or individual has jurisdictional problems in one country's internet space, it is easy enough to set up in a country with a more favorable regulatory policy.

Even so, more and more governments are feeling emboldened to control the internet, while it is still nascent. This trend is occurring even in places that don't have France's strong tradition of state intervention, such as most Anglo-Saxon countries. In the US, privacy advocates don't have much appetite for an FBI web-tapping program called the Carnivore Diagnostic Tool, which sifts through internet service providers' networks to collect data and read the email of criminal suspects. Although it sniffs through all a person's email until it finds what it wants, the FBI insists that Carnivore is used in a highly targeted way, only selecting messages based on criteria expressly set out in a court order—messages transmitted to or from a particular account, for example. It has only been used sparingly since it was initially deployed in 1998, about 25 times in the first two years. Says Donald Kerr, an assistant director of the FBI: "Carnivore is not positioned to filter or access, in a Big Brother mode, all subscriber traffic throughout an ISP network."

There isn't a police force in the world with enough staff or technical expertise to embark on wholesale snooping. The success of online checks and surveillance rests more on luck than on any prepared and researched provision of public service. The haphazard state of web tapping is reminiscent of when wire tapping first appeared. It wasn't clear at first on what conditions police could listen in on a telephone conversation or whether what they recorded could be used in court as evidence.

Today in the US, police require a search warrant from a judge before they can open mail or tap a phone, for which they must show probable cause that the search will uncover criminal evidence. However, access to phone logs for both incoming and outgoing calls is given practically automatically; an officer just has to swear that it is "relevant" to an investigation. In 1979, the US Supreme Court ruled that phone log orders don't violate privacy and protection against unlawful search and seizure under the Fourth Amendment of the Constitution, because phone numbers alone do not reveal who placed or answered a call.

The FBI now considers email addresses and routing information to be equivalent to telephone numbers, even though they reveal far more about a person than does a phone log. In most cases they reveal the names and locations of everybody a suspect has communicated with. And if Carnivore starts tracking web addresses, police will not only know that a person visited Amazon, for example, but also what books she searched for and bought. Some legal experts and civil rights groups say that greater safeguards are needed for policing cyberspace, and that email tapping should at least meet the same court requirements as full-scale wiretaps. Eavesdropping laws are expected to be tested further as the internet goes wireless and cars come equipped with satellite tracking systems.

The situation has been even more draconian in the UK since the Regulation of Investigatory Powers (RIP) Act came on to the statute books in October 2000. It has angered civil rights groups, industry, trade unions, and the media because of the power it gives law enforcement agencies to monitor a person's internet patterns and to intercept and decode email and web content if criminal activity is suspected. The Act gives police the power to force companies and individuals to hand over their electronic keys (encryption codes, passwords, PIN numbers), and gives the government the power to require internet service providers to install interception devices known as "black boxes," which can be used to intercept information on email and internet activity and relay it back to a government monitoring center.

Some of the resentment of cyberlaws stems from frustration that the internet no longer seems to be an open and uncensored network built on mutual trust with control in the hands of its users, not some central authority. However, the internet has expanded through the investments of large companies, and governments, which are building more infrastructure and providing more online products and services, which in turn are prompting more and more people to become cybercitizens. The web today very much reflects the real world and, unfortunately, crime is a major part of that real world. Governments need the power and tools to fight cyber-crime the same as they need the power and tools to fight street crime.

Police forces give assurances that they don't seek blanket authority to view all online communication to monitor law-abiding citizens. But these are words of small comfort to many, who fear that there is nothing preventing police from exploiting opportunities for undue surveillance at some point in the future. When so many police forces and security services have histories of abusing trust, people are naturally suspicious. In the interest of civil liberties, there need to be some checks to ensure that authorities don't abuse power in the virtual world, just as there are checks in the real world.

On the surface, the RIP Act tries to ensure that the authorities' powers of investigation comply with human rights, as communications cannot be monitored unless there is good reason: suspected acts of terrorism, drug dealing, serious crime, tax evasion, and anything in the national interest. It is this last catch-all that has people worried. Too often "national interest" is defined as what's best for the authorities rather than what's best for the people.

Consider when police, acting in the national interest, asked British newspapers to hand over the emails they had received from the former MI5 spy David Shayler. The newspapers refused and the police took them to court. A judge ordered the newspapers to comply, but the ruling was overturned on appeal on the grounds that a free press had the right to investigate matters on behalf of the public without compromising its informants. Had the RIP Act been in effect at the time, the police could have obtained the emails secretly and the case would never have reached the lower court, let alone the appeals court. Had the messages been encrypted, the police could have demanded the key to open them. A legal warrant wouldn't have been needed, as the interception of messages requires only the approval of the home secretary (a government cabinet minister), orders for an encryption key can be made by a customs official, a chief police constable, a magistrate, a judge, or the home secretary, and monitoring of email traffic can be "self-authorized" by any investigating officer.

Roy Greenslade, a British media commentator and former newspaper editor, comments: "The passing of the RIP Act denies everyone the freedom, and the privacy, we thought the internet had provided. It robs journalists and their sources—including that most potent and essential of tipsters, the whistleblower—of their rights and, quite possibly, threatens their liberty."

The internet was the perfect vehicle for anyone wishing to leak official documents into the public domain without leaving any trace of the source of the leak. But with legislation such as the RIP Act (Russia, Singapore, and Malaysia have passed similar laws), governments will inevitably find a way to keep a lid on their secrets. Meanwhile, attempts to intercept email for police investigations will end in futility, because criminals can easily use disguised language, hijacked identities, temporary email addresses, rerouters, and unlisted mobile phones to avoid detection. In France, the Liberty of Communication Act will not stop criminals from posting subversive web content or unleashing viruses, and only those with no intention of breaking publishing laws will register their websites. In the rush to regulate the internet, the only secrets to be exposed in cyberspace will be those of the innocent.

Governments need to find a better balance in order to maintain civil liberties while protecting society against cybercrime. One place they might want to look is technology-friendly Ireland. The government in Dublin has taken a radically different approach from London, Paris, and Washington, with an electronic commerce bill that does not give law enforcement agencies the power to snoop or require the disclosure of encryption keys. Suspects may be required to decrypt their data, on production of a court warrant, but under no circumstance can they be forced to surrender their keys.

COMPANIES SNOOP TOO

Privacy on the internet is a difficult issue and governments sometimes must feel that they can't win no matter what they do. While many citizens fear that government regulation will erode personal privacy, others believe that it's the lack of regulation that's transforming the web into Big Brother. Businesses and governments alike are collecting online data in droves over the unregulated internet by forcing people to provide personal information in exchange for access to services.

While magazine publishers and direct-mail companies have for years been compiling and selling personal information about consumers, the internet makes it easier than ever to collect, analyze, and publish personal data on a massive scale. People give their names, addresses, credit-card numbers, social security numbers, and other personal details over the web without fully understanding how the data will be used. Even many experienced online shoppers are unaware that the websites they visit implant their hard drives with small packets of data called cookies, which are used to "recognize" them the next time they visit so that they do not need to, for example, retype their password. However, cookies also track people's online movements and can be read by other websites that people visit. There is a desperate need for consumer education about e-commerce and the internet, since much of the lack of privacy awareness stems from the fact that the net is a new medium and an increasing number of people with little technical knowledge are going online for the first time.

Most dot-coms merely want to use personal data to get to know their customers better so that, for example, they can put a music advertisement on to the computer screen of somebody who has just done an online search for a particular band. But not many people want to see repeated ads appearing on their computer screens for the latest Britney Spears album just because they once ordered a birthday gift for their niece. They don't want to be permanently trapped in a database they can't get out of, and they don't want to receive unsolicited email (otherwise known as spam). No matter what people do, they can't ever seem to eliminate spam entirely. America Online estimates that 30 percent of its email traffic is spam, and many internet service providers worry about it clogging their systems, causing slower service, and sometimes causing them to crash. Many countries already have laws in relation to unsolicited faxes and phone calls and are now considering legal means to reduce spamming.

Companies don't want to be seen as harassing or snooping on their customers, and e-tailers are starting to realize that they are missing out on sales because of invasive information requests. The majority of purchase attempts on the web are aborted part way through a transaction because shoppers are reluctant to enter personal details. Yet, because companies invest so heavily in e-commerce and want to generate results, there is a temptation to be more aggressive in using data mining techniques to track users' movements around the internet and then aggregate this data with demographic information—age, income, zip code, etc.—to build highly individualized customer profiles. In the US, there has been controversy over companies fusing data collected about people's online buying habits with their purchasing histories in bricks-and-mortar stores. Marketers say that such information allows for more targeted and effective advertising, but it raises sharp objections from privacy advocates who note that less than one-quarter of US commercial websites comply fully with the Federal Trade Commission's voluntary privacy-protection principles.

Even when people are aware they are being monitored, most are powerless to do anything about it. Without online privacy protection, some internet users are resorting to using false names and email accounts to preserve their anonymity (which, of course, encumbers government's own snooping efforts). The internet developed despite the state rather than because of it, and its flexibility is often seen to be in contrast to the rigid and regimented structures of government control. Nevertheless, tired of waiting for the online industry to regulate itself, government debate is growing over whether or not to regulate the corporate use of personal information. And tired of waiting for the federal government to act, many individual states in the US are introducing online privacy laws. The thought of 50 states with 50 different privacy regulations frightens the pants off the dot-coms which, as a result, are starting to come around to the idea that some basic uniform federal rules for commercial websites might not be so bad after all.

Europe is the birthplace of data protection. Believing that privacy is not something that can be left to free-market forces, countries such as Germany, the UK, and Spain have had provisions since the 1980s to ensure access to personal information held in company databases. With an added emphasis on privacy, a European Commission directive on data protection came into force in 1998 requiring European governments to enact individual rights to data access, rights to prevent the processing of information that is likely to cause distress, and rights to object to personal data used for direct marketing and other purposes. National governments must determine conditions under which personal data processing is lawful and establish an independent agency and special tribunals to oversee data protection.

The directive has particularly strict regulations against the transfer of data to any country outside Europe that does not ensure an "adequate level" of data protection. While the definition of adequate level is open to interpretation by the responsible government agencies and the courts, the almost total lack of any American data protection laws would suggest that the US would fall firmly into the "inadequate" camp. Rather than simply highlighting transatlantic cultural differences, the European directive could easily have interrupted the flow of data and even halted e-commerce between the two trading zones. The US government offered a self-regulatory scheme to ensure that data was not misused, but many European countries were wary of how this could be policed. So European and American negotiators spent nearly two years trying to resolve the dispute before establishing that, in order to obtain "safe harbor" from prosecution, American companies would have to seek agreement from European citizens before transferring their personal data.

SIGN HERE DIGITALLY PLEASE

Connected with concerns about privacy is the more immediate fear of being ripped off. The FBI's Internet Fraud Complaint Center received 500 complaints of internet fraud on its very first day of operation on May 8, 2000. Within six months of its launch, the center had received almost 20,000 complaints from 106 countries, with each victim losing on average $665. Almost half of the complaints related to online auctions, and there were also problems with undelivered items, securities fraud, credit-card fraud, identity theft, and bogus business opportunities. Internet fraud has become so pervasive that it has prompted the European

Commission to adopt yet another directive. A sister to the data protection directive, the distance selling directive requires that, in every e-commerce transaction, certain information must be provided to the consumer, including the identity of the supplier, the price of the goods and services, details about delivery costs, and so on. In addition, the consumer has a right to withdraw from the contract within seven days, without penalty.

The more people shop online, the less worried they become about the threat of somebody stealing their credit-card number and running up the bill. As annoying as it may be, they know they are covered by insurance. But they still don't like putting their credit-card number and other personal details on the web too often, because they are concerned about "identity theft." In the US, when a congressional committee posted a list of social security numbers of high-ranking military officers on the internet, somebody was able to aggregate the data to create false identities and then run up their expenses. One retired lieutenant colonel had $50,000 worth of goods charged to accounts in his name.

For e-commerce to flourish, citizens need a higher level of confidence that they are conducting transactions in a secure environment. Computers and networks must be able to confirm that people are who they say they are. It is anticipated that digital signatures will provide an appropriate level of authentication for most online services, augmented by additional proof of identity where necessary.

Parliaments around the world have been scrambling to pass laws to grant legal recognition of digital signatures, mainly for the purpose of accelerating the development of e-commerce. The e-Sign Act in the US states that an electronic signature is whatever two entities agree it to be: "an electronic sound, symbol, or process, attached to or logically associated with a contract or other record." This means that people could enter into a legally binding contract simply by typing in a name attached to an email message, clicking on a web page hyperlink, or pressing touchtones on the phone. It could be a PIN identification or disclosure of a specific, personally submitted password. Or it could be something more sophisticated, such as a digitized image of a signature that's linked to a mathematical algorithm that verifies the authenticity of an online document.

Data security and authentication issues affect e-government as much as they do e-commerce, because public-sector organizations are often required to obtain personal signatures before processing or delivering services. Governments will likely use a range of authentication levels depending on the service provided. Issuing a passport, for example, requires a closer identity check than issuing a fishing permit. Many governments seem happy simply to follow the lead of the private sector in determining security and authentication techniques and technologies. If it's secure enough for a bank, then it's secure enough for government. This makes sense, because people have no trouble using bank machines—they trust bank security a lot more than they trust government security. However, government could do the financial and other sectors a favor by taking some initiative itself to stimulate the use of digital signatures.

It's no coincidence that the new economy is strongest in countries where government is active in driving and accepting technological standards, such as Scandinavia, and weakest in countries where it provides less direction, such as in southern Europe. Finland proves the point. In December 1999, it became the first country to implement a national online identification system to transact government business over the internet. A smart card issued by the Population Registration Center allows citizens to access services and notify the government of a change of address—a legal requirement in Finland—over the internet using a smart-card reader, a PC peripheral that in Finland is becoming as common as a mouse. (Readers will also be attached to telephones, digital TV sets, and counter tops in stores.) To establish a cardholder's identity, the card incorporates authentication and digital signatures on a microchip, as well as certificates for a public key infrastructure (PKI) that allows different parties working in an open environment to complete secure transactions.

It is not mandatory for Finns to possess a smart ID card (although everyone has a national identification number), but the government

221

expects widespread takeup once people are able to use the card to access more services. The cards are an integral part of Finnish plans to put all government services online by the end of 2001, and in the future they will work with third-generation cellphones and digital interactive television. Prime Minister Paavo Lipponin was the first person to sign up for a card and the respected outgoing president, Martta Ahtisaari, used his to register his change of address when he moved out of the presidential residence in February 2000.

HOW COMETH THE TAXMAN?

With a critical mass of people now shopping online, governments are starting to look at e-commerce as a business activity that should be taxed like any other business activity. But as with everything in the new economy, the tax authorities are entering an era of confusion where all the rules are changing, and the internet is eroding their traditional revenue base. Governments like to levy taxes on things that they can easily measure and count. Early taxes concentrated on things like plots of land or the number of windows in a building. Today, most government revenue comes from direct taxation on the income of individuals and companies, or indirect taxation such as customs and excise duties and sales or value-added tax (VAT). All of these tax regimes depend on government being able to identify people, time, value, and location.

Globalization and e-commerce make it much more difficult to monitor transactions and identify the parties involved. It is easy for a company to have a direct relationship with a customer in another country without the need to establish a presence in that country. For governments, profit margins relating to such transactions cannot easily be taxed because the activity can't be attributed to their specific jurisdiction. The owner of a commercial website may be registered in one country, the server located in another, and the customer transaction take place in yet another. This raises questions about double taxation and which jurisdiction's taxes should apply to business conducted over the internet. Governments aren't sure if a website constitutes a taxable presence or, since online traders can easily disguise their whereabouts, if the internet service provider that hosts the site should be considered a taxable agent.

Just as politicians and economists 200 years ago debated the merits of a corn tax, they are today weighing their options about whether or not to levy cybertaxes to stop the loss of revenue from the flow of digitized goods, services, information, and money over the internet. For fear of stifling innovation and economic progress, many governments are adopting a wait-and-see approach to online taxation. They have threatened, but not acted on, proposals to levy internet access fees, such as a percentage of the monthly rate that consumers pay their internet service provider, or so-called bit taxes, a percentage fee based on the amount of data bits downloaded from the internet.

Typical of the confusion, in the summer of 2000, Germany's finance ministry suggested that private use of the internet while at work amounted to a fringe benefit and should be taxed. By the autumn, however, the government had done a complete U-turn and was proposing to make the private use of office computers tax free as a way to help people acquire the necessary skills to become knowledge workers in the information society.

Since e-commerce was not envisaged when today's tax rules were established, online services generally remain exempt from duty if they originate from outside a tax authority's jurisdiction. If this trend continues, governments fear that businesses in their countries will be at a competitive disadvantage in both domestic and world markets. At an OECD ministerial conference in Ottawa in 1998, agreement was reached on the principles that should apply to e-commerce, including that taxation should occur in the jurisdiction where goods and services are consumed. The European Union enshrined the OECD principles in an electronic commerce directive, adopted without amendment by the European Parliament in May 2000 after being agreed to by the EU heads of government just two months earlier. The speed of the decision-making process and the fact that it passed unamended, a rare occurrence in the European Parliament, illustrates the importance European politicians attach to the need for uniformity in electronic trading.

Under the directive, European companies are no longer obliged to levy VAT on e-commerce products sold to consumers outside the EU, but foreign dot-coms must levy VAT on products sold to consumers within Europe. This means that any company with a website may have to research the tax laws of multiple jurisdictions and put in place a system of collection for each. Companies might as a result confine their business activities to only a few profitable markets, and some US dot-coms have complained that they should not be tax collectors for European governments. The European Commission says that vendors could have the option of registering in a single EU member state, but this could give rise to tax competition between countries in Europe. The Commission hopes that member states will understand.

Says Frits Bolkestein, the commissioner in charge of taxation and the European internal market: "Many of the old and established certainties no longer hold. E-commerce in particular has highlighted deficiencies in existing tax systems worldwide and forced administrations to consider long-overdue reform and simplification."

He might have added that the US is in a complete state of disarray. Each of the 50 states has responsibility for collecting its own sales tax and each has different rates, ranging from 3 to 25 percent of the sales price. Five states levy no sales taxes at all. Business-to-business e-commerce is exempt from sales tax, but final products are taxable and businesses must register with the states of companies from which they buy as consumers. Sales tax is paid on purchases if the retailer has a store in the buyer's state. If it doesn't have a store in the state, purchasers are required to pay a so-called use tax, but only if their home state levies sales taxes. This tax already applies to mail-order purchases, but it is not enforced and payment is almost always ignored.

Some states and municipalities also tax telecommunications properties at higher rates than other commercial properties, and e-commerce is further affected by a 3 percent federal government excise tax on telephone service, originally introduced to help finance the Spanish-American War a century ago. There are an estimated 7,000 different taxes in the US, most of which retailers are responsible for collecting. Before dot-coms are dropped into this mire, the whole American tax regime needs to be dramatically overhauled and simplified.

In 1998, the US Congress passed the Internet Tax Freedom Act, which put a three-year moratorium on the imposition of internet access taxes, bit taxes, and multiple or discriminatory taxes on e-commerce. It also set up a 19-member multiparty, public–private Advisory Commission on Electronic Commerce to investigate the impact of international, federal, state, and local taxes and tariffs on internet transactions. Reporting in April 2000, a deeply divided commission recommended an extension of the moratorium for another three to five years.

Tax harmonization in the US isn't going to come easy. As the commissioners found out, no government will quietly surrender its right to tax. States that don't collect income tax don't want any decrease in their sales tax, while states that don't charge sales tax are concerned about any change in their ability to raise income tax revenue. Studies show that people living in jurisdictions with high sales taxes are much more likely to buy online—but if states and local authorities try to tax across their borders, it might as well be teatime in Boston all over again. Many Americans feel that the imposition of tax-collection responsibilities on dot-coms would violate the sacred principle on which the country was built: no taxation without representation.

Already, lobby groups representing consumers, taxpayers, and public policy organizations are popping up across the country calling for a permanent ban on sales and use taxes for e-commerce transactions. Many also want clearer rules to ensure that only companies with a physical presence in a state are compelled to collect sales taxes. One Pennsylvania group, the e-Freedom Coalition, argues that e-commerce empowers consumers to take advantage of competitive tax rates in other jurisdictions and therefore serves as a necessary constraint on excessive government. Says Sean Duffy, president of the Commonwealth Foundation thinktank, one of the e-Freedom Coalition's founding members: "Too many in government see the explosive growth of the internet and electronic commerce as a new opportunity for tax collectors instead of an exciting new opportunity for consumers and taxpayers."

Yet, many US government officials fear that they are setting a dangerous precedent by exempting internet purchases from sales and use taxes, even on a temporary basis. Exempting e-commerce from taxation simply because the opposite is impractical is unfair, in that it places a higher tax burden on traditional suppliers of goods and services. If the internet evolves into a permanent tax-free zone, main-street retailers will go online en masse. They will end up placing web kiosks in their stores where customers can purchase items tax free, and then walk over to the counter to pick up their order. If that happens, the entire concept of transaction taxes may as well be abandoned and governments will have to find other ways to raise revenue.

FROM TAX COMPETITION TO TAX COOPERATION

The old, easy option of increasing corporate and income taxes has pretty much been exhausted. Too many taxation-heavy countries are facing a potential citizen's tax revolt, like the one in the US during the 1980s when Californians voted for the tax-cutting Proposition 13 and Ronald Reagan was swept into the presidency on a platform to slash federal taxes. American citizens now carry an enviously low income tax burden and they are not in a hurry to see their rates inch back up. More significantly, taxpayers in the new economy are becoming more elusive. New models of business and employment are further contributing to the internet's overall effect of blurring established boundaries of geography and jurisdiction.

Companies currently pay corporate tax to governments in countries where they are registered and where they operate through a subsidiary or agent. This has traditionally worked well for governments but, in the digital age, local offices become unnecessary and some firms won't need a physical presence at all. Teams and individuals from around the world, some on the company payroll and some not, pass projects back and forth over the internet, making it difficult for tax authorities to establish where the business is conducted and who should pay how much tax to which treasury. Companies can also easily move their registration to low-tax countries and tax havens; bookies and gambling houses are especially active in setting up their online operations offshore.

The internet causes the tax authorities further grief by cutting out their usually reliable intermediaries: the retailers that collect taxes on goods and services and the companies that deduct income tax from employees' pay. Increasingly, companies are downsizing their staff and contracting work out to self-employed contractors and consultants from whom they do not collect income tax. Globalization and the internet increasingly allow individuals, especially knowledge workers and high earners, to work from anywhere in the world, or to make it seem as if they are working from anywhere. People can work in several countries at the same time without ever leaving their desk.

It has become nearly impossible for tax authorities to track down unwilling taxpayers or "electronic emigrants." People bent on tax evasion have the means for it at a mouse click. Even if people themselves don't move abroad to take advantage of lower taxes, they can move their money overseas. Internet banking allows people to move their money quickly, cheaply, and often anonymously, and tax havens are increasingly marketing their services to individuals. This means that it's getting more difficult for tax authorities to dig up useful pieces of information from banks, brokers, and other third-party institutions. Given that governments tend to tax residents rather than nonresidents on their investment income, there's a possibility that every country will become its neighbor's tax haven.

As companies and individuals shop around for the best tax deals, there is bound to be increasing tax competition between countries, and also between regions within countries. This will force governments to lower or even forgo taxes to attract wealthy and skilled individuals, business, and capital. This might not be such a bad thing. Tax cuts are usually accompanied by a widening tax base, as demonstrated by economic booms in places such as Ireland and Malaysia. Whether many taxpayers pay a little or a few taxpayers pay a lot, it adds up to roughly the same thing. But too much tax competition carries the risk of a "race to the bottom," in which public services will deteriorate and it will become difficult to redistribute national wealth from the rich and mobile to the less well-off.

As the internet forces the reduction of taxes on income, company profits, and consumption, government may take a look back at those things they can more easily measure and count. Land taxes may regain their historical pre-eminence, but they won't affect the virtual company and the cybercitizen. Environmental taxes such as road pricing and carbon emission taxes could become popular, but the more they achieve their goal the less income they will generate. Auctions such as those held for third-generation mobile communications licenses are generating great windfalls for public treasuries, but these are one-offs. The emerging pattern of "stealth taxes"—fees and charges for passports, driving licenses, building permits, and the like—will continue, but these can only raise so much.

Benjamin Franklin once famously remarked that nothing was inevitable except death and taxes. Although the internet hasn't yet enabled immortality, the idea that governments could be left with close to zero income is something that doesn't seem so far-fetched. Nation-states were built on the belief that they had the power to decide for themselves how much tax to collect from their people and businesses. When governments lose that power, the theory goes, they lose their authority and reason to exist. In the digital age, they will lose their power of taxation unless all individuals and all companies and all goods and services in all nations are subject to equal tax laws and enforcement. A global tax system that can be applied to both individuals and companies will only ever come about by unprecedented cooperation between nations, most likely with the support of, initially, regional organizations such as the EU, NAFTA, Mercosur, and ASEAN, and then through supranational organizations such as the OECD or WTO. There are even proposals for a World Tax Organization.

Unlike in most countries, the Internal Revenue Service assesses American citizens on their global income whether or not they reside in the US, allowing them to offset income tax paid in other countries to avoid double taxation. This initially prompted some wealthy "tax-patriates" to renounce their American citizenship in order to avoid paying tax at home, but the government responded, penalizing them by, for example, making it difficult to enter the US for a visit. However, global assessment still doesn't work very well because the IRS depends on other countries to share tax data, which most aren't eager to do. Yet, if other governments were to do the same thing, it would open the doors to information exchange and conceivably lead to different countries working together to share the spoils of tax revenue from online and global trade.

In June 2000, European leaders agreed to end bank secrecy in their respective countries and to share information on nonresidents' savings. This is a small beginning, but it shows that tax cooperation can replace tax competition. The next step, as the US has done, is to disregard the country in which people actually live and tax them based on their citizenship. Linking taxation with citizenship rather than residency will ensure both the supremacy of the nation-state and the compliance of the taxpayer.

10 Universal Access: Spreading the Web Worldwide

ENTRENCHING INEQUALITIES

Every day, about 150,000 people log on to the internet for the first time in their life. Content on the web increases by almost two million pages a day. The hours children spend in front of the television are declining for the first time. The internet is the defining technology of today's generation and it is the fastest-growing medium ever. Yet, despite its rapid growth, there are discrepancies in adoption rates between gender, levels of education and literacy, income, language, race, and ethnicity. The typical web user is a white English-speaking male under the age of 35 with a university education, a high income, living in an urban center, and with no physical disabilities. More than half of all internet users live in the United States although that country makes up less than 5 percent of the world population. There are more web hosts in New York City than there are in all of continental Africa.

The gross disparity in the spread of internet access is resulting in an uneven distribution of the economic and social benefits derived from technology, entrenching existing inequalities between and within countries. People who can't access the internet in the new economy are the equivalent of those who can't read and write in the old. Like wealth and mobility, access to information is becoming a critical factor by which countries, regions, sectors, and socioeconomic groups are judged by society as either haves or have-nots—information rich or information poor.

There is also not much point embarking on the whole e-gov adventure if it's destined only to provide greater access to those who already have no trouble accessing the halls of power. The web provides the opportunity for government to become more inclusive. But in order for e-government to fulfill its vast potential, the internet has to become as omnipresent in society as telephones and electricity—even more so, since half the world still can't make a phone call.

People are prevented from going online by the expense or absence of telecommunications, web connections, and computers themselves. Many countries lack basic infrastructure, or it is limited to the larger cities. An internet account in Argentina can cost as much as $78 a month, compared to less than $20 a month, or even free of charge, in North America and Europe. While there is a trend in the West toward un-metered flat rates, metered internet charges run to about $10.50 an hour in Chad, where the average annual GDP per person is $187. And while the price of a PC has fallen dramatically in recent years, even at $500 they are unaffordable for most people.

Another obstacle to universal internet access is the perception that the technology is too complicated. There are people who will never want to use a computer to communicate with government, or with anybody else. This will force government to keep public services offline even after they are all available online. Running parallel services indefinitely will only add to the complexity and cost of government, further defeating one of the primary purposes of e-government. Agencies must look beyond the standard PC and find alternative electronic delivery channels to allow even the most technophobic citizen to benefit from the e-gov transformation.

Even then, there will be people who think that the internet isn't all that necessary—a billion channels and nothing's on. The World Wide Web is caught in a chicken and egg situation, where people won't start using it until there is relevant and local content, but there won't be relevant and local content until people start using it. Since the disenfranchised and minority interests are almost always the lowest priority for industry, market forces alone will not address the ever-widening gap between the winners and losers of the information age. Governments need to step in and take the lead to bridge the so-called digital divide.

COMPUTERS IN THE CAR WASH

Highway 101 slices through Silicon Valley in California, with Palo Alto on one side of the road and East Palo Alto on the other. There couldn't be a greater symbol of the digital divide. Palo Alto is home to the dot-com millionaires and its municipality's website has a full array of interactive services, from online submissions to the planning department to library searches. East Palo Alto is a deprived town with one of the highest murder rates in America. Its municipality's website consists of only three pages, containing outdated population figures and city hall's address. It wasn't even created by the town itself, but by the regional planning agency on behalf of the town.

A similar situation existed in Kista, one of Stockholm's 18 boroughs that is sometimes referred to as Cellular Valley or the Scandinavian Silicon Valley. Every day about 30,000 people commute in to work there, at one of the world's most dynamic high-tech company parks. There is also a substantially underemployed immigrant population who never traditionally mixed with the commuters. This began to change when Stockholm decentralized its city administration in 1997 and created borough councils. The new Kista council organized its administration not on traditional departmental lines but rather into eight coordination areas, such as one for the elderly and handicapped and one for children, youth, and recreation. Uniting the factious residential and business communities was given top priority and a number of programs were introduced.

The biggest unification project was the Kista Portal, a website linking all companies, institutions, community organizations, and the council itself. There are interactive information and services, a chat room with scheduled visits from local politicians, video streaming of public-interest events, and live web cameras permanently focused on five roundabouts used to enter and leave Kista, so commuters can see when and where traffic is heaviest and plan their route home accordingly. The site is also used for free telephone contact with borough personnel using call-back dialing, and the unemployed can sign up to be matched with one of the companies on a training program.

If people in Kista don't have a computer at home or at the office, they can go to the public library to access the web. Libraries have long been a champion of lifelong learning and an important knowledge source for the community. The internet, however, makes even the best stocked public library seem hopelessly under-resourced, and one might have expected them to fade slowly out of existence. Instead, many public libraries are being rejuvenated by combining their services with those of their online competition. The familiar library environment attracts many who are reluctant to use other community services, and people are comfortable with walking in off the street, sitting down at a computer, and surfing the internet unrestricted and usually for free. Thanks to their web-connected computers, libraries have been able to uphold their public-service duty to provide access to information that people can't find elsewhere, and they are able to offer more services and advantages than ever before.

Incredibly, web-connected libraries have their critics. There are frequent complaints that the computers are monopolized by youths who come to take advantage of higher access speeds than they have at home, and in the process prevent net novices and others from having a go. Some people worry that the computers are used for playing games and surfing pornographic sites. The National Library of New Zealand has been accused of being a free cybercafé where foreign backpackers can check email at taxpayers' expense. And cybercafés themselves sometimes see them as unfair competition.

The truth is that while very few libraries install web-filtering products, abuse of public internet access terminals is minimal and, when it does occur, users are generally warned once and ejected if they continue. The vast majority of library internet users go online for reference and research purposes. Cybercafés, on the other hand, are commercial operations in urban areas frequented most often by young people who want to access the web in a social setting—the very kind of person the critics don't want in the libraries. There are also telecottages, usually run by volunteer groups in rural areas where there often isn't a library. They provide more formal training courses and business services, and many make deliberate efforts to provide access to the elderly and disabled. Again, they complement rather than compete with libraries. That's not to say that governments couldn't do more to support cybercafés and telecottages. They could, for example, use their services and facilities for public training programs, buying time and space the way that schools buy slots at private leisure centers and swimming pools.

Further complementing libraries and cybercafés are web-enabled touchscreen kiosks that have sprung up in the most unlikely places: shopping malls and stores, train stations, airports, hotels, sports stadiums, laundromats, and even car washes. Many retailers find that kiosks help attract people into their stores, and they can be used not just to provide customers with internet and email access, but to merge their offline and online shopping habits and build customer loyalty.

Public-sector agencies, especially local governments, have for some time deployed multimedia information kiosks in claims offices, city halls, and post offices, but their usefulness for e-government can be limited. The Spanish citizens who happily access welfare information and benefit payments from kiosk terminals are probably the exception, as most people will not attend to personal matters in public. They're not going to apply for unemployment benefits or file income tax from a laundromat anymore than they're going to surf porn sites in the public library. To do all that, people will want to access the web in the privacy of their own home.

MORE GIVE, LESS TAKE

Since the most common way to access the internet is with a home computer, the price of PCs needs to fall to encourage more buyers. This is happening, with promotional offers such as cheap computers in return for online subscriptions becoming more popular and, in some places, consumers can get a PC for free if they don't mind being constantly bombarded with online advertising. While most governments are happy to let the free market take its course, others see a need to give it a bit of a push. The Singapore government has equipped 30,000 low-income households with secondhand computers bundled with free internet access and basic training. This was done through community self-help groups and, to encourage industry participation, tax incentives were given to vendors and service providers to donate equipment, professional services, and internet access to the community through civic organizations.

The province of New Brunswick, Canada, issued a $500 rebate to anyone buying a new home computer, while its local telephone operator, NBTel, pitched in with three months' free internet service. Frank McKenna, the premier of the government that introduced the rebate, says that it turned out to be the most massively popular thing he ever did as a politician, although he wasn't sure why at the time. "I understood it better later," he says. "What they would tell me privately is that you've always been taking from us and this is the first time that you've ever given us anything so we're going to take advantage of it. And they did. We sold every computer in every store in our province."

Some governments have toyed with the idea of exempting computers from taxation. The US state of Pennsylvania proposed two one-week opportunities a year to purchase a personal computer without having to pay state or local sales taxes, but this simply promises two weeks of Boxing Day madness every year. The Swedish government feared that a straight tax exemption would have been used by people who already had a computer. The government wanted to find a way for employers and employees to develop IT skills together, thereby building the knowledge economy. So, in 1998, the government made company-provided home computers a tax-free benefit, on condition that they were offered equally to all employees. Companies rushed to dole out web-connected PCs to staff. With their employers deciding specifications, negotiating good rates and setting up internet accounts, it became cheap and easy for Swedish workers to obtain a home computer. PC sales boomed in Sweden and the country was pole-vaulted into first place in the internet league tables, with about 60 percent of the population online.

Because the information society benefits from having more participants, the high number of Swedes with internet access has driven the demand for electronic trade and online services. Internet banking took off soon after the home PC program. There is also a payoff for the government in providing its own online services. Says Leif Pagrotsky, Sweden's trade minister: "What it does to help us develop e-government is an extra bonus. Our focus on education and learning and closing the skills gap is not only a democratic issue of haves and have-nots, but primarily an economic issue of increasing productivity and competitiveness by investing in human capital and by helping new structures to develop."

With more people now online than off, the Swedish government is shifting its attention to increasing levels of always-on, high-speed internet connectivity as opposed to regular dialup phone service. Broadband access is limited mainly to urban areas in the south of the country through cable television lines. In 2000, the Swedish government announced a strategic policy objective to build a nationwide broadband infrastructure. The public–private project will wire every home and business in the country with high-speed internet access.

New Brunswick had the first fully digital telecommunications network in North America, with every phone line in the province running on fiberoptic cable by 1993. At the time, neither the government nor the phone company could make a strong business case for the investment; they did it more or less to see what would happen. What did happen was that 80 companies came in to set up call centers, the province's IT industry grew from three small companies to more than 200 five years later, and educated people who had left for jobs elsewhere came home. Shackled with high levels of unemployment among a small population in a remote location with depleting natural resources, New Brunswick used technology to enable its inhabitants to escape to the knowledge economy and become part of the world's major markets without having to leave home.

About 10 percent of US internet users—four million consumers— were connected through high-speed broadband by the end of 2000. That is double the previous year, with the biggest growth coming from internet service provider subscriptions. This is generating—or, perhaps, degenerating into—a debate over whether consumers should have the right to choose which ISP they want to use over cable lines. Attorneys at the Federal Trade Commission threatened to block the AOL–Time Warner merger unless the companies agreed to open their cable lines to competitors. Meanwhile AT&T, the country's largest cable company, went to court to stop the city of Portland, Oregon, from imposing an open-access requirement. Being in America, it looks as if this will all be decided by the lawyers rather than the politicians, but it needs to be settled quickly one way or another.

Internet users need greater capacity for data transmission to cope with all those video and audio streams, flash pages, and web designs that emphasize style over substance. Certainly, television would never have become the dominant and widespread medium it is today if people had to wait as long for a channel to come on as they do for a web page to open, and then for the whole system to crash without warning.

ANTISOCIAL GEEKS

If every invention reflects the values and needs of its inventor, there's no doubt that most computer products on the market today were conceived by men. If the PalmPilot and other personal digital assistants had been invented by women, they wouldn't have been designed to fit into a breast pocket and the technology wouldn't keep track of just one person's schedule. A woman probably would have designed a family computer (FC?) rather than a personal computer (PC) limited to one keyboard and one mouse. Says Anita Borg, president and cofounder of the nonprofit

Institute for Women and Technology: "What if only 30-year-old women developed technology—all of it—and that technology was geared mainly for 13-year-old girls? Technology would be out of whack, out of balance. But that's the world we live in: Men hold the power, and boys drive the market."

Girls tend to reject the repetitiveness and violence of computer games, which essentially are virtual equivalents of GI Joe: high kill rather than high skill. They also often get bored with school computer classes, which focus too narrowly on the technical rather than exploring innovative uses of technology for different subject areas. Those girls who do well in math and science are often then put off by computer science lectures in university dominated by male students and male teachers. Women who do graduate and pursue a career in technology frequently change their minds once they start their first job, sickened by the male corporate culture. Go to a conference on e-business or a new media networking group, and there will only be a handful of women in attendance.

Women account for roughly 35 percent of internet users in the US and western Europe, 25 percent in Brazil, between 15 and 20 percent in Japan, South Africa, and Russia, 7 percent in China, and a mere 4 percent in the Arab states. These statistics are unfortunate, especially because women are one of the groups in society who could most easily and quickly be empowered through greater web access. The internet affects all of society and computing skills will be required for all future professions. So if women are left out of the digital revolution, then all the strides for political, economic, and social equality that they have achieved in the twentieth century will be lost to them in the twenty-first.

Too often, girls and women see internet users as antisocial geeks. This is partially because there are too few powerful, articulate, computer-savvy female role models. Governments could do more to recognize the achievements of women such as Anita Borg, and they could create greater opportunities for women to emerge as technology leaders and visionaries by reviewing their own hiring practices. The National Security Agency (NSA), an arm of the US Department of Defense, is not the sort of organization where one would expect to find a lot of female employees, but it has successfully attracted many women to its staff through offering continuing-education programs, onsite childcare, flexible work arrangements, and fitness centers. This kind of benefit is usually more enticing to women than to men, who are mainly just after a big paycheck. Women now account for 41 percent of NSA's computer scientists, 31 percent of its mathematicians, and 11 percent of its engineers—all well above the national average.

Governments can also promote and support initiatives such as the Virtual Development Center, set up by the Institute for Women and Technology in 1999 to develop internet technology designs and prototypes based on input from women. Bringing together industry, community, and academia, development centers at the Massachusetts Institute of Technology, Purdue, Texas A&M, and Santa Clara universities hold brainstorming workshops with girls and women, who consider such questions as: What are the issues that will face our families and communities in the future? and What can technology do to help?

Workshops have proposed the development of family information systems, including a scheduler that lets family members see who is doing what at different times of the day. There have been suggestions for a personal health assistant to keep track of all aspects of a user's health, including stored information about medication and treatments, online access to medical files, and a function to dial 911 automatically in an emergency. The results of the workshops are intended to be used to design projects and prototypes by faculty and students from the universities and engineers from sponsoring technology companies, including IBM, Sun Microsystems, Compaq, Hewlett-Packard, and Xerox.

Male techies and industry types often dismiss women's concerns, claiming that they will "catch up" with the technology once they start to "get it." Yet it's the techies who don't get it. Women are highlighting many of the major deficiencies in today's technology, and in the way in which society sees technology, and their views resonate with the concerns of many would-be users of the internet. To many senior citizens, for example, a computer is more complicated than a VCR, and they still haven't figured out how that works. An over-60 is therefore less likely to have web access than an under-30; someone with a disability is less likely to have access than someone without. Among people with disabilities, those who have impaired vision and problems with manual dexterity are less likely to have web access than those with hearing difficulties. Again, one of the underlying reasons is that little consideration is given to these people when designing either computer equipment or computer education.

Many community groups are developing innovative programs to broaden internet access to so-called late adopters, and governments need to support these projects. The US government, for example, supports Generations Online, a self-teaching program to help people over 65 learn to use the internet. It provides seniors with customized software in plain English with step-by-step instructions for going online, and is designed so people can work individually or in classes. It is used across the country in libraries, retirement homes, elder housing estates, and senior centers.

In the Czech Republic, a program called PCs Against Barriers aims to increase the employment rate of long-term and recently disabled people by improving their IT knowledge and skills while at the same time preparing them psychologically to re-enter mainstream society. This recognizes that it's not enough to provide recently disabled people with computer skills if there isn't an equal effort made to help them accept their disability. The initiative is run by Charter 77, a foundation cofounded by Czech President Vaclav Havel, and has developed since 1997 through a public–private partnership between the Czech Ministry of Labor and Microsoft. The ministry provides participants with job placement assistance, while Microsoft offers support through donations of money, software, and hardware. After three years, PCs Against Barriers had provided skills training to more than 700 people in four regional centers, with more than two-thirds finding employment immediately afterward, most as software specialists.

FROM TECHIE TO TREKKY

The day will come when every home is connected to the internet, but it will be an internet not as we know it, Jim. The clunky beige box and monitor taking up space on the desk will still be around, but most people will be connected through their television sets. Says André Arsenault, business development director at Innovatia, a company that develops software to deliver web content to non-PC devices: "There are a lot of people who just don't want a PC. They don't want one in their home, they don't want to deal with this whole internet thing. In the meantime, these people have been sitting in their living rooms with a remote control in their hand changing TV channels. They're very comfortable with that tool. Well, one of the channels happens to be this thing called a portal and all of a sudden they are doing internet things without internet skills, and without that psychological barrier of not understanding computers."

The first commercial digital television service was launched in France in 1996 and tens of millions of people in many countries now subscribe to direct-to-home satellite, cable, and terrestrial digital TV services. In Europe, the market for digital TV is doubling and even tripling every year. TPS in France, Open in the UK, and Teledanmark in Denmark offer interactive and online services including email, home shopping, banking, and games.

While some public-sector agencies are looking to pilot digital TV services, viewers remain seated in their armchairs, remote controls on stand-by, waiting to access a government portal through their television. There are unresolved but not insurmountable matters, such as whether or not the TV portal should be an original design or replicated from the web. It will be a while yet before both government and broadcasters are able to coordinate the delivery of online services through the tube on a large scale, but most agree that digital TV is a prerequisite for achieving universal access and, by extension, e-government.

Governments can take a number of intermediary steps to close the technology gap before digital television replaces analog. For those citizens with chronic technophobia, a single point of contact to government can be provided through one-stop shops. Portugal opened its first Citizen's Service Center in Lisbon in 1999 and has since spread many out around the country. They are open 24 hours a day, seven days a week, and cut across organizational boundaries to provide the services of 21 different government departments, including public records and notary registers, driver's licenses and vehicle registration, passports, social security, and even the coin mint. There's also the water and electricity boards, telephone company, post office, and a bank so people can pay their bills. Essentially it's a portal, except a civil servant is there to tap the keys and click the mouse for the citizen.

New Brunswick also started with one-stop service centers with flexible opening hours and in locations that the public often frequented, such as shopping malls. In addition, the one-stop service is provided over the web itself and over the phone using interactive voice response (IVR). The government had initial fears about applying a new IVR system to issue hunting and fishing licenses, because hunters and fishers in the province tend to be rural and older people with little proficiency in technology. But as it turned out, some people who phoned in didn't even realize they were talking to a computer.

Traditionally, to apply for a hunting or fishing permit, New Brunswickers would have to drive perhaps 30km to a wildlife office to fill in a paper form, giving their hair color, height, and weight so that a wildlife officer in the woods could identify them if necessary. In changing over to the new system, the government instead simply asked people to phone in and give their government health card number, from which the government could access all their personal details. As well as making the procedure easier, to encourage people to use the new system, the government dropped its fees so, for example, an application to hunt moose was reduced to $6 if submitted electronically compared to $10 if done in person at a wildlife office. While some governments charge citizens a "convenience fee" to use online services, New Brunswick believes that government ought to share the spoils of going online with its citizens.

In the first year, 84 percent of hunters and fishers applied for their licenses over the phone. In the following year, the takeup rate reached 98 percent. It costs the government more to process the remaining 2 percent of paper forms than it does to process all the others. The government received no complaints about the change of procedure because the old process was left intact. If the paper forms were removed now, it wouldn't cause much of a problem.

The emergence of third-generation wireless devices and smart phones promises to usher in new applications and more internet users. At first the preserve of the rich and famous, cellphones are now carried by everyone from the student to the cleaning lady. Already, residents of Berlin use their *Handi* to pay parking meters and access traffic and travel information. Students at Eichstätt University in Germany use wireless devices to register for exams and obtain results and search for library books. Passengers on Austrian Railways can buy tickets remotely and simply show their cellphone with the booking confirmation to the conductor.

There are half a billion mobile phone subscribers worldwide and their number will soon surpass conventional fixed telephone lines. Europe may be the world leader, but mobile communication is also becoming the primary telecommunication service in developing countries without sufficient land-line infrastructure. It has been estimated that by 2003 half of all people accessing the internet will do so using a cellphone. By that time, wireless devices will carry a $5 Bluetooth chip to connect a range of hardware solutions, including PCs and notebook computers, printers, scanners, digital cameras, thin clients where application processing is done on a central server, and other consumer devices. The Bluetooth standard, developed by more than 500 technology firms, defines how data can be transmitted between devices using single short-range radio links rather than a tangle of cables. It also ties in the internet.

Eventually, everything that can be transmitted, will be transmitted. The internet penetration statistics that are rolled out today, based solely on access through a PC, will become totally irrelevant as computers become so much part of people's everyday lives that they don't even realize they are using them. Refrigerators will email orders for anything that's been removed. Lavazza has devised a web-enabled coffee machine that sends and receives email requests for restocking or maintenance.

It's not all gimmicks and gadgets. Public services can be provided through a range of electronic delivery channels, so fears that the advent of digital television will make current investments redundant are unfounded. Since all online services are based on the same integrated, web-enabled underlying technology, one project can be leveraged to develop the next. New Brunswick hunting or fishing permits can now be acquired over the web. It's a different front end and a new delivery channel for the citizen, but the back-end technology doesn't change and requires no new investment. Government in the information age is about providing a choice to citizens of how they want to get online and access public services, tailored to individual and family needs at different times, in different places, and in different situations.

CONTENT COMPLEMENTS CONNECTIVITY

In the film *Field of Dreams*, a farmer hears voices telling him that if he builds a baseball diamond in his cornfield, then Shoeless Joe Jackson, one of the greatest players of all time, will appear. "If you build it, he will come," the farmer is told. Some information-age enthusiasts see cyberspace as a field of dreams, claiming that if everyone has access they will come to use it. They won't. They're not going to log on to the web just because it's there, like some kind of cyber Edmund Hillary. They need a reason, and that means content—culturally relevant content in their own language. Without the local development of digital materials, most people in the world will not and cannot digest anything that the internet has to offer.

The internet was born in the USA and Americans make up most of its users. As the web is above all a product of each user's contribution, the

US is therefore the biggest producer of internet information and services. Seven out of the ten most visited sites in Britain and Germany, and six out of ten in France, are American. Some 87 percent of all websites are in English, a language which more than three-quarters of the world doesn't read. A survey for the *Los Angeles Times* showed that 92 percent of Hispanic web surfers in the US, most of whom were born outside the country, accessed predominantly English-language sites because they could not find what they were looking for in Spanish.

The Francophiles of Canada, long noted for their fervent defense of their linguistic heritage against the supremacy of English in North America, are doing their best not to yield to a unilingual, monocultural internet. Quebec has less than 5 percent of the world's French-speaking population, yet it hosts about 30 percent of French-language websites. The province's controversial French Language Charter, also known as Bill 101, states that French must be at least twice as large as English on commercial street signs. In 1998, it was decided that this law also applied to websites. E-commerce sites that serve the Quebec market are usually bilingual anyway, because it's good for business, but there are exceptions. The Office de la langue française, Quebec's "language police," has sent out a number of cease and desist letters to companies with English-only websites. Most orders are ignored. One was sent to a Montreal-area computer store whose web page was 99 percent bilingual, with 1 percent in English only to intentionally not conform with the law. The store manager said: "We think the whole thing is stupid. The internet isn't their problem."

Stupid, true. Not their problem, not true. It is the case that if any Quebec company wants to circumvent the language law, all it has to do is situate its web server one inch outside the province in the English-speaking part of Canada. There is also the reasonable argument that, while a store sign or billboard is there for all to see, nobody is forced to look at a website. Internet users designate a domain address or conduct a search in the language of their choice. On the other hand, the internet is a headache not just for Quebec, but for any government that traditionally makes an effort to protect its local culture. By its very nature, the internet stimulates freedom of communication, and because of its global reach, governments won't be able to impose quotas on foreign or language content as many do for radio and TV.

But fear not Quebec, succor is on its way from the motherland. The Académie Française and other state institutions in France have been busy inventing their own jargon to replace the Americanisms of cyberspace and e-commerce. The French finance ministry has stopped referring to new dot-coms as *les start-up* and now calls them *jeunes pousses d'entreprises* (young sprouts of companies). FAQ does not stand for frequently asked questions but *foire aux questions*. The French word for a computer bug, *bogue*, comes from the skin covering an acorn. Quebec had already coined *courriel* for email, but France rejected it in favor of *courrier électronique*, although most French people just say *e-mel*.

A war of words doesn't necessarily lead to a culturally and linguistically diverse cyberspace, but the French government has so far matched its rhetoric with programs aimed specifically to promote the presence of France and the French language on the web. It has redirected cultural funds to take into account new technology producers, such as multimedia publishing and internet content creators. It has digitized and distributed online cultural materials, including its National Library collections, and there is also an initiative supporting foreign-language sites about France and French culture. The government's own websites are often translated into English and German and sometimes Japanese, "to encourage the international dimension of the internet." More countries ought to do the same. More websites offering an alternative view to the regular diet of American junk-food culture would be no bad thing.

As the number of non-Anglophone websites increases, so too will the number of non-Anglophone internet users. Experience bears this out, without exception. The introduction in 1997 of a computerized Cyrillic alphabet set brought about an immediate growth of websites in Russia; now 60 percent of all internet traffic there takes place within the country. Before Chinese character sets were introduced in 1996, mainland China had 300,000 web-connected computers and 1,500 local websites. By the end of 1999, there were more than 9 million Chinese internet users, including 200,000 connected by cellular phones or PDAs. There were 35.6 million email accounts, about 50,000 top-level registered domain names, and 520 internet service providers. (Private ISPs are permitted in China but they must connect through one of five large state-owned ISPs.)

The market rather than government intervention drives such rapid expansion, but governments can help by removing unnecessary regulatory obstacles. Good conditions for local digital content industries can be established through the legal protection of intellectual property rights, promotion of multilingualism, and support for the use of new technology in the arts and cultural heritage. The single most important step that governments can take to create useful, compelling local content on the web is to move their own information and services online.

LEAPFROG AND INNOVATE

It's often said that a lack of basic infrastructure and existing technology need not be an impediment for developing countries, because they can "leapfrog" more industrialized nations that are being held back by outdated but entrenched analog and legacy systems. The Baltic country of Estonia had virtually no modern technology when it regained its independence in 1991. Government offices and some companies were sparsely equipped with old mainframe minicomputers and there were just two mobile phones in the entire Ministry of Foreign Affairs. There were no computers in private hands.

Today, Estonia is one of the most wired nations in the world, with internet penetration ranking among the world's top 20 countries. All schools are connected, 80 percent of bank transfers are made over the internet, and 30 percent of the population has web access. Per capita income in Estonia has increased from $600 in 1991 to $5,000 in 2000. These astounding results were achieved through a concerted national effort based on a belief that improved connectivity could contribute to the survival of a small, newly independent country and help it find its place in the wider world.

Estonia initially sought help from its neighbors, reaching an agreement with Swedish and Finnish telecommunications operators to install a telephone network in exchange for profits from the business. It now has one of the most modern, and least expensive, dialup services in Europe. The government also provided grants for communities to obtain hardware and software, with the stipulation that recipients pay half the cost in order to create a sense of ownership. To de-politicize the issue, a NGO called the Tiger Leap Foundation was given control of distributing the funds and determining who should benefit. The foundation also organized an annual roadshow in which up to 100 web-connected computers were placed in a big tent in a town square and made available to all who were interested. Instruction and lectures were given throughout the day. Teachers who use computers in their classes worked with less computer-literate colleagues in a teachers' tent. A strategy seminar introduced IT-based management skills to company and local government managers.

Estonia is in an excellent position to e-gov itself. A government portal called the Estonian State Web Center was created in 1998, standardizing and linking existing agency websites. This is making information more accessible to not only citizens but also civil servants. By 1999, government offices were fully computerized and 80 percent of public officials had their own email address. The United Nations Development Program (UNDP), which once had a dozen staff in Estonia, wound up its operations there at the end of 2000 when the country graduated from being an aid recipient to a donor country. The UNDP resident representative said that the country had been a "textbook success story," particularly in its use of information technology for development. Estonia also provides IT training and supports a Tiger Leap project to connect schools in Macedonia, aiding that small, newly independent country to find its place in the world.

Investment in technology is correlated with investment in education and literacy and should be at the heart of any strategy to bridge the digital divide. Much of Costa Rica's economic growth—8.3 percent of GNP in 1999, the highest in Latin America—can be attributed to its determination to put computer laboratories in all high schools, which are kept open after school hours for anybody in the community to use. As a country without an army, and therefore no military spending to drain the public coffers, Costa Rica has been able to invest more per capita than most developing countries on school computers and on training its teachers, the country's so-called soldiers of knowledge.

Its national IT strategy includes a determined effort to integrate isolated rural communities into the national economy. To tackle rural citizens' fears of technology and increase their motivation, the government set loose a fleet of self-contained multipurpose, multimedia mobile units, called LINCOS for "little intelligent communities." They travel around the countryside like a digital-age bookmobile, powered by their own generators and providing a variety of functions, including internet access, email facilities, computer training, and a small lecture theater.

Connecting the rural poor requires innovative approaches, and usually a shift of emphasis from individual connectivity to community connectivity. Integrated multipurpose community information centers, often known as telecenters, are increasingly providing technology and internet access to residents of remote communities who cannot individually afford the equipment or who don't have the skills to use computer tools. Telecenters typically provide access to the web, email, and other data networks such as electronic libraries and government and community information systems. Many include shared office space for local small businesses. Some also provide facilities and training for local radio and TV production and broadcasting programs. And since, to close the digital divide, it is as important to teach people to use technology as it is to give them access to it, most telecenters try to add value with training in computer literacy and distance learning programs.

Shared information and communication facilities were first introduced in Scandinavia about two decades ago as means of improving access to telematics in rural and isolated areas. The concept spread to other isolated parts of Europe, such as Scotland and Ireland, and also to remote areas of Australia, Canada, and the US. Brazil has implemented hundreds of centers and aims to have 3,000 established by 2004, often located in buildings that also include postal, banking, and other public services. The first Brazilian telecenters were in rural townships of between 50,000 and 100,000 inhabitants with poor infrastructure. More recently, they have been introduced to extremely remote and isolated areas. Brazilian telecenters are entirely self-supporting in spite of—or perhaps due to—relatively low tariffs.

Telecenters are emerging as the primary mode of internet connectivity in Africa. South Africa established 55 centers, which include an element of e-government as citizens are able to access and print out application forms for identity documents and trading licenses. Innovative approaches are being found to deal with inadequate telecommunications infrastructure and limited human resources.

Manguzi is a rural community in the Maputaland region of the KwaZulu Natal province of South Africa, where most people are subsistence farmers and where there is almost no infrastructure. CSIR icomtek, formerly the information and communications unit of the South African Council for Scientific and Industrial Research, established a telecenter in the town in 1998. It is managed by a local person trained by the CSIR and provides various services, including dialup internet access. The center has one of the few telephone lines in the area.

However, because there is no public transport and most people don't even own a bicycle, many people have to walk long distances to reach the telecenter. Since it was too far for many students to walk from school, a local headmaster asked if a relay connection could be made to the school. In a place with a well-developed telecommunications infrastructure, this would have been no problem. But while each school in Manguzi was given a computer, there were two schools that, for technical reasons, could not be linked by fixed telephone, cellular, ISDN, spread spectrum, or leased lines. A direct satellite link was technically possible but financially prohibitive. So instead, the CSIR attached a radio with antenna to the computers in each of the two schools, along with a satellite receiver card and broadcasting dish. When school users want to access the internet, they relay their request to the telecenter via the radio link, where a fileserver dials on demand and the requested information is downloaded directly to the school's PC using satellite broadcasting technology. The radio link to the telecenter requires no monthly payments, and the price of the telephone call from the telecenter to the ISP is covered by the income generated by the telecenter's activities.

LET THEM EAT CYBERCAKE?

Most of the world's rural poor have little, if any, money to spend on luxuries such as information and communications. There are other divides more important than the digital one: healthcare, education, human rights. There are countries, especially in Africa, with chronic food shortages, low rates of life expectancy, high rates of illiteracy, few natural resources, and poor soil. Many people have argued that the internet cannot change the lives of the world's poor and reject the notion that they can ever be considered a market for high-tech products. Philanthropists have warned that an overemphasis on the technology gap could undercut the urgent provision of aid for food and medicine.

At the first Worldwide Forum on Electronic Democracy, held in Paris in March 2000, a speaker from a wealthy west European country argued passionately that the poor could not eat cybercake and that the internet was only creating greater inequalities between rich and poor nations. Shortly afterward, Ibrahim N'Daye, mayor of Bamako, capital of Mali, one of Africa's poorest countries, stood up and replied: "To access the internet, people have to have a computer, which nobody has in my country. And even if they had a computer, they would need a telephone line, which is also a rare commodity in Mali. And even if they could somehow get online, all the languages on the internet are unknown to most people in my country. And even if the languages were known, half our population is illiterate... So before you ask me, 'Well, what the hell are you doing here?', let me say that I believe technology can adapt to take into account even our situation. For IT companies, there are huge opportunities in developing countries. We're convinced that researchers will find solutions to many of our problems. I am encouraged to hear about the way mobile phones are going... maybe we won't need decades to set up a telephone network. And for the half who can't read or write, maybe researchers will come up with some tools to help them communicate, something like voice-recognition technology that they have for blind people."

Thabo Mbeki, the president of South Africa, also argues passionately that, while poor countries must be selective in which technologies they embrace, they cannot wait until poverty and illiteracy have been eradicated before plugging into the web. He says that the internet could be more useful for poor countries than it has been for rich ones, and that unless Africa especially taps into it, the continent will face new barriers and be left disenfranchised in all walks of life. UN Secretary General Kofi Anan also warns that the world's poor must not be cut off from the digital age. He says: "People lack many things: jobs, shelter, food, healthcare, and drinkable water. Today, being cut off from basic telecommunications services is a hardship almost as acute as these other deprivations, and may indeed reduce the chances of finding remedies to them."

These views from Africa, often in sharp contrast to some of the deep thinkers of the North, underline the point that developing countries should not have to choose between health and technology. The two are not incompatible if the deployment of new technology is viewed as part of an overall solution to global problems. The North talks about the digital divide, the South wants to hear about "digital dividends." Rather than focus on the divisiveness of the technological gap, the international community should consider the internet as a source of opportunity to uplift the impoverished people of the world from the lowest rung of human development. The web doesn't directly put food into mouths, but it can improve the distribution and quality of food and other basic needs. It can provide access to telemedicine and healthcare specialists. It can create the opportunity to access and exchange information on agriculture, animal husbandry, basic hygiene, literacy, water management and environmental protection, handicrafts, and business administration.

With the personal engagement of both the Bamako mayor and the country's president, Mali advanced from 800 internet users in 1997 to 4,500 in 2000; a small but significant achievement. To compensate for a lack of phone lines to homes and businesses, support was given to the growth of public access points such as cybercafés. In March 2000, an event called Bamako 2000 was organized, bringing together 2,000 participants from 48 countries to share positive experiences. Mali now has telemedicine, distance learning, and even e-commerce. The impact of information technology on economic and social development has been so positive that there are now plans to connect all 701 villages throughout the country. In getting this far, one of the most important policy decisions taken by the government was to create a competitive environment for the telecommunications sector, freeing it from the exclusivity and control of the country's élite.

For them to become more self-sufficient and part of the global economy, it helps if poor countries have transparent democracies that promote education rather than corrupt dictatorships that wage war. The internet is used daily to help suppressed people in their struggles for human rights, and its ability to act as an agent for democratization can be seen by the lengths to which dictators go to ban the medium from their countries. Fearing an unrestricted, uncensored flow of information from across its border, the military junta in Myanmar (Burma) imposes prison sentences of between 7 and 15 years for any unauthorized use of a computer or modem. A citizen who wants a legitimate internet account must apply to the state-run Myanmar Posts & Telecom, which has the only web server in the country, and pay anywhere from $300 to $1,000 to get connected, plus a monthly fee of $65 and perhaps a usage charge of $3–5 per hour. The Myanmar junta has no interest in bridging the digital divide, and no interest in ending four decades of repression, poverty, and isolation.

THE RIGHT TO COMMUNICATE

Article 19 of the Universal Declaration of Human Rights states: "Everyone has the right to freedom of opinion and expression; this right includes freedom to hold opinions without interference and to seek, receive and impart information and ideas through any media and regardless of frontiers."

This right to communicate arose out of a postwar concern for free speech and a free press. There have been attempts by the United Nations to secure the right to two-way communication, but proposals have always collapsed due to ideological differences, first between East and West and then between North and South. However, it is on the basis of Article 19 that national post offices and the Universal Postal Union (UPU), the UN agency that oversees the global postal system, have defined their social obligation to provide universal access to a mail service, allowing citizens to send and receive goods and messages from any point in the world to any other point. It is this need to fulfill broader social interests that makes the post office different from companies like FedEx. But if the ability to send and receive snailmail is a fundamental human right then, in the digital age, shouldn't it also be a right to send and receive email?

In July 2000, a panel of independent experts drawn from government, business, and civil society reported to the United Nations Economic and Social Council and recommended that the UN should link the right of universal access to information and communication services such as the internet with existing principles and conventions on human rights and development. The panel challenged the international community to ensure that there was universal access to the internet by the end of 2004.

While not completely accepting the dare, the United Nations Millennium Declaration includes a commitment to ensure that the benefits of new technologies are "made available to all." This declaration, which states the values, principles, and objectives of the international agenda for the twenty-first century, is the main document to come out of the Millennium Summit, the largest ever gathering of world heads of state and heads of government, held in New York in September 2000. The summiteers agreed with a further panel recommendation to form a UN taskforce on information and communication technology to facilitate the expansion of new technologies in developing countries. Jose Maria Figueres, former president of Costa Rica, heads the group of international agencies, private industry, and foundations and trusts. The G8 countries have also established their own Digital Opportunity Taskforce (dot) aimed at helping developing countries join the internet age, as a result of campaigning from Thabo Mbeki and fellow African leaders Olusegun Obasanjo of Nigeria and Abdelaziz Bouteflika of Algeria.

While all this sounds like yet more talk and still not much action, the work of these groups is important, because the international donor community does not have a well-coordinated, strategic approach to addressing the digital divide. Stronger partnerships are needed to avoid duplication, foster collaboration and openness, and share best practice and experience. Developing countries often learn best from each other since they face similar problems, so there need to be programs to facilitate South–South information flows. Some modest technology investments in developing countries have paid huge dividends, but experiences have not been shared and projects not replicated because nobody hears about them. The donor community needs to help disseminate this knowledge.

The North also has to make sure that the rules governing the emerging networked global economy are fair so that the South can become contributing participants rather than exploited spectators. Currently, the US operates as the hub of internet interchange and developing countries have to make US dollar payments for online exchanges and connectivity to North American telecommunications carriers, which carry 98 percent of global interregional traffic. This contrasts with the accounting rate system for the international telephone network, in which developing countries receive cash transfers from developed countries. Therefore, a shift from voice-based telecommunications to the web results in not only prohibitive connection costs but also a loss of revenue for developing countries.

People want a useful and affordable internet, businesses want to expand their markets, education wants to change the way it teaches, and government wants a more efficient and cost-effective way to deliver public services. All of these different interests are converging to create a greater awareness of the digital divide and to lift it on to the global political agenda. With a concerted international effort, universal web access is achievable. However, it is not necessarily inevitable, and failure to act does not bode well for a future knowledge-based global society.

11 Smart Communities: Better Places to Live and Work

SMART COMMUNITY SPIRIT

A few well-publicized cities and towns have thrived in the prosperity of the new economy, becoming exciting and vibrant places to live. Established financial centers such as New York, London, and Amsterdam have also largely succeeded in attracting digital-age growth, because the financial sector has a huge appetite for information technology. But the vast majority of cities haven't been so lucky. Most only watch the images of success elsewhere, while they suffer from a decline in their traditional manufacturing or agricultural bases. Small businesses that once competed locally with just a few other companies are now up against companies of all sizes from all around the world. New jobs that might be created in the service sector don't go to displaced factory workers, resulting in social divisions within the community. Skilled and educated people find work elsewhere, leaving behind their dreary city with its dirty streets, rundown and graffiti-covered buildings, high rates of unemployment, crime, homelessness, and drug and alcohol abuse.

Local governments can no longer make their municipalities appealing to companies simply by lowering business rates. Today, high demands are put on the quality of the working and living environment, and a council must find innovative ways to improve the attractiveness of its town as a place for companies to locate, for individuals to live, and for tourists to visit. Industry and investors want access to good public and private-sector services, a modern communications and transportation infrastructure and, most importantly, a large pool of skilled labor. In a world where people can live anywhere and still do the same job, earn the same wage, and buy the same goods and services, local governments also have to compete for residents by offering good schools, healthcare, parks, leisure facilities, cultural activities, public safety, housing, and overall quality of life. Tourists have to be tempted by easy access to attractions, events, and hotels.

Municipal governments are marketing themselves as never before. Many act in near desperation to keep existing firms from closing, and compete feverishly with other towns and regions to attract new businesses and new industrial sectors, especially in high technology. The enormous impact of globalization often makes local leaders feel powerless, even though communities have their own visions and aspirations. In an attempt to combine the realities of the global economy with community values, many municipalities, volunteer groups, and local businesses are joining forces to use the internet to create smarter and more sustainable communities.

The growing international smart community movement aims to use new technology to transform city life in deep-seated ways rather than incrementally. The internet can drive urban renewal by making everything more accessible. E-commerce makes shopping more accessible, e-government makes public services more accessible, teleconsulting makes healthcare more accessible so that a disabled person, for example, doesn't have to travel to a distant hospital for a simple diagnosis. For culture, leisure, and tourism, the web enables customized information and online reservations. A smart city integrates e-commerce, e-government, online healthcare, and education, often through a single community portal. Says John M. Eger, president of the San Diego-based World Foundation for Smart Communities: "Unlike towns and cities of an earlier era which were built along railroads, waterways or interstate highways, these cities of the future—smart communities if you will—will be built along information highways."

A smart city has exceptional cultural and community spirit. It boasts close partnerships between education, business, city hall, and the voluntary sector. Every home, business, and service site has high-speed internet access. No longer satisfied with national one-size-fits-all programs, residents of a smart community know how they want to put technology to use in their neighborhoods. Citizens participate as the designers and suppliers of online information and services, which reinforces civic life and local democracy. Through its schools, businesses, sports groups, cultural associations, and individual initiative, a smart community mobilizes people to articulate their expectations and needs in respect to the information society. Municipal leaders assume responsibility for ensuring that the infrastructure and support systems are in place to create local jobs and ensure sustainable economic growth, seeking input from the community and pursuing constructive policies regardless of any unhelpful shenanigans going on upstairs in parliament or the president's office.

AN URBAN LABORATORY

Parthenay is a small city in rural western France that in the early 1980s, due to a decline in its agricultural industries, was in deep economic crisis with no community assets, spirit, or identity. Local leaders resolved to revitalize the economic, cultural, social, and political life of the city by helping citizens set up associations, activities, and exhibitions. This involved relinquishing the kind of political control in which the council decided everything, in favor of encouraging citizens to become active participants in the development of their community. The local council acted as a catalyst by contributing funds or facilitating relations between community groups. This approach brought tangible results. With a population of just 18,000, Parthenay now has more than 250 community groups in various fields of endeavor. It hosts 150 annual cultural events and festivals, and the city hall doesn't organize or set the schedules for any of them.

As part of its support function, the local council saw how new technology, specifically the internet, could be used to stimulate initiatives and improve dialogue between citizens. A Digital Town project was launched in 1996 and it became the community's ambition to be an "urban laboratory of the information society," to find out what would happen if new technology was suddenly introduced to the everyday lives of citizens and society at large. Says Parthenay's philosophical mayor, Michel Hervé: "We say 'laboratory' because the city is sufficiently small for one to observe the complexity of interactions at the everyday level, and to understand the effects of these technologies. By starting small, the information society can be experimented with and truly take form."

Visionary leadership, from the mayor, local councilors, and city manager, is vital for a smart community project. If these people don't even know how to turn on a computer, they aren't going to think about using the internet to improve the quality of life in their communities. Too often, smart community projects are isolated initiatives, undertaken by an individual department with no support from the top and with no connection to other parts of the public administration, let alone the wider community. A citywide action plan or e-strategy has to be put in place to define the vision, identify funding, and establish the steps to be taken for implementation.

Parthenay's plan was simultaneously to connect schools, businesses, cultural associations, public administration, and individual citizens. Its first step was to open a public "digital space" in the local social services office, with 20 computers and free internet access and multimedia learning. Soon there were 11 digital spaces around town, with a total of 80 computers, scanners, a video database, and high-speed cable access. With more than 200 visitors every day, the spaces helped introduce people to new technology and ensured equal opportunity to access the technology.

In 1997, the council launched a "1000 micros" (one thousand PCs) initiative, which allowed residents to pay FF300 ($40) per month over two years for a home computer and internet connection. Frustrated that no private internet service provider wanted to set up shop in the city, and regarding the web as a kind of public utility that should be accessible to all, the council gave all citizens free internet connection and email accounts through the city hall's server. Local residents, associations, and SMEs could have their computers and modems configured by a town technician. At around the same time, Parthenay established In-Town-Net, a citywide intranet intended to be an "electronic mirror" of the real city with which local companies, associations, and individual citizens could create their own websites (with personalized management tools allowing people to generate pages without knowledge of a specific programming language), hosted for free on the city's server. In-Town-Net also includes public discussion forums, a diary of local events, and free classified ads. By 2000, there were more than 400 local organizations publishing 55,000 web pages.

Just as corporate intranets have changed the way employees work within their companies, a city intranet can change the way citizens live within their communities, says Hervé. "Company intranets have created a homogeneous space, generally around a common project, to which everyone can contribute. Interrelational complexity has also been increased and intranets allow regeneration, thanks to a certain amount of dismantling and reconstruction which allows the web to be set up outside the scope of hierarchical systems."

Before the Digital Town project, most of Parthenay's community groups and volunteer associations struggled, because people could not find mutually convenient times to meet and the cost of mailing information to members was too expensive. Now, online communication is free and business can be conducted at any time and from anywhere. In local commerce, a shoe store owner started to promote his range of oversized shoes on his website—he now takes orders electronically from around the country. Each week, the local movie theater decides which film to screen by asking movie goers to email in their choice from a selection of films listed on its website, bringing democracy to the cinema.

OUT-OF-TOWN ASSISTANCE

Rejuvenating and transforming an entire city is a mammoth undertaking, thus it helps to have private-sector partners and support from a higher level of government: state, central, or supranational. Parthenay's Digital Town project was local in nature and execution, but it could not have progressed as far as it did without assistance from outside the community. The town volunteered to be a guinea pig for three continuous European Commission research and development projects, from 1996 to 2000, through which it worked with various prominent high-tech companies, including Siemens, France Telecom, Microsoft, and Philips. Previously, large global corporations expressed no interest in small-town projects, but through its European pursuits, Hervé was able to convince enough firms that petite Parthenay was the ideal place to test new technologies before applying them on a grander scale.

The three-year (1998–2000) Integrated Multimedia Applications Generating Innovative Networks in European digital towns (IMAGINE) project aimed to develop a European model for a smart community with online services in education and training, employment, regional economy and e-commerce, public administration, and democracy. Besides the full complement of industry partners, the project involved local SMEs and teams of social science researchers from several universities, who identified user requirements and monitored the success of applications. Different services were rolled out in four similar-sized towns: Parthenay, Casale Monferrato in Italy, and Torgau and Weinstadt in Germany. Siemens now packages all the applications and offers them for sale to other communities as a sort of smart city toolbox.

A number of countries have showcase towns and test sites where technology is integrated into the community to see what happens. In May 2000, after a nationwide competition, the Canadian government awarded matching grants of C$5 million ($3.3 million) to 12 smart community demonstration projects, one in each of the country's 10 provinces, one in its northern territories, and one in an aboriginal community.

One recipient was the remote, far north city of Yellowknife, a government administrative center and mining town, similar in size to Parthenay. Its smart city initiative was sponsored by 22 public, private, nongovernmental organizations, and voluntary agencies covering the full spectrum of economic, social, and cultural life in the city. With 40 percent of the local population already connected to the internet, Yellowknife aims to become the first community in Canada to achieve 80 percent access. The smart city project establishes a community information network where cultural and geographic communities can exchange content, products, services, and ideas. The network includes a HelpNET to simplify access to social services and promote improved collaboration and cooperation among caregivers, and a LearnNET to provide an education forum accessible to all residents.

A BusinessNET works to create a new image of Canada's north as a place to do business. Local companies get a listing on an electronic directory, as well as email, voice, and fax buttons to allow web surfers to contact the business. Companies can join an e-commerce virtual incubator mall that allows full-service order, delivery, and payment services. Through BusinessNET, consumers get better access to local products and access to banking services, as many Yellowknife business customers live in far-flung Arctic villages where there are no banks. A separate website provides a range of services to tourists, including online booking and reservations.

In Ireland, the former state-owned telecom operator, Eircom, contributed I£15 million ($17 million) to bring the town of Ennis in rural county Clare into the information age. A company set up with the Ennis town council oversees all aspects of the Information Age Town project and connected 4,500 of the town's 5,600 homes (83 percent). Every household was offered a multimedia PC and software, valued in total at I£1,500 ($2,000), with free internet access; people were simply asked to make a contribution to an account fund to be reinvested for additional local information-age projects. Residents with little or no computer skills were given an eight-hour basic familiarization course to ensure that at least one member of every household could use their machine. People were also given a chance to qualify for the European Computer Driving Licence, a self-paced module computer training course.

Prior to 1998, when the project began, over 600 Ennis homes didn't even have a telephone. Now, many households have network-based voice-mail, prompting the local *Clare Champion* newspaper to declare: "No more busy tone in Ennis." All 12 schools and more than 400 small businesses were given high-speed telecommunication connections and, to further encourage e-commerce, shops were offered subsidies to buy computers, database and application development, website design, consultancy, and training. The local musical instrument store set up a web page in Japanese to serve customers in Tokyo where traditional Irish folk music is incredibly popular. The local pharmacist used the internet to lower his costs for prescriptions by teaming up to purchase online with other independents, allowing them to compete more effectively with the prices of large drug-store chains such as Boots that are moving into Ireland.

Local sports and voluntary groups were all given free web hosting for one year and website templates to simplify data input and mainte-nance. The local St Paul's Catholic church has a website that allows parishioners to book masses. The community library has a public inter-net terminal, but since many people already have a PC at home, this is used mainly by asylum seekers arriving at nearby Shannon airport to keep in touch with home. Tying the whole project together is a commu-nity website that includes an interactive map that people can use to surf around town, accessing local businesses, public bodies, and community groups. The site includes a live link to the Clare FM radio station as well as live broadcasts of music events and the local arts festival.

VIRTUAL SHOPPING MALLS

Even if they're not going all the way to becoming a smart city, reaching out to all aspects of society, many municipalities are at least building virtual shopping centers where local businesses can display their wares. A virtual mall usually sits on the city intranet, or there can be hyperlinks from a community portal. The purpose of these is to stimulate e-commerce and help old-economy firms, especially SMEs, to improve their competitiveness in the new economy. Just as a municipality might build and maintain a shopping precinct for bricks-and-mortar stores, it can build and maintain one for virtual stores. And just as citizens can walk along city-maintained streets and window-shop, they can surf a city-maintained virtual mall and browse through the online stores without having to purchase anything.

It is up to the companies' offers and advertisements to encourage shoppers to enter and buy. Most companies offering products and services over the internet are continually on the lookout for ways to reach their target groups. Simply being on the web works only for large global firms with a well-known name or strong brand. So, just like being on Main Street or in a shopping center, local firms benefit from having a spot in the same virtual neighborhood as municipal services and cultural groups and clustered with other shops.

A local business can usually plug into a municipal virtual mall free of charge, which has led to cries of unfair competition from dot-coms that could be providing the same services through a commercial portal. These criticisms tend to fall on deaf ears in most city halls, where officials believe that the private sector has had ample time and opportunity to set up community portals but has done nothing about it. Meanwhile, local businesses struggle to survive and make the transition to the new economy. Some cities, such as The Hague in the Netherlands, even go as far as to help small firms go online by offering them free consultancy.

In the same way that city tourist departments and commercial map-makers both produce street maps, there is no reason that public and private portals can't coexist and complement each other. The bigger difficulty for local councils is to determine which businesses should be eligible for a place in a virtual mall or for a link from the city hall website. Parthenay has so far been able to accommodate all its businesses, while

Yellowknife leaves the decisions and management to the local chamber of commerce. The city of Siena, Italy, wants its virtual mall to uphold the image of Tuscany and thus only accepts businesses specializing in the region's culture, food and wine, handicrafts, and tourism. While many cities have quality criteria that companies must meet, any approval process to filter out certain businesses has to be approached with caution. If a Christian bookstore is given a link, for example, a council could be obliged to give equal space to a Jewish, Muslim, or Buddhist bookstore, or even, for that matter, to an adult bookstore.

The city of Cookeville, Tennessee, found out that it couldn't play favorites when the editor of the *Putnam Pit*, a small, muckraking tabloid and website, took the council to court for refusing him a hyperlink from its website. The city already had links to several for-profit and nonprofit sites, including internet service providers, a law firm, and a truck product manufacturer and distributor. However, it had no stated policy on who could be linked; the city's computer operations manager merely added links as they were requested.

When the *Putnam Pit* editor asked for a link, the computer operations manager referred the decision to the city manager, who refused because he "didn't care for" the editor's published opinions. The city manager decided it would be best to limit links to nonprofit websites, but indicated that he would not allow a link to the *Putnam Pit* even if it were nonprofit. This prompted the city to adopt standard criteria requiring linked sites to promote the economic welfare, industry, or tourism of Cookeville.

The editor went to court claiming that his First Amendment right had been violated, because the city had established a public forum by allowing web links and he was unconstitutionally discriminated against because he was unable to be represented in that forum. A federal appeals court judge said that while the editor wasn't entitled to a link from the city's website, he could not be denied one solely based on his controversial views. "The requirement that websites eligible to be linked to the city's site promote the city's tourism, industry, and economic welfare gives broad discretion to city officials, raising the possibility of discriminatory application of the policy based on viewpoint," ruled the judge, before sending the case back to district court for further proceedings.

One way around both "must link" rulings and criticisms of unfair competition is to open and market a local portal to everybody, running it as a private enterprise for which companies are charged a competitive hosting fee. This was the approach taken by Berlin when its official city site was set up in 1999 as a public–private partnership, to provide value-added services and a broad range of online content reflecting all aspects of life in the city. The site includes information and services from more than 250 cultural, media, and public administration organizations. There is an opinion forum where Berliners can pass judgment on local restaurants or the latest movies, and a dating page where residents can meet, according to the promotional brochure, "irrespective of whether it is for romance, a pleasant group of inline skaters or the search for a partner to go to Hawaii with."

To pay for this added-value excitement, the Berlin community portal has more than 500 local companies paying for a listing in the online *Marktplatz*. They can pay more for banner advertising and promotions aimed at specific target groups. The virtual market includes a variety of payment options, and consumers can search the site by product or company and have items delivered directly to their door.

INFRASTRUCTURE, ENVIRONMENT, AND ATTITUDE

The new technology industry is a highly networked sector in which firms enter into continually changing strategic alliances with other technology companies and create one-off partnerships for specific projects. They therefore like to be located close to each other, not only virtually but also physically, in the same city, the same industrial park, even the same building. Many city councils look to match urban renewal projects with efforts to attract high-tech companies, and city centers are becoming high target areas for both.

The Helsinki City Council took a dilapidated inner-city building constructed originally as a recreational center for the 1952 Olympic Games, and slated for demolition ever since, and converted it into a high-tech media and culture center. Besides reviving the old building and its immediate surroundings, the renovation of the Lasipalatsi ("glass palace") serves to showcase and disseminate new media, and brings together technology developers, content developers, and technology users. Because it was important to have complementary companies and organizations, the city held a competitive bid to select the most suitable tenants. One of the criteria was that the business had to make use of the internet.

Opened in 1998, Lasipalatsi contains several TV production companies, a bookstore, a public library with 20 web-connected PCs, a florist, bars, cafés and restaurants, and a cinema that hosts IT seminars during the day and alternative films at night. Everywhere in the building, people are confronted with technology. Even the cafés and restaurants have touch-screens inserted in the tables from which customers can order drinks.

Lasipalatsi has a social goal to stress the human side of technology and make it more accessible to all, thus contributing to the city's transition to a smart community. The building and land are owned by the city administration and managed by a city-owned company with a board comprised of public officials and tenants of the building. This helps create synergy in the building and coordinates projects between the tenants. The board's mixed public–private composition has helped city officials gain a better understanding of not only technology but also general business needs, while the private firms have a better appreciation of the social role of technology.

The Lasipalatsi project is part of a wider vision for the economic development of Helsinki and is designed to complement an Art and Design City, an 85-hectare site of experimental media production and testing located 6km from the city center. In early 2000, an audiovisual complex was completed that is due to continue expanding until 2014, when the number of residents is expected to increase from 4,000 to 8,000

and the number of jobs from 3,000 to 12,000. It will feature a sophisticated broadband fiberoptic network accessible to all residents, schools,
and businesses. Helsinki also boasts the Otaniemi Technology Park,
home of Nokia, and one of Europe's most extensive commercial science
parks with 5,000 researchers and 200 companies.

Concentrated science parks, offering high-speed, low-cost
telecommunications infrastructures, are becoming the most popular way
for municipal governments to convince modern firms that their city is
the place to locate or expand. The Dubai Internet City opened in October
2000, a year after its conception, with 200 leading technology companies
taking up immediate residency. Dubbed the world's first e-business free-
trade zone, the technology park provides an "infrastructure, environment, and attitude" to enable technology firms to operate locally,
regionally, and globally out of Dubai, with significant competitive advantages including corporate tax exemptions, no personal income tax, waiv-
ing of currency restrictions, land with a 50-year renewable lease, and a
single online window for all government clearances such as trade licenses
and work permits. After China, the Middle East is the fastest-growing
region in the world for new technology growth, and Dubai is determined
to become the regional hub, with the Internet City the first step to
putting the emirate on the world IT map.

Technology parks are often seen as the key to giving traditionally
low-tech cities an instant high-tech image. The TeleCity science park in
Manchester, cradle of the industrial revolution, provides the UK's only
transcontinental internet exchange outside of London, with much
cheaper rates. Manchester's biggest asset is arguably its university, which
supports new technology startups by providing access to its labs and
powerful computers, as well as office space and legal and financial aid. In
return for its support, new companies pay royalties to the university after
three years of profitable operation. In the late 1990s, the university supported 50 startups, creating 200 new high-tech jobs for the city.

Many of today's most successful technology companies were
started by ambitious university students, and they also provide the skilled

workforce needed to attract companies locating to a city. It is no coincidence that Boston, with all its universities and colleges, is so reputedly high-tech. In some cities, university campuses are tying in with local technology parks. The Dubai Internet City is home to the Dubai Internet University, which has a curriculum covering e-business, e-finance, e-marketing, e-design, e-management, and e-everything else.

In Sweden, the Royal Institute of Technology is locating its IT campus in Cellular Valley, the Stockholm suburb of Kista that is home to Ericsson. About 10,000 students will study, conduct research, and train with companies in the area. This in turn will help to urbanize Kista, which is a traditional industrial zone with few services and amenities. Says Stockholm Mayor Carl Cederschoid: "Modernizing Kista means joining the adjacent housing areas to the growing center for new technology and getting restaurants, libraries, theaters, cinemas, pubs into the area. I think the students will be very helpful in that respect, at least when we're talking about the pubs."

If all else fails, a city has to go out and sell itself. The Hague was in the unenviable position of lacking both a high-tech image and a major university, and it faced fierce competition from other large cities within its own country: the financial center of Amsterdam, and Utrecht and Rotterdam with their good universities. The city also competes with smaller municipalities and university towns in its own region. To attract foreign high-tech firms and new jobs, the city council works with a private-sector organization called The Hague Development Foundation, which identifies and targets specific North American companies looking to establish themselves in Europe. It helps companies find an appropriate office location and staff, and takes care of the legal aspects of setting up a business in Europe. In this way, combined with a good telecommunications infrastructure, the council has been able to entice such firms as Amazon and MapQuest to establish their European headquarters in the city.

Ultimately, a smart community requires broadband internet access for all citizens, businesses, educational institutions, hospitals, and other community members. A digital broadband infrastructure enables the high-speed transmission of all kinds of data, such as architects' drawings, high-definition photographs, medical x-rays, audio, video, and graphic art images. It enables a fully networked business community to form partnerships and consortia and compete regionally or globally. It allows people to work from home or on the road, and it provides citizens with the opportunity to develop new-economy skills and to link their activities with the wider community to create a better quality of life.

Telecommunications infrastructures were traditionally built and maintained by state-owned monopolies that provided national service without discrimination between communities or regions. With telecom liberalization and privatization, new providers are constructing the key digital infrastructures, such as fiberoptic networks, that the information society requires. However, private firms follow market demand, which can leave great swathes of a country unconnected.

Similarly, in many countries, municipal governments once owned local cable TV networks, but these too have been privatized and small cable companies everywhere are being swallowed by global telecom giants. With the emergence of the new economy, the wiring of a city is becoming a key municipal infrastructure concern, as important to urban prosperity as are its telephone lines, electricity grid, water mains, sewers, roads, and public transport. Many authorities now regret having sold off their cable networks and are starting to reinvest in broadband infrastructure to speed up the development of online services or to help specific groups.

Other municipalities, perhaps more wisely, are working with or leasing lines from telecom operators whose core business is to provide telecommunications infrastructure. As part of the Information Age Town project, Eircom laid Ireland's first local digital broadband ring around Ennis, which in turn is linked with other towns through the national ring. The Ennis ring connects all areas of the town and carries enough capacity to handle the equivalent of 250,000 telephone calls simultaneously.

In the Netherlands, under a national government initiative to provide access to disadvantaged communities, the city of Eindhoven has provided broadband access to a designated "knowledge neighborhood," an area of the city with 84,000 inhabitants and 38,000 households. The city worked in partnership with KPN, the former state telephone company, to speed up its DSL infrastructure; a mobile operator to test GPRS, WAP, and Bluetooth services; and the local cable operator to increase its data capacity. Philips was asked to supply set-top boxes so that people could access the internet through their TV sets. By reaching a critical mass of broadband users, Eindhoven's e-city project, as it is called, is serving as a testbed for a new generation of digital services. These include e-commerce, online booking for travel and cultural events, the establishment of virtual communities, healthcare services, and education and training. Most importantly, the e-city has allowed the municipality to provide public services online.

VIRTUAL CITY HALL

The postwar world required strong central governments to drive through the universal provision of major common needs such as healthcare, social welfare, and national infrastructure. However, with people today having more diverse needs, the centralized approach to governing no longer works as well. The nation-state is drowning in a vast network of interacting public, private, and nonprofit organizations, and it has become too large and too far removed from people's daily lives to solve local problems.

As such, central government is beginning to see that, after decades of neglect, local government is the most useful delivery channel for the provision of seamless, citizen-centric public services. Central government services, for example, would be made more widely available if they could be accessed through a community portal. Localization is an essential part of e-government. As the level of government closest to the people, the municipality is well poised to emerge as a citizen's entry point to the entire public administration. Whether cosmopolitan or rural, local authorities have lots of public access points—schools, libraries, leisure centers, municipal offices—ready to be wired up. Citizens should be able to arrive at city hall to pay a parking fine and also take the opportunity pay an overdue water bill, apply for a passport, renew their voter's registration, and be reminded that their property tax is due—all in the same visit and without being pushed from pillar to post.

Partnership working with different public, private, and voluntary agencies is already a significant factor in the provision of local services, but if municipalities are to fulfill a wider leadership role in guiding their towns and cities smoothly into the information society, they must set an example and adopt the same technologies used throughout the community and in business. Some fear that otherwise central government will look for other partners, perhaps in the private sector, to deliver services at the community level and local councils will be side-stepped once again.

The computerization of local council offices to enable e-government comes part and parcel with any smart community initiative. Even tiny Ennis allows its residents to apply for car tax and planning permission online. In Parthenay, requests for alcohol sale licenses or birth certificates can be made electronically and local taxes can be paid online. Archives can be accessed, as can job-search assistance and job applications. Suppliers to the local administration are able to check the internet to see the progress of their invoice, from receipt to approval to the issuing of the check, so that they are not always calling the accounts department.

Smart cards are becoming the citizen's key to unlocking the smart community. Often used together with digital signatures to ensure the confidentiality of electronic transactions, multifunction citizen cards can be used as proof of identification to obtain public information and to access services over the internet from PCs, digital TV, mobile phones, multimedia kiosks, one-stop shops, automatic bank tellers, or any electronic device with a smart-card reader. Smart-card technology has been around for some time now, and its success in the banking sector provides an example of how it can be applied as an electronic purse to pay for public services, utilities, property taxes, fines, building permits, registry certificates, public transport, parking, hospital services, admission to events and museums, registering for classes, and so on. Most cards work like credit cards and many can be recharged or used for cash withdrawals at any bank machine. Some cities are working with the business community so that citizen cards can be used to pay for goods and services and to sign contracts. In the future, they might double as a driving license or even house keys.

To minimize costs, the city-state of Bremen, Germany, did not develop its own citizen card but worked with a local savings bank to launch a smart card with debit and pre-paid functions and an integrated digital signature function. By providing the service to other cities and regions, it is expected that by 2002 there will be some 35 million Bremen-Eurocheque (Mastercard) smart cards in circulation. Says Herbert Kubicek, professor of applied computer science at the University of Bremen, which is involved in the development: "The government does not have to produce the cards and, most important, we can benefit from the trust and habits citizens already have in electronic banking."

In a smart community, web-connected citizens can easily access public information, official documents, and administrative proceedings. It is through the municipality that citizens can best feed back their opinions to enable all levels of government to be more responsive. With the help of the internet, citizens can interact more easily with public authorities, generate interactive public debates, and have a greater say in issues of governance.

The Barcelona City Council has an official program to use the internet to facilitate the exchange of information and opinions between citizens and the administration, involving the entire municipality rather than a single department. The city holds an electronic town hall meeting with different discussion topics each month: social welfare in January and public transportation in February, for example. The city presents a topic two months in advance, and outlines how the subject will be approached and who from the council will participate in the discussion.

Specialized municipal staff and political officials responsible for the subject under consideration participate in each forum, and experts from outside the municipality are brought in to contribute their ideas. All are available for direct discussion with citizens, and individuals can exchange information and points of view with each other. Topics can be proposed by the citizens themselves and there is a separate forum with school students. Citizens can actively contribute their ideas and suggestions about the issue under discussion, or they can offer their opinions passively by choosing specified voting options during online polls. The contributions are not binding on council decisions, but they are taken into consideration in the drafting of proposals.

Brisbane City Council in Australia has a similar Your City Your Say online community consultation process, in which citizens register to participate in online mediated discussions on subjects that change weekly. A CityNET application, developed as part of its smart city project, broadens Yellowknife's existing virtual city hall to enable people to influence council priorities. A bulletin board tracks progress, answers questions, and engages debate on a variety of issues, including the smart city program itself. Nonresidents are even asked for their views.

In Parthenay, council reports and minutes posted on the web are eagerly awaited by people who previously would never have dreamed of making the trip to city hall to read them. In Weinstadt, Germany, citizens are asked for their views on city proposals, and they can then see the tallies of online public opinion polls, sometimes prompting councilors to shift their positions. Says Weinstadt Mayor Jürgen Hofer: "If you get opinions directly and more precisely than you ever thought possible, this will surely influence the decision making within the town council."

As globalization makes it more difficult for national governments to influence political and economic conditions, the wellbeing of citizens will increasingly have to be addressed at the local level. To rise to this challenge, local leaders must recognize the value of collaboration and cooperation, grasp the importance of new technology, and use it in meaningful ways to create smart communities. Smart communities do not exist in cyberspace, populated by cyborgs. They are real places inhabited by real people who are making the most of the opportunities the internet has to offer. With a shared sense of mission, they are forging links and relationships like never before and, in the process, improving the economic, social, and cultural fabric of their communities.

12 Cyberdemocracy: Onward to Electronic Suffrage

THE BODY POLITIC

Franklin Delano Roosevelt was the first American politician to use radio to reach the masses. John Fitzgerald Kennedy was the first to benefit from television. In what may yet be another sign of the times, Jesse "The Body" Ventura was the first to achieve electoral success with the help of the internet.

In 1998, this former pro wrestler used the web to organize a long-shot, independent bid for governor of Minnesota, and ended up beating two established politicians. Ventura spent a paltry amount on his campaign and only accepted contributions of $50 or less, most of which came in through the Ventura for Minnesota website. He sold bumper stickers, baseball caps, and t-shirts, and recruited volunteers online. Digital pictures of Ventura were uploaded on to the website in almost real time, so voters could see where he was and what he was doing on the campaign trail. The website included Ventura's position on the top 50 or so campaign issues, from education to gun control, and he daringly provided a forum to let citizens debate. In the final week of the election campaign, the Ventura website received 1.2 million hits. It cost about $700 to build and the webmaster had no previous experience in web design. It wasn't slick, but it was innovative and it worked. It got The Body elected.

Less than two years later, in March 2000, John McCain used the web to raise $1 million in just 48 hours after his strong showing in the New Hampshire primary for the Republican presidential nomination. He raised a total of $6 million online and attracted 110,000 volunteers. McCain's popularity was due largely to his plan to reform the US's corrupt system of election campaign financing. He still lost the nomination to the party establishment favorite, George W. Bush, but all the new ideas in the presidential campaign came from the outsiders.

Meanwhile, in February 2000, shockwaves were being felt around Europe as the far-right Freedom Party of Jörg Haider entered government in Austria after a successful internet-driven election campaign. This has led to fears that the web will give rise to extremist politics by providing an equal platform to every racist, fundamentalist, and nutcase. Yet most who voted for the Freedom Party were motivated less by racism and more out of attraction to the party's opposition to the country's time-honored system of *Proporz*, in which the established center-right and center-left parties shared power and patronage, appointing between them all public-sector jobs from garbage collector to ambassador.

In the same month, next door in Croatia, Stipe Mesic went in three weeks from rank outsider among nine candidates to the winner of the presidential election to succeed the late Franjo Tudjman. At the start of the campaign, Mesic posted a website so flashy it would have humbled even the most high-tech American politician. It included an hour-by-hour schedule of his public appearances, streamed speeches and interviews in both RealVideo and QuickTime with cached clips that visitors could view later on, and an interactive section where anyone could email a question and read Mesic's replies.

With fewer than 200,000—only 4 percent—of the country's 4.6 million people having internet access, his opponents thought he was wasting his time. But word got around and the very idea of the site appealed to many voters; even if they couldn't see it, they thought it complemented Mesic's aim to create greater transparency, and to end Croatia's nationalism and isolationism by opening up to Europe, NATO, and the wider world. The website wasn't aimed so much at people living inside Croatia; it was for people outside. Croatian expatriates, of which there are many, are allowed to vote in national elections and their worldly opinions tend to carry sway with friends and family back home. Mesic knew that, and he knew that the internet was the best way to appeal to the expat vote.

In Slovakia, nine men lined up in May 1999 to run for its first free election for president after the country's velvet divorce from the Czech Republic—nine men, but not a single woman. That is, until groups of citizens and nongovernmental organizations identified Magda Vasaryova, a former Czechoslovak ambassador to Austria, as a qualified independent female candidate, persuaded her to run, collected the necessary signatures for her petition, and supported her election campaign, all through the internet. Without the financial backing of any political party, Vasaryova finished third. While the campaign aimed to provide an inspiration for Slovakian women in their struggle for gender equity, it also demonstrates the political impact that the internet can have even in countries with low access. At the time, less than 1 percent of Slovakia's population was connected.

Third-party candidates traditionally have little luck getting elected unless they have a super-rich supporter bankrolling their campaign. Legislators never seem to get around to reforming election financing rules, because it is their parties' money machines that ensure their re-election. So it remains politics as usual, with the party establishments forever keeping their grip on power. Meanwhile, democracy continues to deteriorate. Democratic societies today are characterized by the emergence of extremist parties, low voter turnouts, negative election campaigning, corruption, patronage, sex scandals, and disillusionment about politics and government in general, especially among the young. High-caliber people are reluctant to enter public life because they don't want to be hauled over the coals, and increasingly society is left with spineless politicians who tend to their own narrow interests rather than taking care of the common good, supposedly the primary task of representative democracy.

As Jesse Ventura and a growing number of others are proving, the internet can help break the mold of cozy, soundbite politics. (It is probably no coincidence that of all the American gubernatorial elections in 1998, Minnesota had the highest voter turnout.) The web brings new and unknown rules to the game of politics. It drives down the cost of campaigning and makes it more democratic by allowing any candidate to raise campaign funds, attract volunteers, organize themselves, and reach voters in a way that was previously only possible through the support of established party machines. Anyone with a computer and an internet connection can now make themselves look like a presidential contender.

STRANGE WEBFELLOWS

The web's biggest impact on democracy is its ability to allow people to organize. When political activists had to communicate by phone or fax, it was too difficult and expensive to build alliances and share information. On the internet, it is easy to disperse information widely and quickly. This allows for all kinds of strange bedfellows and new partnerships, including those between developed and developing countries.

In 1998, an NGO published on the web a draft copy of the Multilateral Agreement on Investment, or MAI, which was being negotiated behind closed doors by the 29-member club of rich countries, the Organization for Economic Co-operation and Development (OECD). A well-organized *ad hoc* coalition of consumer-rights activists, environmentalists, and developing countries quickly mobilized, passing the word by email and setting up websites providing copious amounts of information about the proposed international treaty to harmonize rules on foreign investment. The attacks left negotiators confused about how to proceed, and ultimately foreign investors lost interest in the MAI and talks dithered.

Similarly, the 1999 World Trade Organization (WTO) summit in Seattle was derailed by an unusual coalition of trade unionists, environmentalists, human-rights campaigners, consumer-rights groups, nationalists, protectionists, and anarchist youths sensing an opportunity for violence. Everyone from Friends of the Earth to Pat Buchanan was alerted to the protests by the web. The problem with the MAI negotiations, the WTO trade round, and similar initiatives isn't necessarily that they aim to advance globalization, but that they are conducted behind closed doors by faceless technocrats with no public accountability. In this sense they're not much different to an authoritarian regime, and even these must eventually listen when the people speak. The internet helps people to be heard by allowing them to speak louder, and with more voices.

In December 1996, demonstrators took to the streets of Belgrade and other Serbian cities after Slobodan Milosevic nullified local elections won by the pro-democracy opposition. An independent radio station, Radio B92, broadcast regular updates and announced meeting points for the protestors. So Milosevic closed it down. This prompted Radio B92 to reroute its programming to the internet, along with text messages and pictures of the demonstrations, ironically helping it to vastly expand its reach to a global audience. As a result, people from around the world inundated government officials, state-controlled media, and other Milosevic supporters with email protests. Within two days Radio B92 was allowed back on the air.

B92's internet broadcasts were a continuation of earlier tactics used by campaigners in other parts of eastern Europe prior to the fall of the Berlin Wall and by the students in Tiananmen Square, who bypassed official communication channels by sending faxes to the West. The difference with the internet is that text messages, as well as photos, audio, and video, can be sent to an unlimited number of recipients in one click. Worse news for dictators is that the web answers back. The internet's ability to disperse ideas instantly at little cost makes it a medium of unprecedented power, a threatening tool to the authority of popularly elected and despotic regimes alike.

With many in eastern Europe, Latin America, Asia, and Africa now enjoying the political freedoms already well established in western Europe, North America, and Japan, democracy in many ways risks becoming a victim of its own success. A free press and a better-educated public expose government failures that previously were left covered up. Greater transparency brings closer public scrutiny and citizens are better prepared to question and demand explanations from government.

The basic premise of politics-as-usual representative democracy is that full-time professional legislators are needed to assess priorities, reach compromises, and make smart choices. Citizens are traditionally too ill-informed about the intricate details of public policy, and too much public discussion limits the ability of politicians to pore over government legislation, conduct intelligent debate and, essentially, do the jobs they were elected to do. Yet, elected officials don't fulfill this idealistic function, because no one human can pay attention to every issue affecting their constituents. Instead, they become pawns of their party or more powerful interests. However, any party beholden to special-interest groups, be they fundamentalist Christians, big business, trade unions, or whoever, will not survive the digital age. Online communities are replacing ideology, religion, geography, race, gender, and other traditional divisions as the primary force behind political and social attitudes.

The internet is the place to go to find other people who share common views. Citizens connected to the web are by far the most conversant with the issues confronting the digital age (privacy, social exclusion, cybercrime, and so forth), much more than politicians, who still largely "don't get it." When *Wired* magazine conducted surveys in 1997 and again in 2000 on Americans' views of democracy, knowledge of current affairs, and voting habits, it found that internet users were, by huge margins, better informed, more opinionated, more likely to believe in democracy and diversity, and more likely to have faith in the future.

Governments cannot expect to govern a society where knowledge workers drive economic success but remain clueless on political matters. People are more dexterous and aware than most politicians realize, which begs the question: Why do we need politicians? Cybercitizens want to worry less about who is leading them and more about leading themselves. They want to be more directly involved in the actual governing process. Rising up like some modern-day Jeffersonian yeoman farmers with their laptops and wireless devices, they want to set their own political agendas, establish government priorities, and even help implement policies. They want to transform the representative democracy of today into a new form of participative democracy for tomorrow.

VOLUNTARY REALLOCATION OF POWER

Niccolò Machiavelli's *The Prince*, published in 1513, warned rulers not to embark on institutional reform, because they would only make enemies of those who profited from the old system and receive only lukewarm support from those who might profit from the new system. "There is nothing more difficult to execute, nor more dubious of success, nor more dangerous to administer than to introduce a new system," he said. Most leaders have since followed Machiavelli's advice, as history shows that political power only ever changes in one of two ways: either the system becomes corrupted at the core and it collapses, or there is a revolution outside that forces a collapse. The internet is driving an unstoppable political change that in theory could lead to a collapse if the transition to participative democracy is not made smoother through a genuine political will to let and make it happen.

Disregarding Machiavelli's warning, a 1999 report for the G8 Government Online Project suggests that governments consider the so-called third alternative. Auli Keskinen, director of research and development for the Finnish Ministry of the Environment, wrote: "The voluntary reallocation of power for the benefit of a citizens-steered society is very challenging indeed. It would really need a new kind of understanding of shared societal power to be a worthy goal."

Referendums, plebiscites, and ballot initiatives are increasingly being used as a form of direct participation in the democratic process. Traditionally used primarily to approve constitutional amendments, referendums are now relied on to make many of society's difficult choices. The Irish are asked if they want to legalize abortion, the Danes are asked if they want to trade their kronas for euros, and Alabamians are asked to decide to eliminate a ban on interracial marriage. In the 2000 US

283

presidential elections, there were more than 200 referendums on ballots across 42 states.

It has been argued that referendums requiring voters to choose a simple yes or no do not permit a deliberative process and well-reasoned policy, or that eccentric millionaires are too often encouraged to promote pet causes. During the Canadian election in November 2000, a briefing document for candidates of the right-wing opposition party foresaw referendums on such questions as abortion and capital punishment if just 3 percent of the voting population demanded one. That brought much public ridicule, with a political satire TV program launching a petition to collect the required 3 percent—400,000 signatures—for a referendum to change the first name of the opposition leader, Stockwell Day, to Doris. This figure was reached through a website within hours. Yet, it is because politicians are too afraid to take controversial stands or make unpopular decisions that referendums are so necessary today.

It was through referendums that voters in Oregon decided to legalize doctor-assisted suicide for terminally ill patients, Californians got rid of their government's politically correct bilingual education system, and seven states and the District of Columbia approved the use of marijuana for medical reasons. In each case, the public debate that preceded each vote was more in-depth than any deliberative process undertaken by a legislative committee. As the Italians have long understood, if there were no referendums, nothing would ever get done and the country would become politically gridlocked.

Many countries are also reviewing the roles of their parliaments so that backbench legislators can make a more meaningful contribution to the governing process. Furthermore, some are giving the judiciary new powers to review political decisions, while others are introducing changes in their electoral systems, including new rules on the financing of candidates and political parties. One of the best ways to involve the citizen in the decision-making process is to integrate any reforms with new technology. The internet makes it easy to start discussions, establish agendas for debate and deliberation, and bring in experts and interest groups, thus allowing concerned citizens to have a role and make an impact on issues from the very beginning. This leads to a better understanding between government and citizen, with less apathy, cynicism, and confrontation all around. The World Bank, for example, took the hint that seemed to escape the WTO and OECD and now involves NGOs in many of its debt-relief and environmental projects. Despite its own share of policy disasters, because of its greater transparency and more democratically enacted measures, it is not surprising that the World Bank has not been confronted with anything like the battle of Seattle.

While it is difficult to say if they are merely paying lip service, some unlikely world leaders and organizations are lending weight to the view that a new political order is required. In a digital message made available to the AOL community in March 2000 following a visit to Virginia's high-tech corridor, Egyptian President Hosni Mubarak said that while governments are the only representative institutions who can speak for their peoples, there was certainly a growing role for other actors. "The challenge is to allow for room for the new changes, accommodating the new online communities and the transnational networks," he said.

As governor, Jesse Ventura receives 13,000 emails a week from citizens telling him what they think of certain issues. He encourages the correspondence, saying that there is no better way to get so close to so many people so easily and inexpensively. Communicating through email and internet discussion groups tends to be less formal and more conversational, and therefore more egalitarian than the usual ceremonial protocols and bureaucratic procedures of government. Says Helene Falch Fladmark, a young technologically aware member of the Norwegian parliament: "For me, this is a way to give the public a more friendly picture of an MP."

Of course, the sheer volume of email communications makes it almost impossible to reach the ideal of an on-going, easy-going dialogue between the elected and the electors. With citizens also expecting faster responses to an email than they do to a letter, many politicians tend to moan about information overload. Public officials are also among the most vulnerable to email hoaxes, spam, and virus attacks. However, these merely add up to a need for further innovation, such as installing security filters and replacing sticky notes with citizen relationship management systems to ensure that requests and complaints don't go unanswered. There are systems in place where little flags pop up on employees' computer screens to remind them to follow up on emails, letters, phone calls, and faxes. The technology exists to ensure that the most important messages get through; as always, the most significant factor for effective communication is what people say rather than how they say it.

If the public has better access to quality information, people will form better-quality opinions. The internet facilities this by providing a simple way to access official documents, budgets, proposed legislation, committee meeting hearings, parliamentary proceedings, and so on. Anyone who believes in a more open and accessible public administration should fight all temptation to maintain proprietary islands of data or paper files locked in cabinet drawers. In the future, online information will be a defining characteristic of democracy. The effort and costs of publishing information electronically are modest and well within the means of any public agency.

As the poorest country in the Americas, making a difficult transition to democracy, Haiti is trying to help its people make more informed decisions about their country's development by disseminating social and economic data over the internet. The Haitian Institute of Statistics, the official government agency responsible for data collection, in collaboration with a national NGO and a private consulting firm, launched a website in March 2000 to provide country statistics and analysis together with a discussion list. This kind of information was never before widely circulated and is important for political transparency and for the country's reintegration into the international community. Greatly increasing the number of users and range of statistical data also improves strategic decision making at all levels. For Haiti, the unique aspect of the project was that it involved a tri-partite partnership between public, private, and nongovernmental organizations that is serving as a paradigm for wider participation in the political process.

The model was replicated in the runup to local and parliamentary elections, when the national research network REHRED (Réseau Télématique Haïtien pour la Recherche et le Développement/Haitian Telematic Network for Research and Development) brought together national and international institutions to set up an online network to inform the public about the upcoming electoral process. A website made available the programs of political parties and individual candidates, official election documents, reports on campaign activities, and actions taken by the provisional electoral council that was governing the country. (Haiti had been without a parliament for 16 months.)

Few Haitians have internet access, but local journalists and aid workers were given computer training and they used the site extensively to help them report and monitor the election and contribute to the fairness and transparency of the electoral process. Despite political violence in which 15 people were killed and concerns that people would be too scared or cynical to vote, close to 60 percent of registered voters turned out, and monitors from the Organization of American States (OAS) declared the election fair.

MORE ACCESSIBLE PARLIAMENT

A country's parliament is its shrine to democracy and it is here that citizens in a participative democracy should be able to get the information they need to make educated decisions. Yet, many people see their legislatures less as a chamber for serious deliberation of a country's laws and more as a venue for shouting matches, childish name-calling, and even punchups between opposing sides. With government controlling legislative timetables, the powers of committees, and the voting behavior of backbench members, the average politician's only chance to influence policy is by lobbying the executive branch behind closed doors.

Part of this cynicism stems from the public's lack of opportunity to witness directly the way the legislative process works. While many parliaments have set up websites, the purpose of most is to ease the workload of parliamentary administrative staff and to provide a more effective service to politicians, journalists, civil servants, solicitors, and interest groups. Sites are not usually designed with public convenience in mind, as users are assumed to have a detailed knowledge of legislative processes, with documents, debates, and proposed legislation left as unedited abstracts. Some parliaments are starting to stream live debates over the internet, but these too are intended primarily for traditional users of parliamentary information. Essentially, they are the same as a parliamentary TV channel, with the only added benefit that debates can be followed from abroad.

Few citizens have more rights than the Swiss to participate directly in their nation's political affairs, so it should not come as a surprise that the parliament of Switzerland's website is unique, in that it was set up primarily to make the institution more open and accessible to the public. The Swiss parliament had always rejected the idea of broadcasting its debates on TV because a television transmission, even for politically astute viewers, is difficult to follow if no explanatory commentary is made available about the speaker or the subject being discussed. Nevertheless, demand for more transparency was coming from the cantonal authorities and media as well as the public at large, who wanted to follow the work of the federal parliament without having to make a trip to Berne. So parliament decided to approve live broadcasts, but only if additional information was made available to put the debates in context. The only way this could be accomplished quickly and cheaply was with a live internet relay.

In 1999, a system called Live+ started streaming video and sound from the debates of both upper and lower houses, together with a technique known as patching that provides two additional information windows simultaneously on a PC screen. Web users can interactively call up additional information relating to any MP, the composition and work of parliamentary committees, and the issue being debated. It is up to them to decide how deeply they want to investigate a particular subject, digging into a database containing all the information on parliamentary business since a piece of legislation began.

Petitioning parliament or a legislature is another important aspect of civic participation in a democracy. The new Scottish parliament is improving this function with a website called E-Petitioner, which allows citizens to create an official public petition, set up an online debate, and encourage supporters to sign. The first e-petition to be accepted by the parliament was in March 2000, initiated by the the World Wildlife Fund to ensure that marine parks are included in a national park system for Scotland. The 337 people who attached their names to this petition had to log on to the internet and digitally sign the petition, giving their name and address. E-Petitioner weeds out duplicate and fictitious names like McDonald Duck and provides further authenticity by checking postcodes. In this way, an electronic petition becomes more credible and carries more weight than a piece of paper thrust into the hands of passers-by in the street.

In Finland, through backing from the Ministry of Education and private enterprises such as Compaq, Nokia, and the Helsinki Telephone Corporation, the City of Espoo youth council has set up a website via which young citizens can petition municipalities and various public authorities. The youth council is a public body that can submit motions directly to the city council and be represented in city committees. Its IdeaFactory website allows youths to make proposals that are debated by other young people. Debates are assessed by elected moderators, who then prepare motions that are sent back to participants for a vote. If a proposal is endorsed, with virtual signatures from often hundreds of young people, it is forwarded to a city board, different municipalities, or the local media. The initiative not only gives youths an influential role in the political process, it also provides a way for decision makers to have genuine contact with young voters and their way of thinking.

WEB CAMPAIGNING: IT'S ONLY NATURAL

The way politics works today, party candidates go out and try to win enough support for their positions and ideas. In the future, it will be the people who go out and seek political support for their beliefs. They will shop around on candidate, party, and nonpartisan political websites to see whose positions match their own views on the issues important to them. This will force politicians to speak to society, not merely to their party machines, enabling citizens to get closer to the ideal of making an informed choice.

This was the aim of Minnesota E-Democracy, a nonprofit, nonpartisan, issue-neutral organization established in 1994, when it put up a website with information about Minnesota candidates from impartial sources and the candidates themselves. There was also official government election information, online candidate debates, and an email forum for people to discuss election issues. The discussion forum soon took on an agenda-setting role in the state as political activists, journalists, and politicians joined in to share exchanges. Minnesota E-Democracy was probably the first election-oriented website, and it gradually replicated itself across a number of states and nationally.

By the time the US elections of 2000 rolled around, the internet had become a major electoral factor, with a plethora of campaign portals, election news sites, and sites serving targeted groups such as women, youth, minorities, and so on. The Freedom Channel, supported by grants from foundations including the Robert Wood Johnson Foundation, the Carnegie Corp. of New York, and The Freedom Forum, provided 90-second video clips of the presidential and congressional candidates discussing different issues and also carried candidates' TV commercials.

The Markle Foundation's nonpartisan, nonprofit Web White & Blue 2000 project was a collaborative effort of a number of online media organizations to stimulate debate and interest in the electoral process. It included electronic access to the presidential campaigns, additional election information, and behind-the-scenes articles, and it provided an opportunity for the public to voice their opinions and ideas.

Democracynetwork.org and the League of Women Voters provided information on candidates from all 50 states as well as links to advocacy groups. Issues2000.org provided presidential candidates' positions on issues in a cross-referenced hypertext grid. USA Democracy let users know by email how their elected representatives voted on particular bills in either the House or the Senate. Other sites included Civil Rights.org, Women Count, vote-smart.org, grassroots.com, iVillage, and Rock the Vote. All of these sites made the job of being an informed citizen much easier.

Similar voter watchdog sites have emerged in other countries, particularly in Japan during its general election in June 2000. The site of the People's Movement not to Elect Defective Lawmakers included a blacklist of 26 Lower House members whom the movement believed should not be re-elected because of their involvement in corruption scandals, failure to keep promises, and lack of engagement in parliamentary debates.

Political parties and individual candidates for anything from county sheriff to president are also going online with their own websites. Most are rudimentary "brochureware" sites that invariably include photos of the candidate, their biographies, positions on certain issues, and perhaps some recent speeches. Too many are in the vein of the "Widdy Web," the site of Ann Widdecombe, the British opposition spokesperson for home affairs, which features photos of the MP out Christmas shopping and another with her cat Pugwash. She provides snailmail contact details but no email address or links to other sites such as the party leadership. Then again, there's not much point connecting to the opposition leader's website, because it contains the party logo and the words: "The Rt Hon William Hague MP, Leader of the Conservative Party" and absolutely nothing else. This is slightly better than Prime Minister Tony Blair, who doesn't have a personal website.

The site of another British opposition MP has the word "claptrap" flashing beside a list of government policies. US politicians don't usually mention their opponents online and prefer to use their websites to recruit volunteers and solicit donations. The exception was the 2000 presidential campaign sites, which essentially were an extension of the two lead candidates' negative billboard and TV advertising campaigns. George Bush's site counted down "the end of the Clinton–Gore era," while Al Gore's site counted the number of days that Bush had refused to debate him. American politicians often have their sites designed and produced by one of a plethora of new political dot-coms that materialized in the runup to the 2000 elections. These companies often take perhaps a 6 percent cut of any credit-card donation made over the web to the candidate. Says Phil Noble, president of PoliticsOnline.com: "You can now do everything but kiss babies online. And I'm sure someone, somewhere is developing cyberlips."

Back in Europe, Helene Falch Fladmark is not an average politician in that she is the only graduate engineer in the Norwegian Parliament and one of the few to use the internet actively in her professional career before becoming a full-time politician. She says it was "only natural" for her to include the internet when planning her first election campaign in 1997, and in so doing became one of the first Scandinavian politicians with their own website. Her intention was to create a window where she could display her thoughts and beliefs, and a forum where people could react. Falch Fladmark also used email to solicit votes but, in order not to alienate people, she was careful to avoid mass distribution and ensured that every email she or her campaign workers sent was a personal message. She spread the news about her website launch by sending e-cards to friends and acquaintances and asked them to pass them on. Says Falch Fladmark: "I don't know how many votes I got through the internet but it certainly was one way to show the image of me as a young and modern alternative."

There is little doubt that the internet is a new, powerful form of communication that politicians can no longer ignore. Future candidates will win or lose an election by the way they use the internet, in much the same way as they can win or lose today by how they come across on television. A web surfer spends an average of 20 minutes looking at a political website—compare that to a TV commercial.

However, the use of the web as a campaigning tool gives rise to new dilemmas for election regulators, particularly in respect to rules covering campaign expenditures and contributions:

> News articles about parties and candidates printed in newspapers and magazines or broadcast on television and radio are not normally considered an election expense, but it is unclear if this should apply to articles published on a party or candidate website.
> Costs incurred by candidates for soliciting contributions are often exempt from expenditure limits, so should the cost of establishing a campaign website be exempt if it includes an application for people to make donations?
> Sometimes a company will provide a hyperlink from its website to a candidate's site, or a candidate will link to the sites of other candidates or a political party. Links provided at no charge could conceivably be considered a contribution in kind. A vendor selling bumper stickers, pins, and t-shirts might pay for a link from a politician's website, but it is not clear if that payment should be considered a corporate donation. The cost of making a link from one site to another is negligible or nonexistent, so if they are treated as contributions, their value must somehow be determined. And since a link can remain on a site for an extended period, it would have to be determined in which reporting period the contribution should occur.
> Regulators must also consider websites created by campaign volunteers or "fan sites" put up by individuals to urge support for, or opposition to, one or more candidates. These could be construed as donations in kind but, if so, the value of this expenditure would have to be determined.
> If a site contains both candidate information and other unrelated information, then presumably only a portion of the costs of the site could be treated as a contribution.

There are concerns that grassroots activities will be driven offline and that the development of the web as a participatory, democratic medium will be impeded if candidates are made to pay for any kind of internet exposure. In the US, the Federal Election Commission applied its standard donation limit and disclosure rules for the 2000 elections, but monitored that year's cybercampaigns and sought public input into the issues before reviewing if there was a need to modify its regulations for future campaigns.

In Japan, election officials are in a quandary over whether or not to allow internet campaigning at all. The issue came to a head during the June 2000 general election over a law preventing campaigns from using visual images that reach a large, unspecified number of viewers, put in place to ban election TV advertising because it gave an advantage to wealthy candidates. Although the original intent of the law suggests that it should not apply to the internet, which offers a cheap mass-communication medium, candidates were required to stop updating their home pages at the start of official campaigning. With more underdog opposition candidates maintaining websites than the old guard of the ruling Liberal Democratic Party (LDP), there were complaints that the incumbents were simply trying to limit opportunities for the public to become better acquainted with new leaders. The LDP hung on to power but lost its majority in face of increased voter frustration, and the Japanese government is reconsidering its ban on internet election campaign use. The fact that all Lower House members have now been provided with a laptop with internet connection in their offices should further help them to come around to the idea.

VOTE EARLY AND VOTE OFTEN

Brazil was ruled by a military dictatorship for two decades, and there were widespread allegations of fraud and corruption when elections were restored in the 1980s. Today, the country is a vigorous democracy with 80 percent of its 106 million voters regularly turning out to cast ballots in general elections. Yet, the world's third largest democracy is not an easy country to govern at the best of times and, given its past, the integrity of the electoral process is a key concern for many.

Entering the 1990s, the Brazilian authorities embraced the concept of electronic voting to help ensure that elections were conducted fairly. In the 1990 general election, a trial was held in the state of Santa Catarina where citizens cast their votes using paper ballots and local election workers entered the results into a computer system for tabulation. In 1994, computer-based tabulation expanded nationwide. In 1996, about one-third of the voting population cast their ballots electronically in local elections, and in 1998 almost two-thirds cast electronic ballots for the election of president, 27 senators, 27 state governors, and over 2,000 state and local officials.

Voters arrived at a polling station and presented their identification so that an election official could verify their eligibility. They then approached a voting kiosk, which prompted them to choose a candidate. The local computer registered the vote and automatically informed national election headquarters, which kept a running tally of all the votes cast. With votes tabulated in real time, it was no longer necessary to wait days after the polls closed for a winner to be declared. Instead, results were published immediately on the internet. In 1998, more than 5,000 voting centers in 2,800 cities across Brazil were linked together, making it essentially the largest intranet in Latin America. By 2002, Brazil plans to have a totally electronic national election.

Let's compare Brazil with, say, Florida. Statistical analysis suggests that if there had been an accurate count of all Florida votes in the 2000 election, Al Gore would have won the state by up to 20,000 votes, giving him the presidency. Yet, George W. Bush is in the White House and there are valid questions about whether he got there fairly. Probably nobody will ever know who won the most number of Florida votes on November 7, 2000, but the biggest loser, according to one of the many judges who issued an opinion on the matter, was the American electoral system. The court battles for and against manual and partial recounts took vote-counting and certifying authority away from election officials and gave it to the judiciary. More than a month after voters had gone to the polls, history was made when the US Supreme Court intruded into the political arena to hear an appeal from Bush against a ruling made five days earlier by the Florida Supreme Court to allow a partial manual recount of Florida votes. For the first time, a US election decision was pushed out of the voting booth and into the country's highest court.

The Florida recount put the Supreme Court in a difficult position because there had been constitutional violations with the on-again, off-again manual recounts. Partial recounts were conducted only in selected counties and arranged under varying standards for counting ballots, seemingly flouting Florida law saying that manual recounts must include all ballots. However, while a full manual recount may have meant that the final decision rested with the voters, carrying this out would have prolonged the election battle indefinitely and, in practice, would have been impossible. When Palm Beach County started its manual recount, it took 11 hours to tot up just 1 percent of the ballots.

By the narrowest possible majority (five to four), the US Supreme Court issued a convoluted ruling ordering the Florida Supreme Court to establish new voting standards consistent with the equal protection clauses of the constitution, after which the votes could be recounted and reviewed. All this had to be done before the electoral college met to certify the votes nationally, which it was scheduled to do just two hours after the ruling was issued. In effect, that decision ended the election.

The court was roundly criticized for its lack of impartiality and for issuing instructions it knew were impossible to carry out, but the ruling did challenge election officials to create uniform standards for casting ballots so that, in the future, every vote should count. If ultimately no action is taken, the door is open for almost anybody to go to court over an election dispute involving differences in ballot design or voting methods. This could have disastrous consequences for a country such as the US where the electoral system is highly decentralized. Yet, bizarrely claiming that one electoral system will not work for all voters, many American citizens' coalitions remain adamant that elections should continue to be conducted as locally as possible.

Nonetheless, if the 2000 election was decisive about anything at all, it was that the country's voting methods and procedures are in serious need of re-examination. Several states, including Florida, appointed commissions soon after the election to improve their electoral processes. The Federal Election Commission (FEC) planned to review standards on voting equipment, which it had not done for a decade even though voting errors are often much higher in elections than is allowed in testing. Voting machine certification is voluntary and about 20 states have not adopted federal certification standards. Voting system failures are not always reported to the FEC. The controversy of 2000 raised countless issues about voting technology, certification of voting equipment, and the human element in the voting process.

Like most states, Florida used a dizzying array of vote-counting systems, mainly punchcards and optical scans of paper ballots, but also mechanical lever machines and manually tabulated ballots. Immediately following the election there were allegations of widespread irregularities, including the confusing butterfly ballot paper that led many people to spoil their ballots or accidentally vote for an unintended candidate. When there are 19,000 spoiled ballots in one county, as there were in Palm Beach, something is seriously wrong.

In the now infamous punchcard system used in Palm Beach, voters use a pointed instrument to knock out a tiny perforated rectangle alongside their choice of candidate. When the rectangle isn't punched through cleanly and manages to cling on to the card, it becomes a "chad." When a card with a chad is fed through a vote-counting machine, it is often smoothed back into the hole, nullifying the vote. About 35 percent of American voting districts use this unreliable, antiquated system, and there isn't a single US state where ballots aren't overpunched and thrown out. Precinct workers have been arrested for punching extra holes into ballots, but their guilt is difficult to prove in court. With optical scanned paper ballots, such as those used in many other Florida counties, voters might have to darken out a box or oval, but many voters will instead simply make an X or check mark. Some scanners will still count these votes, others won't. Often if a paper ballot is folded or if a voter momentarily pauses with a pen over an oval, a scanner will record a multiple vote or even register the vote for a different candidate than the one intended.

No voting system is perfect and that is why countries have laws to allow recounts, but recounts using paper-based punchcard and optical scanned paper ballots are not any more precise than the original count. Manual recounts are open to human error and fraud and, as Florida too easily demonstrated, they take an unrealistically long time to complete.

Elections are traditionally expensive endeavors at the best of times, even more so when there is the added overhead of a recount. Paper and printing costs of ballots are also escalating. Election authorities must ensure that there are sufficient ballots for the whole electorate even when only 50 percent or sometimes less turn out to the polls. Extra ballots end up being destroyed—or stuffed. In 2000, one state governor joked about the need for his supporters to vote early and vote often. There were cases of poll workers receiving ballots at their homes on the day before the election, absentee ballots that were not counted because they were discovered too late to be certified, and allegations that some people voted twice, once in person and once by absentee ballot. In Florida, ballot boxes were discovered in a hotel and a church. There were reports that black voters in Tallahassee were turned away from polling stations because the polling station had supposedly run out of ballots, and some voters complained that they could not vote because polling stations had closed early. These kind of election irregularities are not unique to Florida, nor are they unique to the United States.

Governments and their election authorities are under increasing public and judicial pressure to make every vote count. They are expected to provide increasingly lengthy ballots, often in multiple languages, while delivering fast and accurate tallies. They must do all this in a cost-effective manner while ensuring voter privacy and election integrity. It seems incredible that, in the twenty-first century, the world's most technologically advanced democracies still play around with bits of paper every time they hold an election. Voting has remained basically unchanged for centuries, despite the fact that fewer and fewer people bother to turn out to vote and many groups of people, especially the young, are not adequately represented in the polls. Elections are most definitely broken, and the internet is a tool that can help fix them.

TWO KINDS OF E-VOTING

Elections are becoming more web enabled through candidate campaign sites, online voter registration, and the posting of election results. Using the internet to facilitate the voting process is the next logical step in order to improve voter convenience, revive voter interest, and increase voter participation. If there is to be no more tampering with ballots, no more controversial recounts, no more false exit-poll predictions, no more electoral farces, then all votes ought to be cast through a secure website.

There are two kinds of online voting: one where election officials control the computers used for voting, such as in Brazil; and the other where election officials don't have control of the computers, so people can vote from home, work, school, the public library, or half-way around the world. Initially, most authorities will simply install computers in polling stations, because they will only trust what they can control. But in time, people will demand a choice of e-voting. There is no point maintaining other paper-based voting options, because then internet voting would become a supplementary added expense rather than an aid to increase the integrity and reduce the cost of elections.

Direct recording electronic (DRE) machines with touchscreens located in polling stations have been around for some time and voters generally react positively to using them. Yet, they have been deployed only sparingly in very few countries because, as special-purpose machines, they are expensive. A general-purpose machine, such as a web-connected computer terminal, is more cost-effective because it can be used for other things between elections. Voters must also be shown how to use a special-purpose machine and there never seem to be enough workers at a polling station to do a complete demonstration. DRE machines record votes randomly on a memory disk that is transferred to a central computer facility to be read so, in the event of a recount, it is difficult to prove that the machine recorded a particular vote accurately.

The internet can leave an audit trail that can be examined instantly, especially if the two end points of the transaction are under the control of a single authority. The Brazilian system records every access to every computer, program, and file, thereby allowing officials to conduct a review after the election to prove that the system was secure at all times. The system, installed by a Brazilian company that provides network system integration for online banking, also carries out checks during the voting itself, alerting election officials to any sign of an intrusion or cyberattack.

Currently, with any election system, voters can only cast their ballot at the polling station where they are registered, which they might not be able to reach due to time constraints, poor weather, transportation or health problems. With internet voting, people can go to any polling station, allowing them to choose a place that may be closer to their home, work, school, or wherever. Computers, still under the full control of election officials, could be located at convenient places all around a voting district—in libraries, shopping malls, on the street. They could be put in the back of a vehicle and driven around a neighborhood like an ice-cream van. They could be open to the public for days or weeks prior to election day, allowing more locations and more time for voting than is currently the case.

Several countries such as Brazil have already proceeded with online voting in their polling stations, while the counties of San Diego and Sacramento in California and Maricopa in Arizona introduced the concept to the 2000 US presidential election with nonbinding online trials held in parallel to conventional ballot voting. Those who participated in the shadow elections found the online system easy to use and most people said they would prefer to vote online.

Arizona and the 2000 presidential campaign are also famous for hosting reputedly the world's first legally binding internet election when nearly 40,000 voters in the Arizona Democratic Party primary cast their ballots online. With only 12,800 in total voting in the 1996 primary, Arizona Democrats were getting discouraged. The state had twice as many registered Republicans as Democrats and the governor, both senators, and five of six members of the House of Representatives were all Republican. To rejuvenate their party, Democratic officials concluded that it had to make voting easier and more convenient for its members.

In 2000, voter participation increased by 660 per cent even though the outcome counted for nothing, since Al Gore had already locked up the nomination and his main rivals had dropped out of the race. More than 40 percent chose to vote over the internet from their home, work, school, library, community center, or Native American reservation. Another 35 percent voted early by mail and less than 20 percent went to a designated polling station. Of those who did vote in person, about one-third cast an online ballot at a computer terminal in the polling station.

VOTE WITHOUT LEAVING HOME

Someday people will log on to a website, establish their identity with a password and digital signature, and cast their vote in a binding election for president or parliament. Voting might take place over several days during which people can vote at any time of day or night, and they can take as much time they need to cast their ballot. The website will provide online help as people go through the voting procedure. Online voting will allow more people to participate in elections, particularly those who are homebound, travelers, and expatriates. People will no longer be constrained from voting because they are stuck in a hospital bed or a snow storm. Web-savvy but politically indifferent young people will be more likely to show an interest. While online voting itself is not a cure for political apathy, it can help enfranchise people by letting them vote more easily.

The public may love the idea of voting online from home, but most government and election officials remain skeptical. Voting convenience is important, but elections also need to be secure, free, and fair to ensure the legitimacy of government. Currently, there are too many serious, valid concerns about security and privacy. These need to be addressed and overcome before home voting from any web-enabled device is possible on a large scale in binding public elections. If anything, standards for e-voting need to be higher than those used currently for conventional paper ballots, because a general election marred by a cyberattack or hijacked by a hostile nation is too frightening a prospect to contemplate. Internet voting could be open to generic hacking and denial-of-service attacks such as the kind that have brought down many dot-com sites, as well as Trojan horse attacks that could allow someone to see how people voted and perhaps even change their choice without detection.

Dot-coms and credit-card companies tolerate a degree of fraud in their online transactions as the cost of doing business, which is anyway partially covered by insurance. But online voting is not an e-commerce transaction. No amount of election fraud can be tolerated; the system must be absolutely fail-safe. While there are techniques to avoid these problems, they are not readily available to the average computer user. Digital signatures can be used to authenticate a voter while at the same time protecting their privacy, but the cost of the technology needs to fall dramatically before governments can consider providing one to every voter. In the Arizona Democratic primary, there were problems with bottlenecks on the system due to a high volume of voters all trying to log on and cast their votes at the same time. Users of Macintosh computers and some older PCs also had difficulty linking to the website.

Other concerns about internet voting are less technical and more value judgments. There are fears that by allowing the casting of ballots outside an institutional setting, a person could be pressured and coerced by their boss, colleagues, union officials, or family members to vote a certain way, or even to sell their vote. However, submitting absentee ballots in advance by mail is becoming increasingly popular and in some jurisdictions it is already the way in which the majority of people vote. Driven by the desire to provide more convenient voting options, some governments are conducting entire elections through the post. The acceptance of voting from home by mail makes the idea of voting from home by the internet less controversial.

The bigger problem with online home voting is the contention that it discriminates against elderly, minority, and low-income voters who generally have less access to the internet than young, white, middle-class voters. There was a legal challenge to the Arizona Democratic primary on the grounds that it was a new-millennium version of the literacy test and was unfair to those without web access. Nevertheless, it can be as easily argued that the web increases access by allowing on-screen ballots to be presented in a choice of languages, and sites can have the flexibility of larger font sizes and an audio component for the visually impaired.

Rather than derailing the online voting movement with legal challenges, projects should be made to work in tandem with other government and community efforts to close the digital divide. Placing online voting points in traditional polling stations is part of the answer, as are initiatives to increase voter turnout in communities such as lower-income neighborhoods where computers are not part of everyday life. Internet voting could even stimulate civic participation projects, much like Rock the Vote, the nonpartisan, nonprofit organization that helps young people realize and utilize their political power. For the US elections in 2000, it collected more than 160,000 voter registrations online.

While the technical arguments against online voting are compelling, given time they are not insurmountable. Building trust and confidence in online voting will require a large effort, and until this happens, most election authorities will prefer internet voting in the controlled environment of a polling station. According to a state of California taskforce on internet voting that published its opinion in January 2000, achieving the aim of providing voters with the opportunity to cast ballots at any time from any place over the internet would best be served by "a strategy of evolutionary rather than revolutionary change."

This makes sense so long as achieving home voting is indeed the ultimate goal. Home voting experiments should continue, otherwise the problems will never be resolved—besides, somebody has to try it to see if it works. The risks and challenges should be seen as action items to be addressed in trials by online voting proponents, including online voting industry startups such as Election.com, which conducted the Arizona primary vote; VoteHere.net, which conducted the Sacramento and San Diego trials; and Safevote, which provides the internet technology for Brazilian elections.

Online voting will happen first in jurisdictions that don't have a lot to lose because their political machinery has already reached a point where it isn't working very well. Countries with a long history of corruption and a short history of democracy could easily find internet voting a vast improvement on existing election integrity and security measures. Online voting will also receive a boost from those countries that give the vote to citizens living abroad, yet these people remain disenfranchised because of voting logistics. In its 2000 presidential elections, Croatian expatriates were allowed to cast their votes from anywhere in the world over the internet, and no doubt people within the country itself would have wanted the same opportunity, since many had to stay home due to blizzards and high winds.

As part of a larger parliamentary reform package, the state of South Australia has proposed reserving one or two seats in its legislative council to be voted for by a "virtual electorate" comprised of South Australians living outside the state. A legislator who specifically represented the interests of the expatriate community would give nonresidents a reason to stay connected to the state and provide a platform for bringing them home when their skills are needed, claim government officials. Nobody knows how many expat South Australians are out there, but it's a lot. Out-of-state enrolment and elections would help identify the "global tribe," so the internet would not only facilitate the vote but also link up the extended family and build a stronger community. Says Michael Armitage, minister for the information economy: "Most South Australians will have expatriate family members or know someone who has moved out of state. This is about Mr. Citizen's daughter or niece, or Mrs. Citizen's brother or son or grandchild."

Referendums also provide ideal testing grounds for internet voting because the ballot questions usually require a simple yes or no. In September 2000, after casting their traditional paper ballot in a French national referendum on whether the presidential mandate should be reduced from seven years to five, voters in the city of Brest were asked to go home and vote again over the internet in a mock reenactment. Even though the trial meant nothing, 35 percent of the voters did so.

Municipalities also tend to be more interested in internet voting than do higher levels of government because local elections often have abysmally low voter turnouts, and the whole internet voting concept fits in neatly with that of the smart community. Says André Santini, mayor of the high-tech Paris suburb of Issy-les-Moulineaux: "The technological revolution is creating a new kind of citizen, capable of monitoring the activities of their elected representatives, of expressing their opinion in real time, and of forming themselves into pressure groups, leading one to foresee the changeover to electronic suffrage."

The evidence is there to suggest that the internet will play an increasingly important role in democratic elections, and there is clearly a demand for greater voting convenience. Governments must address demands for the provision of a better election service in the same way that they are answering calls to improve the provision of other types of public service. If the internet can help engage the electorate and bolster a rotting political system, it will be well worth the effort.

Bibliography

AAUWEF (2000) *Tech-Savvy: Educating Girls in the New Computer Age*, Washington DC: American Association of University Women Educational Foundation.

Agarwal, P.K. (2000) "Portals: the path to e-everything," *Government Technology*, March, www.govtech.net.

Akdeniz, Yaman (1997) "The regulation of pornography and child pornography on the internet," *Journal of Information, Law and Technology*, 28 Feb, http://elj.warwick.ac.uk/jilt/internet/97_1akdz/.

Alexander, Kim & Jefferson, David (2000) "Internet voting: proceed cautiously," *San Jose Mercury News*, May 16.

Atkinson, Robert D. & Ulevich, Jacob (2000) *Digital Government: The Next Step to Reengineering the Federal Government*, Washington DC: Progressive Policy Institute, March 1, www.ppionline.org.

BBC News (2000) "Technology in schools: ask Michael Wills," BBC News Online, May 10, www.bbc.co.uk.

Bellamy, Christine & Taylor, John A. (1998) *Governing in the Information Age*, Buckingham: Open University Press.

Bentsen, Cheryl (2000) "Why women hate IT," *CIO*, September 1, www.cio.com.

Bishop, Matthew (2000) "The mystery of the vanishing taxpayer: a survey on globalisation and tax," *The Economist*, January 29, www.economist.com.

Bolkestein, Frits (2000) *VAT on Electronic Commerce*, Brussels: Transatlantic Policy Network, Sept 20.

Booz Allen Hamilton (2000) *Achieving Universal Access*, London: Booz Allen Hamilton, www.bah.com.

Breslau, Karen (2000) "Digital citizen 2000: one nation, interconnected," *Wired*, May, www.wired.com.

Britton, Eric (2000) *The Bogotá Challenge*, Paris: EcoPlan International, May 23, www.ecoplan.org/carfreeday.

Brooks, Michael (2000) "A case for the digital detective," *Guardian*, February 3, www.guardianunlimited.co.uk.

Brown, John Murray (2000) "Small town enjoys big connections," *Financial Times*, October 3, www.ft.com.

Brown, William (2000) "A war of words," *Electronic Telegraph*, February 3, www.telegraph.co.uk.

Brumby, John (1999) *Connecting Victoria: Ministerial Statement*, Melbourne: Government of Victoria, November.

Butler, Kevin (2000) "Is Big Brother surfing the Internet?", *Investor's Business Daily*, August 9.

Cabinet Office (2000) *E-government Interoperability Framework*, London: Office of the E-Envoy, Cabinet Office, September.

Caldow, Janet (1999) *The Virtual Ballot Box: A Survey of Digital Democracy in Europe*, Institute for Electronic Government, IBM, www.ibm.com/government.

California Internet Voting Task Force (2000) *A Report on the Feasibility of Internet Voting*, Sacramento: California Internet Voting Task Force, January, www.ss.ca.gov/executive/ivote/.

Carrell, Severin (2000) "Police turn to the internet with secure website for informants," *Independent*, May 5, www.independent.co.uk.

Central IT Unit (2000) *Benchmarking Electronic Service Delivery*, London: Central IT Unit, July, www.citu.gov.uk.

Cezanne, Thomas (2000) "US ecommerce companies struggling in Europe," *Business 2.0*, September 5, www.business2.com.

Cohen, William S. (1997) Remarks, National Defense University Joint Operations Symposium—QDR Conference, Washington DC, June 23, www.defenselink.mil/speeches/index.html.

Cohen, William S. (2000) Remarks, Center for Strategic and International Studies, Washington DC, October 2, www.defenselink.mil/speeches/index.html.

Commonwealth of Australia (2000) *Government Online: The Commonwealth Government's Strategy*, Canberra: Department of Communications, Information Technology and the Arts, Commonwealth of Australia, April, www.dcita.gov.au.

Council for Excellence in Government (2001) *E-Government: The Next American Revolution*, Washington DC: Council for Excellence in Government, www.excelgov.org.

CourtLink (2000) "Colorado courts first in nation to offer statewide e-filing in civil and domestic cases," *CourtLink*, August 7, www.courtlink.com.

Coyle, Kevin (2000) "Common myths about paperwork elimination," *E-Gov Journal*, www.e-gov.com/egovjournal.

Daté, Shruti (2000) "Do CIOs have enough power to do their jobs?", *Government Computing News*, April 17, www.gcn.com.

Davies, Linda (2000) "Digital democracy," *IBM Government Journal*, www.ibm.com/government.

de Leon, Rudy (2000) Remarks, European Institute Roundtable, Washington DC, October 17, www.defenselink.mil/speeches/index.html.

Denning, Dorothy E. (1999) *Activism, Hacktivism, and Cyberterrorism: The Internet as a Tool for Influencing Foreign Policy*, Nautilus Institute,www.nautilus.org/info-policy/workshop/papers/denning.html.

Denning, Dorothy E. (2000) *Cyberterrorism*, Special Oversight Panel on Terrorism Committee on Armed Services, US House of Representatives, May 23.

Department of Information Services (2000) *Washington State Digital Plan*, Olympia: Department of Information Services, February.

Department of Justice Initiative (2000) *Integrated Justice Information Systems*, Washington DC: Department of Justice Initiative, April 12, www.ojp.usdoj.gov/integratedjustice/.

Department of State and Regional Development (1998) "Online Government 2001," *Multimedia Victoria*, Department of State and Regional Development, Government of Victoria, May 6.

Department of State and Regional Development (2000) "Government Logs on: Victorian Government Agency Case Studies," *Multimedia Victoria*, Melbourne: Department of State and Regional Development, Government of Victoria, January.

DETR (2000) *Cross-cutting Issues in Public Policy and Public Service*, London: Department of the Environment, Transport and the Regions, February 2, www.local-regions.detr.gov.uk/cross.

Donahue, Sean (2000) "Red tape busters," *Business2.com*, June 13, www.business2.com.

Doyle, Charles & Morris, Hugh (1999) *The Net Effect*, London: Fabian Society, March, www.fabian-society.org.uk.

Dugas, Tim, Green, Lyndsay & Leckie, Norm (1999) *The Impact of Technologies on Learning in the Workplace*, Office of Learning Technologies, Human Resources Development Canada, March, http://olt-bta.hrdc-drhc.gc.ca.

Dunleavy, Patrick, John, Steve & Margetts, Helen (2000) *Beyond the Fine Words on the Web*, Institute of Public Finance, www.ipf.co.uk.

EC (2000) *A European Way for the Information Society*, Brussels: Information Society Forum, European Commission.

EC (2000) *Strategies for Jobs in the Information Society*, Brussels: European Commission.

Economist (1999) "The people's choice," *Economist*, August 12, www.economist.com.

Economist (1999) "The non-governmental order," *Economist*, December 9, www.economist.com.

Economist (2000) "Opening a gavel of worms," *Economist*, December 14, www.economist.com.

EDS (2000) "EDS awarded $6.9 billion Navy Marine Corps intranet contract; largest government information technology pact ever," EDS news release, October 6, www.eds.com.

Eger, John M. (1999) Letter, *Time*, March 18.

Electronic Government International (2000) "Finnish citizens begin using smart ID card," *Electronic Government International*, January 28, www.kablenet.co.uk.

Elliott, David M. (1999) *Examining Internet Voting in Washington*, The Election Center, www.electioncenter.org.

Evans, Mark (1999) "Quebec must learn to speak the language of the Web," *Globe and Mail*, September 16, www.globeandmail.com.

Federal Computer Week (2000) "E-voting: worth the work," *Federal Computer Week*, September 4, www.fcw.com.

Federal Election Commission (1999) "Use of the Internet for campaign activity," *Federal Register*, Vol. 64, No. 214, November 5.

Financial Times (2000) "Governments go shopping online," *Financial Times*, March 15, www.ft.com.

Fine, Sean (2000) "Net gain accrues to innovative schools," *Globe and Mail*, December 15, www.globeandmail.com.

Freeman, Alan (2000) "Cybercrime meeting moves at bureaucrat, not Internet, speed," *Globe and Mail*, May 16, www.globetechnology.com.

Gansler, Jacques S. (1998) "Affordable weapons systems: a design for the future," *Defense Issues*, Vol. 13, No. 35, www.defenselink.mil/speeches/index.html.

Gates, Bill (1999) *Business @ the Speed of Thought: Using a Digital Nervous System*, London: Penguin.

Gerck, Ed (2000) "From voting to Internet voting," *The Bell*, Vol. 1, No. 1, May, www.thebell.net.

Government Computing News (1999) "EPA's IT edge man," *Government Computing News*, January 11, www.gcn.com.

Government Information Department (1999) *France in the Information Society*, Paris: Information and Communication Legal and Technical Department, Government Information Department, www.internet.gouv.fr.

Government Technology (2000) "The lease we can do," *Government Technology*, July, www.govtech.net.

Grande, Carlos (2000) "Cyber criminals likely to strike," *Financial Times*, October 18, www.ft.com.

Greenslade, Roy (2000) "I arrest you for emailing," *Guardian*, July 31, www.guardianunlimited.co.uk.

Grove, Andrew (2000) Keynote address, Harvard International Conference on Internet & Society 2000, Cambridge, MA, June 2.

Hamilton, John P. (2000) "International dimensions of organised crime," *Microsoft Combating Cross-Border Crime 2000 Conference*, Cape Town, South Africa, March 23.

Hancock, Julia (2000) "1,491 charged in Internet pedophilia case," Reuters, October 28, www.reuters.com.

Hayes, Heather B. (2000) "Schools supplied," *Federal Computer Week*, October 2, www.fcw.com.

Hearst, David (2000) "Yahoo! enters international legal minefield," *Guardian*, July 24, www.guardianunlimited.co.uk.

Heroux Pounds, Marcia (2000) "All vote-counting machines are vulnerable to errors," *South Florida Sun-Sentinel*, November 14, www.sun-sentinel.com.

Holley, Michael L. (2000) "Combined Endeavor 2000: operation and management of an interoperable multinational network," *TechNet Europe 2000*, Prague, October 19.

Hoon, Geoff (1999) "Crime, criminal justice and the Internet," *British Irish Law Technology Association Cyberspace 1999 Conference*, March 30.

Hyde, Stuart (1999) "A few coppers change," *Journal of Information, Law and Technology*, June 30, http://elj.warwick.ac.uk/jilt/99-2/hyde.html.

IBM, *Open Education: Access to Lifelong Learning for Economic Opportunity*, www.ibm.com/education.

Intergovernmental Advisory Board (1999) *Integrated Service Delivery: Governments Using Technology to Serve the Citizen*, Washington DC: Intergovernmental Advisory Board, August.

Joha, Ghassan (2000) "Cyberwar hackers try hand at systems crash," *Star*, November 2, http://www.star.com.jo.

Jupp, Vivienne (2000) "Implementing eGovernment: rhetoric and reality," *Andersen Consulting Insights*, No. 2, June, www.ac.com.

Kerr, Donald M. (2000) *Statement for the Record on Carnivore Diagnostic Tool Before the United States Senate Committee on the Judiciary*, Washington DC: Federal Bureau of Investigation, September 6, www.fbi.gov/pressrm/congress/congress00/kerr090600.htm.

Keskinen, Auli (1999) "Teledemocracy, Finland," *Democracy and Government On-Line Services Contributions from Public Administrations Around the World,* G8 Government On-Line (G8 GOL), 1999, www.statskontoret.se/gol-democracy.

Kessler, Wayne (2000) *The Microsoft State: Pennsylvania's Powerport Deal,* The Commonwealth Foundation, June 9.

Kornblum, Janet (2000) "Hackers invited to muck up mock ballot," *USA Today,* November 2, www.usatoday.com.

Korzeniowski, Paul (2000) "The XML factor," *Federal Computer Week,* August 28, www.fcw.com.

LaSalle, Luann (1998) "Language laws apply to Internet advertisements in Quebec," *Canadian Press,* April 28, www.cp.org.

Lawlor, Maryann (2000) "Internet tax analysts encounter legislative, regulatory minefield," *Signal,* May, www.us.net/signal.

London Borough of Newham (2000) "Better access to services for Newham residents," *Newham News,* London Borough of Newham, February, www.newham.gov.uk.

Mallett, Robert L. (2000) Remarks, *E-Gov 2000 Conference,* Washington DC: US Department of Commerce, July 13, www.doc.gov.

Matthews, Sally, Mackison, James & Brantley, William (1999) *Integrated Service Delivery: Governments Using Technology to Serve the Citizen: International, Federal, State, and Local Government Experiences,* Washinton DC: Intergovernmental Advisory Board & Federation of Government Information Processing Councils, August, http://policyworks.gov/intergov.

Matthews, William (2000) "Postal Service first to try online reverse auctions," *Federal Computer Week,* April 17, www.fcw.com.

Matthews, William (2000) "Can the Net revive the vote?", *Federal Computer Week,* September 4, www.fcw.com.

McAuliffe, Megan (2000) "Working party to examine CrimeNet," *ZDNet Australia News,* July 31, www.zdnet.com.au.

McDermott, Kevin (2000) "The Web snares more candidates than ever this year," *St Louis Post-Dispatch,* July 17, www.postnet.com.

McDonough, Brian (1999) "Sealing the cracks," *Government Technology,* December, www.govtech.net.

Mieszkowski, Katharine (1999) "Sisterhood is digital," *Fast Company,* September, www.fastcompany.com.

Millar, Stuart (2000) "Sex gangs sell prostitutes over the internet," *Observer,* July 16, www.observer.co.uk.

Monty, Jean (2000) "Brain gain: the ABCs of dot-com," *Globe and Mail*, May 3, www.globeandmail.com.

Mubarak, H.E. Hosni (2000) "Digital Message from the President of the Arab Republic of Egypt," America Online, March 27, www.aol.com.

National Audit Office (1999) *Government on the Web*, London: National Audit Office, December 13.

Newcombe, Tod (2000) "Technology helps states transform welfare," *Government Technology*, April, www.govtech.net.

Noack, David (1999) "Most cybercrime goes unpunished," *APBnews.com*, December 9, www.apbnews.com.

Norman, Michele (2000) "Don Tapscott: man with a message," *Converge*, March, www.convergemag.com/profiles.shtm.

Nunn, Sam (2000) *Get Ready for Cyberwar*, Blueprint, Democratic Leadership Council, February 1.

O'Hara, Colleen & Caterinicchia, Dan (2000) "Government issue," *Federal Computer Week*, April 10, www.fcw.com.

O'Meara, Molly (2000) "Harnessing information technologies for the environment," *State of the World 2000*, London: Earthscan, www.earthscan.co.uk.

Osborne, David & Gaebler, Ted (1992) *Reinventing Government: How the Entrepreneurial Spirit is Transforming the Public Sector*, Reading, MA: Addison-Wesley.

Ostberg, Olov & Clift, Steven (eds) (1999) *Democracy and Government On-Line Services*, G8 Government On-Line (G8 GOL), January, www.statskontoret.se/gol-democracy.

Overland, Martha Ann (2000) "Carnegie Mellon U. to offer online programming classes in India," *Chronicle for Higher Education*, September 11, http://chronicle.com/world.

Owens, William A. (2000) "Revolutionizing warfare," *Blueprint: Ideas for a New Century*, Winter.

Paun, Vasile (2000) "The gap in RMA: options and priorities for the Romanian armed forces," *AFCEA TechNet Europe 2000*, Prague, October 19.

Peters, Erik (1998) *Provincial Auditor's Report*, Office of the Provincial Auditor of Ontario, www.gov.on.ca/opa.

Phillips, Deborah (2000) "Is Internet voting fair?", *Network World*, June 26, www.nwfusion.com.

Porteous, Samuel (1996) "The threat from transnational crime: an intelligence perspective," Commentary No. 70, Canadian Security Intelligence Service, Winter.

Prister, Giorgio, *Digital cities: a fair e-tale in the making*, IBM, www.ibm.com.

Putnam Pit, Inc.; Geoffrey Davidian v. City of Cookeville, Tennessee; Jim Shipley, United States Court of Appeal for the Sixth Circuit, File Name: 00a0235p.06, Electronic Citation: 2000 FED App. 0235P (6th Cir.), July 19, 2000, http://laws.findlaw.com/6th/00a0235p.html.

Raper, Tony & Tyrrell, Patrick J. (2000) "Providing end-to-end information access: from Secretary of State to the foxhole," *AFCEA TechNet Europe 2000*, Prague, October 18.

Reding, Viviane (2000) "Education in the 21st century: education for the knowledge economy," *Conference of the Asia-Europe Foundation*, Luxembourg, May 2.

Reuters (2000) "Japan e-politics ban can't keep candidates off Web," Reuters, Tokyo, June 16, www.reuters.com.

Rudd, Alexis H. (1997) "POLICE-L: the police discussion list," *FBI Law Enforcement Bulletin*, March.

Salopek, Jennifer J. (1999) "Rural electronification," *Training & Development*, October.

Sarkar, Dibya (2000) "Chicago police offer citizens a way to track local crime," *Civic.com*, November 6, www.civic.com.

Shiver, Jube, Jr. (2000) "Many online taking privacy into their own hands," *Los Angeles Times*, August 21, www.latimes.com.

Schultz, James (2000) "Cyberattacks: the worst is yet to come," *Washington Technology*, July 17.

Schulz, Hans H. (2000) "Lessons learnt from current CIS operations," *TechNet Europe 2000 Symposium*, 18–20 October.

Select Committee on Public Accounts (2000) *Thirty-First Report*, London: House of Commons, July 19.

Shaw, Andy (1997) "Divorce Canadian style," *Infosystems Executive*, October, www.plesman.com.

Smith, Ronel (2000) "Overcoming regulatory and technological challenges to bring internet access to a sparsely populated, remote area," *First Monday*, October, www.firstmonday.org.

Street, Terry (1999) *Private Public Partnerships: Briefing for SOCITM Members*, Northampton: Society of Information Technology Management, www.socitm.gov.uk.

Symonds, Matthew (2000) "The next revolution: a survey of government and the internet," *Economist*, June 24, www.economist.com.

Takamatsu, Natsuko (2000) "Hirata gov't tries weekly no computer day," *Mainichi Shimbun*, June 23.

Tapscott, Don (1996) *The Digital Economy: Promise and Peril in the Age of Networked Intelligence*, New York: McGraw-Hill.

Times of India (2000) "Village voices," *Times of India*, January 31, www.timesofindia.com.

Timmins, Nicholas (2000) "Searching for general health issues," *Financial Times*, September 1, www.ft.com.

Towns, Steve (2000) "Digital Justice," *Digital States Survey*, Center for Digital Government, April, www.centerdigitalgov.com.

21st Century Workforce Commission (2000) *A Nation of Opportunity: Building America's 21st Century Workforce*, Washington DC: 21st Century Workforce Commission, June.

Unisys (2000) "Hitching a wagon to e-government," *Exec*, Unisys Corporation, September–October, www. unisys.com.

United Nations (2000) "Development and international cooperation in the XXI century: the role of information technology in the context of a knowledge-based global economy," *Report of the Secretary General*, Economic and Social Council, New York: United Nations, May 16.

Vaas, Lisa (1999) "The Web helps EPA clean up piles of data," *ZD Net*, March 15, www.zdnet.com.

van den Berg, Leo & van Winden, Willem (2000) *ICT as Potential Catalyst for Sustainable Urban Development*, Rotterdam: European Institute for Comparative Urban Research, Erasmus University, October, www.euricur.nl.

Wake, Bev (2000) "Computers E-shape education," *Ottawa Citizen*, September 5, www.ottawacitizen.com.

Ward, Seamus (2000) "NHS becomes an on-line shopper," *Public Finance*, www.publicfinance.co.uk.

Waskell, Eva (2000) "California Internet voting," *The Bell*, Vol. 1, No. 6, October, www.thebell.net.

White, Jason (2000) "Pennsylvania, Washington take different paths to e-government," *Stateline.org*, June 21, www.stateline.org.

Woodall, Pam (2000) "Untangling e-conomics: a survey of the new economy," *Economist*, September 23, www.economist.com.

Web References

Access Washington: www.access.wa.gov

Arizona Democrats: www.azdem.org

Armed Forces Communications and Electronics Association: www.afcea.org

Athabasca University: www.athabascau.ca

Atlantic Canada On-Line: www.acol.ca

Australian Information Industry Association: www.aiia.com.au

Australian Taxation Office: www.ato.gov.au

Berlin Marktplatz: www.berlin.de

Bridges.org: www.bridges.org

Center for Digital Government: www.centerdigitalgov.com

Center for Technology in Government: www.ctg.albany.edu

ChildcareLink: www.childcarelink.gov.uk

Cisco Education Ecosystem: www.cisco.com/edu/

Civic.com: www.civic.com

Connecting Canadians: www.connect.gc.ca

CopNet: www.copnet.com

CourtLink: www.courtlink.com

CrimeNet: www.crimenet.com.au

Cyberspace Policy Research Group: www.cyprg.arizona.edu

Digital 4Sight (formerly Alliance for Converging Technologies): www.digital4sight.com

Dubai Ports and Customs: www.dxbcustoms.gov.ae

Ennis Information Age Town: www.ennis.ie

Environmental Protection Agency, Envirofacts: www.epa.gov/enviro/

Estonian Informatics Center: www.eik.ee

European Commission Information Society: http://europa.eu.int/comm/information_society/index_en.htm

European Commission Information Society Promotions Office (IPSO): http://europa.eu.int/ISPO/

Europol: www.europol.eu.int

Fathom: www.fathom.com

Federal Computer Week: www.fcw.com

Finnish Information Technology Development Center: www.tieke.fi

FirstGov: http://firstgov.gov

First Monday: http://firstmonday.org

Foundation for Information Technology in Local Government: www.fitlog.com

French Government Program for the Information Society: www.internet.gouv.fr

General Services Administration: www.gsa.gov

G8 Global Information Society: www.g7.fed.us

G8 Government On-line Project: www.statskontoret.se/gol-democracy

Government Technology: www.govtech.net

Gyandoot: www.gyandoot.net

Healthfinder: www.healthfinder.gov

IBM Institute for Electronic Government: www.ieg.ibm.com

IMAGINE project: www.imagine.district-parthenay.fr

IndyGov: www.indygov.org

Information Society Commission: www.isc.ie

Information Technology Association of America: www.itaa.org

Intergovernmental Technology Leadership Consortium, Council for Excellence in Government: www.excelgov.org/techcon

International Federation of Workers' Education Associations: www.ifwea.org

KableNET: www.kablenet.com

Kista portal: www.kista.com

Lasipalatsi, City of Helsinki: www.lasipalatsi.fi

London Borough of Newham: www.newham.gov.uk

maxi: www.maxi.com.au

Microsoft E-Government News: www.microsoft.com/europe/industry/government/newsletter

Minnesota E-Democracy: www.e-democracy.org

National Association of State Information Resource Executives: www.nasire.org

National Grid for Learning: www.ngfl.gov.uk

National Telecommunications and Information Administration (NTIA) digital divide website: www.digitaldivide.gov

Office of Intergovernmental Solutions: http://policyworks.gov/intergov/

Office of the e-Envoy: www.e-envoy.gov.uk

Ohioworks: www.ohioworks.com

OneWorld digital divide campaign: www.oneworld.net/campaigns/digitaldivide/

PA PowerPort: www.state.pa.us

Parthenay InTownNet: www.district-parthenay.fr

policity: www.policity.com

QuickLinks: www.qlinks.net

United Nations Development Programme, Information and Communication Technologies for Development: www.undp.org/info21/

UK Online: www.ukonline.gov.uk

Service New Brunswick: www.gov.nb.ca/snb

Singapore eCitizen Portal: www.ecitizen.gov.sg

SchoolNet: www.schoolnet.ca

Science Learning Network: www.sln.org

SkillNet.CA: www.skillnet.ca

Society of Information Technology Management: www.socitm.gov.uk

Stipe Mesic campaign site: www.stipemesic.com

Stockholm Challenge: www.challenge.stockholm.se

Swedish ICT Commission: www.itkommissionen.se

Swiss Parliament: www.parlament.ch

Technology in Government: www.ebusiness.ca/tg/

Telecities: www.telecities.org

Texas Electronic Government Task Force: http://lanner.dir.state.tx.us/egov/

Virginia home page: www.state.va.us

Virginia Department of Motor Vehicles: www.dmv.state.va.us/

Washington Technology: www.wtonline.com

World Car Free Day Consortium: www.ecoplan.org/carfreeday

World Information Technology and Services Alliance (WITSA): www.witsa.org

Yellowknife Virtual City Hall: http://city.yellowknife.nt.ca

Index